# Beyond Monty Karel

## A Gentle Introduction to the Art of Dynamic Object-Oriented Programming in Python

## Volume 2

Joseph Bergin

Published by Joseph Bergin, Slant Flying Press
2023

ISBN: 978-1-940113-10-4

# Beyond Monty Karel
# A Gentle Introduction to the Art of Dynamic Object-Oriented Programming in Python: Volume 2

Joseph Bergin

---

## Preface

A number of users have asked for more material in the spirit of Monty Karel. The original book is intended for only the beginning weeks of a course, which leaves some the dilemma of what to do for the rest of the term. This volume is an attempt to discuss some additional ideas as well as some more Python features. The chapter numbering begins where Monty Karel leaves off and we will frequently make mention of what was learned there. However, we begin to leave the robot world here and will discuss many ideas from beyond that world.

This book is not intended as a Python tutorial, however. It is more about "how to program", especially in an Object-Oriented style.

The two volumes together should form the basis of a first college course in computing using Python.

We will see int, float, strings, etc., but no attempt was made to provide all the rules and caveats of such things. Many books that call themselves text-books seem to me to be, instead, reference works, with everything gathered together nicely to ease looking up information, rather than books to learn from. Instead, I have attempted to show, for the most part, how the features of Python are used to build real programs with a focus on Object-Oriented programming. This is a book about writing programs, including some quite interesting and difficult programs. You may struggle with some of this material, but the struggle will take you to a better place. I hope you agree that it is worth the work you will put in to it.

The Intermezzo sections are just examinations of long programs that use important techniques that the novice must master. Throughout we emphasize good Object-

Oriented development, but also cover many other things as well. Chapter 14 is special. It is not intended to be used after the rest, but rather, along the way. It introduces a term-long project that will build something like the Monty Karel simulator, though in a non-graphical form. In technical terms, it produces the model to which views can be added later. The sections of that chapter are keyed to the other chapters in the book, with many exercises that can be done as the student learns the material of those earlier chapters.

The Appendix offers implementations of some collections classes that are similar to, but simpler than, the classes in the Python libraries. They are intended for reading and study, though we make use of them in the latter part of the book, starting in Chapter 11.

Caveat: The syntax here is from Python 3. It is inconsistent with earlier versions. Note that Python is changing and growing and the developers haven't always kept backward compatibility. I use an early V3 Python and the Eclipse development environment.

Software to simulate Monty Karel is available on the Web.
http://csis.pace.edu/~bergin/KarelJava2ed/downloads.html

---

Joseph Bergin, Pace University (retired)
June 2023

# Table of Contents

# 9 The State of the Computation

What is your state of mind as you read this? As you read, does the state of your knowledge change? What is your state of health? This chapter makes explicit the notion of *state* in computer programs. There are three notions of state that we want to explore here: implicit state, execution position (program counter), and explicit state.

## 9.1 Implicit State

When programming in most languages, including the robot programming language, the programs are "stateful:" they contain a lot of state. For example, when karel puts a beeper down, the "state" of the world changes, as it has an additional beeper at that corner. At the same time the state of the robot changes, as it has one less in its beeper bag. On the other hand, the number of beepers in the system as a whole has not changed: it is *invariant*. Most of your programming in the robot world up to this point has been moving the state of the computation forward in this sense. The world begins in some state, or configuration. Walls and beepers are in initial positions. Robots are placed initially at certain corners with beepers, directions, etc. Then the program begins to execute and the state begins to change with some things varying and some things remaining invariant. For example, the state of the robot nearly always changes when we execute an instruction, but the state of the walls never does.

This idea of an invariant is very important. On one hand it means that there is one less thing that the programmer needs to keep track of in writing the program. That permits you focus on the things that can change: on the sequence of state changes. We have also used the idea of an invariant to help us with the computation itself. For example, when a robot moves toward the Southeast, the sum of its street and avenue numbers is invariant. We used this idea effectively in Section 7.5.

Note also, that in most programs the state changes are locally predictable. You can look at any statement and predict what changes it will make to the state of the computation. That isn't always, the case, however. For example, if you introduce random elements into the program, such as multi-threaded execution, it may not be possible to predict precisely what will occur. That doesn’t mean we have chaos, however. It just means that we have to rely on general, rather than specific, notions of state transition. So, for example, in the Dining Robots example, we can predict what will happen within each robot's execution, though our description is somewhat conditional: If a fork ever appears on this corner, the robot will pick it up… etc. The same is true in the real world, of course: If a bus ever appears on this corner, I'll be able to ride downtown to visit my friend.

There is another situation in which we are able to make only general statements about the state changes in a program. If we have employed dynamic polymorphism, then when we send a robot a message via a reference variable we may not be able to know, in principle, the precise type of the robot that will receive the message, so we don't know the precise method that will be executed in response to the message. All we know is that whichever robot receives the message will execute its own corresponding method, making some changes to the state that might not occur if some other robot received the message instead.

In fact, when any robot, or, more generally, any object, receives a message, the response of the robot will depend on both the type of that object and the current state of the object. For example if we send a *putBeeper* message to a robot it will execute its own version of that method, which may not be the one defined in UrRobot, but the response also depends on whether it has any beepers in its beeper bag at that moment as well. Its state "at that moment" depends on the sequence of state changes that have occurred up to then in the execution of the program. Again, the same is true in the real world. When you ask a friend to perform a service for you, the response of the friend will depend on what kind of friend he or she is, but also on their current state (of mind, of health, of your relationship, etc).

In many ways, your own ability to keep track of the state of a computation defines your true ability as a programmer. Of course you cannot maintain every detail in your head. There is just too much of it. In fact, much of the detail is hidden from you anyway. In the robot world, much of it is intentionally hidden within the simulator that executes your programs. You don't know, or care, for example, how the simulator's author decided to implement walls and beepers as long as you can make accurate assumptions about their behavior as your code executes. But at a different level, you need to do this yourself. Once we have written a new class and implemented methods within that class we can mostly forget the details, unless we learn that there is an error in the program.

Even deeper, if we have created a hierarchy of classes and built polymorphism into our programs then objects of each of our classes can behave differently when sent a given message. Can we forget the details in this case? That depends, of course. If we have used good names for the class, objects, and methods then we have made a good start. More important, though, is keeping discipline in making the actual actions we program within a method true to the idea of the method and the class. If our *turnLeft* method is changed so that the robot turns right instead, then we won't be able to keep general, abstract, notions of the result of a message. We need to guarantee that whenever an object executes an action that it "does the right thing" from the standpoint of the client that sends the message. It means that when we define a hierarchy of classes we need to be true to some concept that makes sense in *our* world, so that our mental ability helps us understand our own work, rather than hindering us, and overloading us with detail. We will return to this idea in Section 9.2.1.

We have tried, in creating the robot programming world, to set a consistent metaphor in which you can think about things. Sometimes it is a bit awkward, perhaps (helicopter pilots), but we needed a way to help you get started thinking about how it works in a way that seemed to us to be natural and not misleading. For example, in the real world physical robots naturally move in parallel. But as we saw in Chapter 8, it is harder to do here, so the helicopter metaphor was set simply to lead you to begin to think naturally about how the program would behave when you execute it.

But you need to do exactly the same thing when you write a program so that your natural innate thinking ability makes it easy to reason about the state of your program and the sequence of state changes you call for in its execution. This means good names, consistent implementation of concepts in hierarchies, metaphors for your objects, etc. Humans are good at abstraction. It is how we deal with complexity overload. We are good at metaphor. It is how we deal with ambiguity. So we need to use these tools to build programs that we ourselves can understand.

It must be pointed out, if it isn't yet obvious to you, that the purpose of writing a computer program is communication. The primary target of communication is not the computer, however. The characteristics of computer languages are designed (usually somewhat poorly) so as to help people organize their own thoughts and communicate them to other people. Most computer programs are built in teams. Most are built for other people than their creators. So good communication is essential. But the primary target of this communication is you, the programmer, yourself. Every program notation and statement is a note to yourself to remind yourself of your intent when you wrote it. That is why naming and consistency are so important. Computers have certain abilities that humans do not, primarily the ability to organize vast quantities of low-level detail. But they cannot "think" in any sense. You have to do the thinking to organize the appropriate series of state changes that will solve your computing problems. To do this effectively, rely on your abilities of abstraction and metaphor.

### 9.1.1 Assertions

One of the things that we humans do is to make assertions about the state of the world. "My computing course is hard." "My computing course is fun." An assertion is simply a statement that may be true or false: a *predicate*, actually. But by making an assertion we are claiming that it is true, in fact. Perhaps you have noticed that you cannot ask a robot which street it is on, or how many beepers it has in its beeper bag. This was intentional because we wanted you to learn to program at a deeper level. It is possible, however, within the robot world, to make assertions about the state of a robot, even though you can't query the robot about the state. The assertion methods are not implemented in the robots, however, but in special objects called TestCases. Perhaps you have already come across these.

There is a class in the robot world called RobotTestCase, discussed in detail in Chapter 12, that permits you to make assertions about robots. This is mostly used with the Python *unittest* testing framework, by creating sub-classes of RobotTestCase and including test methods in your extension. But assertions can be used in other ways. An object of type RobotTestCase can make assertions about robots and about the world in which the robots operate. For example, if *aTest* is such an object, then

```
aTest.assertBeepersAt(5, 3);
```

is an assertion that there are one or more beepers in the world on fifth street and third avenue.

When an assertion "passes" (i.e. the statement of its truth is really true), nothing happens. The program that contains it just continues. But when it fails, it raises an Exception. You have almost certainly seen exceptions by now if you have been executing programs using the simulator. Among the common exceptions that you will see is *AttributeError*, raised when you try to send a message using a reference that has not been made to point to any object. If you include these robot assertions in your regular programs, though they are not intended to be used that way, then your program will terminate whenever any assertion fails. The exception will be AssertionError. However, if you use them in the unittest framework, then the error will be caught by that framework and you will be given messages about which assertion failed. unittest is discussed in detail in Chapter 12. We also note, for completeness, that Python has an *assert* statement that can be used, though it is less flexible than capturing such assertions in a class. Its discussion is also beyond the scope of this book.

However, even if you don't create executable assertions, it is good to get into the habit of making assertions about what you know to be true at each point in a program.

An example might help solidify the ideas here. Suppose we know that a robot has just executed the following instruction:

```
def mysteryInstruction(self):
    while self.frontIsClear():
        self.move()
        self.putBeeper()
    self.turnLeft()
```

We can then assert with confidence (provided that we know that the instructions here have not been overridden to do strange, unexpected, things, that the robot has a wall to its right and to its left there is a sequence of beepers, perhaps of length 0, extending back to the corner just after its initial corner. We cannot assert, however, that there is a beeper on the current corner, just from this. Actually, it is a bit more complicated than this. We made an assumption that the above was executed without error shutoff as could happen if the robot runs out of beepers in the middle of executing it. So it would have been better to say that we can make the above assertion provided that the instruction was executed successfully.

We can also sometimes chain assertions together. Suppose prior to executing the above that we had been able to assert successfully that (a) the robot was facing West, and (b) that there were no walls in the world other than the boundary walls. Then we could additionally assert after successful execution of the above, that the robot was facing South at the West boundary wall.

There are two situations in programming when making assertions about programs and chaining them together in this fashion is especially useful. The first is when you are given an unfamiliar program and asked to determine what it does. The assertions about the state help you understand what is going on from statement to statement as you simulate its execution. We did this, actually, back in Chapter 3, to see how to develop new instructions. The second situation in which this is a useful thing to do is when you discover an error in your program and want to fix it. Before you can intelligently repair it, you need to know where, and probably why, it is broken.

We continue the discussion of state in the next section and what we have said above about assertions, etc., applies there as well.

## 9.2 The Program Counter

When you simulate the execution of a program, you probably use your finger or a pencil to point to the current instruction that you are examining, or perhaps write down the instruction number if you have numbered each one. When a computer actually executes your program it does essentially the same thing.

A program (the *interpreter, or possibly a compiler*) on your computer translates your Python programs into a simpler form that is more difficult for humans to read easily, but is more suitable for computers, since the instructions are extremely simple. One robot program statement may translate into hundreds of "machine language" instructions, in fact. Some versions of Python use an intermediate form, called "byte codes," but they have much of the same characterization of this machine language: they are very simple and easy to execute for a machine that cannot think, but can only manipulate simple data using simple rules. Just as your program consists of a sequence of instructions, so does a machine language program, though the latter can be loaded into the memory of a computer, which you can think of as just a list of symbols encoded in numeric form. The important thing is that they are a *list* of symbols and so a single pointer, like your finger, can be used to tell where in the program is the next instruction to be executed. This place is called the *program counter,* since the value of it will normally advance by one position (counting) unless some logical instruction is executed to make it do otherwise (jump). But you can think of this very low level program counter as being just like what you do when you point at one instruction after another in tracing or simulating the execution of a program. We will look at the details of the pc and machine language in the Secondo Intermezzo.

The important concept of this section, however, is that knowing where the program counter is in a program gives you a lot of information about the state of a computation. Let's see an example or two. We will use our robot language here rather than try to go into the details of machine language, but the idea is exactly the same in each case, though the granularity is much finer in a machine language instruction: the individual machine language instruction does much less than the individual Python instruction. Suppose we examine the following fragment of code in which we have numbered the instructions:

```
1    gil.putBeeper()
2    if gil.frontIsClear():
3        gil.move()
     else:
4        gil.turnLeft()
5        gil.move()
```

Suppose that the program counter is at instruction number 3 and we are about to execute it. Then we can assert that gil is on a corner with a beeper and that its front is clear. However, if the program counter is at instruction 4 instead, then we can assert, instead, that gil's front is NOT clear, but that it is on a corner with a beeper.

In particular, note that when the program counter is within an IF or IF-ELSE statement that you have gained information depending on the test of that statement. You can think of this as "climbing Information Hill" since the level of information has increased. However, once you leave the IF structure you don't know anymore what the state is. The front could be blocked or clear. But the information is deeper than that. Recall that your program will only execute one clause of the IF statement. We write the THEN clause knowing that the front is clear (an assertion we can make) and the ELSE clause knowing that it is blocked. So the program has captured information, by executing the IF, that we make use of.

BUT, once we leave the IF statement, we not only don't know what the state is then, we no longer know what the state was previously, while the program was in the middle of the IF statement somewhere. We have lost the information that we had captured in the IF. We have "fallen down Information Hill." We will return to this idea in a moment.

If we have complex program structure, as was examined in Sections 5.5, 5.6, and 6.5, for example, we gain information as we move deeper into the structures. If we are in the THEN clause of an IF that itself was in the THEN clause of another IF, we know what both of the tests are true unless we have executed an instruction along the way that invalidated one or both of them. However, because of the nature of our thinking processes, it can get harder for us to remember what that information is. This is why we recommended earlier that deep nesting of structures not be employed in your programs.

One useful technique that is often employed successfully is this. Suppose you execute an IF statement and learn something in the process. Even more generally suppose you learn something in any way whatever about the execution of your program, just because you know what happened up to the point of the program counter. Suppose you need to know later in the program what was true back at this earlier moment and act on that knowledge at that later time. One way to do all of this is to create a new object that captures both the knowledge of what occurred at the early point as well as the behavior that will be appropriate later.

Here is an example of this that comes from a program outside the robot programming world. We are going to be moving outside the world of robots gradually in any case. Suppose you want to create a Dungeon Game that consists of Player objects, Place objects, and Thing objects. The players move through the places and may find, and carry things that they employ. One useful Thing is a transporter. The behavior of a transporter is as follows. If a player finds it somewhere the player may pick it up and carry it about. The first time that the transporter is "activated" it remembers the place in which the activation occurs. Then later, whenever it is "activated" again, it immediately transports the player back to the place in which it was first activated.

The transporter needs to remember if it has been activated or not. On the first activation, the program gains information and we don't want to lose it. In particular we climbed *Information Hill* to learn that it had been activated, and we don't want to fall down the other side and have to climb it again to regain the information we had earlier. Objects, especially Strategy objects, are very good at this. Suppose the transporter is given a *remember* strategy when it is created. The activation of the transporter is then delegated to the strategy object. The initial strategy, when executed, does two things. It tells the transporter to remember this place and it also tells the transporter to replace the "current" strategy (this initial strategy) with another: a *transport* strategy. This new strategy will then automatically be the one delegated to by the transporter if the transporter is again activated.

And what does this other strategy do? It causes the player carrying the transporter to go immediately back to the place that is being remembered by the transporter. Thus the information that the transporter was initially activated is captured in the second strategy object and is then itself executed when called for later in the program. In this way, knowledge gained at the site of the program counter can be preserved for later use.

Note that the two strategy objects capture different kinds of information. The first captures the fact that the transporter has NOT been activated and the second that it HAS. But the strategies also capture different behaviors. The first captures what to do if the transporter has not been previously activated, and the second the appropriate behavior if it has been.

When used this way, the strategy object can be though of as a *flag*. In American football, when a violation of the rules occurs, the referee will throw up a piece of cloth (the flag) to indicate the infraction. The play is usually allowed to continue, but the presence of the flag is an indication when it ends that the violation occurred. (Similar things occur in European Football (soccer) though play is normally stopped immediately.) The players can see the flag and know that something out of the normal order of play will happen. But here in our Dungeon Game, the flag itself also carries not just the information that something occurred, but also what must be done in the program later because of it. The behavior. Our flags have behavior. It is as if the referee had a whole bunch of flags, each with instructions about how to proceed after the infraction and was careful to throw the correct one when the infraction first occurred. That would be unwieldy in our world, but it is very useful in the computer world. That is because the referee is a thinking being and won't have to "climb Information Hill" to recover the knowledge of the nature of the rule breaking, but the computer, needs to record it specifically or else recreate it. But if we need to record a bit of information (the transporter was activated) we might as well record more (what to do).

From the standpoint of the strategy objects, each just implements its *doIt* method differently. So each is very simple. At the point at which the transporter is activated the transporter just sends the doIt message to whichever strategy it happens to have current at that moment, so the transporter is very simple as well. But we get polymorphic behavior just by having captured the information that was known at the point of the program counter.

### 9.3 Explicit State (Introduction)

Programs employ a third kind of state, and we have done this already, though sparingly. For example, a Choreographer kept references to the other robots it was directing. Likewise an Adder robot (Section 7.6) knew some helper robots and could send messages to them. Our most sophisticated use, however, has been Strategies. A Spy robot kept changing strategies as it moved through the world. The current strategy that it carries is part of its state. What it does depends on what kind of object it is (Spy) and also on its current state (the strategy it knows about). We have been able to do a great deal without depending too much on such explicit state, and now we will be able to do a bit more using it. It will make some of the things we have done much easier, in fact. Explicit state wasn't introduced earlier so as not to get in the way of your learning of important techniques that might have been masked by these new ideas.

*Instance variables,* sometimes called *fields,* were introduced in Section 4.1.2. We saw there that an object of the Organizer class could maintain references to other objects whose actions it directed. In our case the organizer had three fields, one for each assistant robot. So creating an organizer actually creates three robots. But note that if we create two organizers we actually create six robots. Each of the organizers knows its assistants by the names karel, matt, and kristen, by the way. Since the assistants were created within the choreographer object itself, we were using the *composition* technique to build an organizer: An organizer *has* three assistants. The assistants are not supposed to be used outside the organizer. Only the organizer can. (Actually, since the names of the assistants didn't start with underscores, they actually can be referenced elsewhere. Adjusting those names would improve the encapsulation.)

The situation was a bit different, though, with the StrategyLayer class in Section 4.6. There the initial strategy was given in the constructor invocation when we created a new NullStrategy. Therefore, whatever code creates a StrategyLayer has access to the strategy that it used to create the new StrategyLayer and so can use that strategy itself, perhaps giving the same strategy object to different StrageyLayers. The StrategyLayer, then, doesn't *own* the strategy itself, though it uses it: *delegates* actions to it.

We are used to composition and delegation in the real world also. An automobile *has* pistons. It is built by composition of parts. A person *uses* the services of a doctor to recover from injury or illness. It delegates actions to the doctor. Composition and delegation are two of the most important techniques of the object-oriented programmer, and both are recognized by the presence of fields within the object. The difference between them is a bit more subtle, however and depends at least somewhat about how you think about your program, not just the code you write. It is pretty clear in a few situations, though. If one object, a Choreographer, say, creates an assistant and the program doesn't permit any other code to send messages to that assistant, then it is pretty clearly composition. But if other code can send messages, it may be delegation instead.

But how could other code access the fields within the organizer if the organizer creates them and makes them "private"? One way would be for the organizer to have a method that returns a reference to one or the other of the assistants:

```
def firstAssistant(self):
     return self._kristin
```

That would be poor idea here, since then the organizer or a choreographer couldn't really determine what happens with this assistant. Other code could direct it as well. It is as if the audience at a ballet could shout out instructions to the dancers on the stage and have them followed. It might be interesting to see, but the idea of a choreographer would be broken in this situation.

Encapsulation is the process of guaranteeing that things that should be private are really kept private. The purpose of encapsulation is to let the programmer guarantee that the object (choreographer, say) really can behave according to its specification. In particular it permits the programmer to guarantee invariant properties of the objects created. Here the invariant is that the assistants maintain the same locations and directions as the choreographer, relative to initial locations and positions. If we add the above method, we can no longer make such a guarantee.

Python actually has no way to make things truly private. We indicate, to a reader or user that a field or method is private by using underscore prefixes in a name such as _kristin. One underscore indicates that the name should be used only within objects of the same class. Two underscores indicate the name should only be used within a single object and not shared with other objects even of the same class. However, this is only a convention; unenforced.

There is another, also very important, reason for encapsulation. When you try to reason about a program you have a difficult task as it has so many parts. Encapsulation lets you consider the program piece by piece. As you move to bigger pieces, made up of smaller ones, you can ignore the details of the smaller pieces. For example, when you are driving an automobile, you can ignore the fact that it has pistons. Whether it has six or eight doesn't affect how you drive. At a lower level, repairing the car, it may matter, but you have specifically chosen, then, to look at this lower level. Suppose you needed to keep track of all the details of all the parts of an automobile just to drive it: whether each piston was on the up or the down-stroke, for example. We would find the task impossible. The same is true in programming and especially in reasoning about our programs. Therefore we encapsulate our objects and hide as much information as possible from the rest of our program about the inner workings of each object. Said another way, we give each object responsibility for its own inner workings and we specify these by thinking about their invariant properties as well as their variant properties (how they can change).

The StrategyLayer class has another property that is worth thinking about. Not only could we set its initial strategy in the constructor, it also has a *setStrategy* method by which any code with a reference to a StrategyLayer can change its strategy. We say that the StrategyLayer object is *mutable*: can be changed. We say that the setStrategy method is a *mutator* method for these objects. Thus, another object can change the state of a StrategyLayer by sending this message. So, even though the myStrategy field of a StrategyLayer is "private", the object still isn't very well encapsulated. Therefore, encapsulation is about more than just making your fields private, though you should do that in nearly every situation. (The few cases in which you should use some other *visibility* marker for fields are outside the scope of this book.)

But since a StrategyLayer is not well encapsulated, it will be difficult to create invariant properties for it, and therefore to make assertions about its state without considering larger sections of the program than the class itself. This complicates our reasoning process, especially in the presence of errors in the program. By way of contrast, consider the situation of the BlockWalker in the same section. There, the current strategy was also changeable, but all changes were handled internally. The *walkASide* method, which is also a *mutator* for the __strategy and __otherStrategy fields, does that swap without external prodding, therefore is only be invoked from within the objects of the class themselves. So a BlockWalker object can change its own strategy, but other code cannot.

Actually, in Python, the enforcement of encapsulation is weak compared to some other languages (Java). This capability of peeking into the implementation of an object and changing it complicates our reasoning about our programs if we take advantage of this flexibility. Notice, then, that flexibility in a programming language often leads to complications in its use. While it may be easier to do some things with the added flexibility it may be harder to reason about the effect, and it is this ability to reason about your programs that is your most powerful programming tool.

## 9.4 Primitive Data

In most object-oriented languages (Python, Eiffel, Ruby, and Smalltalk are the main exceptions) not everything is an object. The language also defines more primitive things that can't be extended or receive messages, though they are encapsulated. Normally they can be manipulated in various ways, but using syntax other than message passing, since they have no methods. Even in the robot world, we have walls, which are not objects. They don't have behavior and they can't be manipulated, though the World can place and remove them. Python contains several different types of primitive data, many of which are numeric in nature. We have already used *bool* values of course and our predicates return them and our IF and WHILE statements depend on booleans. The primitives types each form a *data type*. Technically, everything in Python is an object. Execute the command *help(5)* to see how complex things are.

A data type is a set of values, a set of operations on the values, and a set of rules that define how the operations behave. For example, the boolean data type of Python consists of the set { True, False }. The operators are (among others) &&, | | and !. The rules are given by the normal rules of logic (with short-circuit operations, of course).

One major distinction in Python is that values of some types are mutable and others are immutable. An int is immutable as is a String (str type). But lists, which we will see soon are mutable: you can add values to a list.

Many primitives of Python are numeric and they are similar to numbers in arithmetic, though with some differences.

The simplest numeric data type of Python is *int*, and we have used it already, for initialization of the street and avenue of a robot when it is created, for example. Our constructors have all depended on the fact that the first parameter of the constructor has type int. The values of the integers of mathematics are infinite in extent, both in the positive and the negative directions of the number line. That is the first major difference with numbers in (nearly all) computer languages. In most languages the built in types form a finite range of values. In Java, an int is between the value $-2^{31}$ and $+2^{31} - 1$. This gives exactly $2^{32}$ different values (a little bit over 4 billion values), which implies that an integer can be represented in 32 *bits* (base 2 digits) or four bytes, as a byte is 8 bits. The language Python 3 (version 3) doesn't define a maximum or minimum int, so arbitrary integer values can be used. But a computer is still a finite machine, so there are implied limits.

Note that values in Python have a defined type. For example 42 is int and 4.2 is float. However, variables in Python are not associated with a type and so can refer at different times to values of various types. This is called "dynamic typing", as opposed to the "static typing" of Java and other languages. This makes Python more flexible, but, again, leads to the issue that too much flexibility can, when used, lead to confusion.

You can assign an int to a variable variable in Python with something like

```
size = 100
```

This sets up an association between the name "size" and the int value. Note that size is just a name that refers to an int. Reassigning it doesn't change 100, but makes size refer to a different int. This is universally true in Python: variables like size are references to values. The *values* might be mutable or not.

Note that such variables can vary (hence the name *variable*). At a given instant of execution, however, a variable is associated with a single value. At the next instant, it could be changed by the programmer's code. But objects *use* variables to remember things.

Suppose we have two variables with some values assigned:

```
x = 100
y = 200
```

Then, if we say

```
x = y
```

the reference to x will be to 200, the same as y. But it doesn't create a "new 200". It only makes a change in the reference. This is also true universally in Python and will be important when we use more complicated types as values: the second statement of

```
name = 'Monty'
name = 'Karel'
other = name
```

wont change the string 'Monty'. It will just make the variable *name* point elsewhere. And the final statement above won't create a new string, just make *other* refer to the same string that *name* does.

Changing an int variable by incrementing it (giving it a value larger than the value it currently has), which you can write

```
size = size + 3
```

is very common. So common, in fact that there is a shorthand for it:

```
size += 3
```

In either case the value *size* + *3* is computed and the variable size is then given this new value. Think of a variable as an association between a name and a value. You do this. Your name may be Mary, but YOU are not Mary. Mary is just a name (identifier) that people use to designate you. You are YOU. There is an association between the word Mary and the person you. Note that the name can actually refer to different people at different times and in different contexts. There are lots of "Marys" in the world. The same is true of variables. We have seen this before with reference variables that refer to robots. All variables have this property. A variable is associated with a single value at any time, but it can be changed.

You can, in fact change the value of size to 4.12 if you like. The value has float type and so the variable refers to a value of float type, but the variable itself has no type.

Conversely, several variables can denote or be associated with the same value, and at the same time in this case. You could also have the name "dear," as your parents might denote you. Multiple names for the same value. The same is true with variables in Python and most computer languages as well. Associations size = 6; and age = 6; can be simultaneously in effect. Likewise different reference variables can refer to the same objects simultaneously, as we have seen before.

Python has a number of binary operators that work on numeric values. They don't require that the values have the same types, but discipline in their use will make some things easier.

```
x + y # sum of x and y

x * y # product

x - y # difference

x ** y # exponentiation x^y

x % y # remainder when x is divided by y: modulus 11 % 3 is 2

x // y # integer quotient: 8 // 5 is 1
```

The appendix has a list of Python operators.

So far the only variables we have used (Monty Karel) are references to robots and strategies as fields of our classes. We can actually use any types that we like.

For example, a robot could be made to remember the location at which it was delivered to the world, like this:

```
class Rememberer(UrRobot):
    def __init__(self, street, avenue, direction, beepers):
        UrRobot.__init__(self, street, avenue, direction, beepers)
        self.__initialStreet = street
        self.__initialAvenue = avenue
```

We made the instance variables private since we don't want other parts of the program to ever change them. Of course, we would want to take advantage of this new knowledge. Such a class could provide an *accessor* for the information. For example:

```
def initialStreet(self):
   return self.__initialStreet
```

Then a client of this code could know where the robot was created. Note that we can have both fields (instance variables) and methods with the same name. Python has no trouble with this, and it lets us associate a single name with a concept, which can be very helpful.

## 9.5 Making Use of Arithmetic on int Values

What we say here will also apply to other numeric values, actually, but we will use int as a sort of standard primitive value. Later we shall see some primitives with very different characteristics, though.

Lets suppose for a while that we are putting robots into a world without walls other than the boundary walls. Having created a robot somewhere, we can make it move to the origin by having it execute the following sequence of instructions. Note that we shall assume a few simple instructions exist in the class of this robot. We have built these in the past, so it won't be difficult to provide them if you want to execute this code.

```
self.faceWest()
while self.frontIsClear()
   self.move()
self.turnLeft()
while self.frontIsClear()
   self.move()
```

Let's illustrate simple arithmetic with robots, though we will use a technique that is too simple for general use since it will only work once for a given robot.

Suppose we have the Rememberer class from the previous section, but we also give it two additional fields:

```
__westDistanceWalked = 0
__southDistanceWalked = 0
```

The intention is that the robot will record the distance it walks toward the west in the first of these and the distance it walks toward the south in the other.

We can take advantage of these by overriding the move method of this class as follows:

```
def move(self):
    if self.facingWest():
        self.__westDistanceWalked += 1
    elif self.facingSouth():
            self.__southDistanceWalked += 1
    super().move()
```

Then, every time the robot steps west, it increments that variable. We will ignore here the problem of what gets recorded if there is an error shutoff, but you can think about that on your own.

Given this framework, we can have the robot go to the origin (but only once) with this instruction:

```
def goToOrigin(self):
    self.faceWest()
    while self.__initialAvenue-self.__westDistanceWalked > 1:
        self.move()
    self.turnLeft()
    while self.__initialStreet-self.__southDistanceWalked > 1:
        self.move()
```

Note that the overall structure is like what we have done before, but instead of using external sensors (frontIsClear()), the robot uses internal counters. It depends on the fact that when it is created its current corner is (initialStreet, initialAvenue). The reason it only works once (and even then, only if it hasn't moved previously) is that the current corner changes and this only works from the initial corner. Still, it illustrates the counting principle. The westDistanceWalked is initially zero. Each time the robot walks toward the west this is incremented by one. The expression `initialAvenue-westDistanceWalked` is its current avenue number and when this reaches 1 (first avenue) we must stop.

You may like to know that hidden inside the Python Karel simulator that you have probably been using, there is a more sophisticated version of the above so that the program can keep track of where all the robots are as the execution of your program progresses. (Execute *help(robota)* to see what features are basic to robots.)

Of course it is possible to make errors in this sort of programming as in any other. Suppose we replace the > (greater than) operator with >= (greater than or equal to)? The program will break and the robot will experience an error shutoff. An error in counting in which the result differs by one from the desired result is called an *off by one error*. It is very common in programming. The same thing happens when you use the wrong stopping condition in a FOR-LOOP.

Note the six numeric binary comparison operators (==, !=, <, <=, >, and >=) require numeric arguments[1] and produce boolean results. Python is pretty forgiving, actually, if you use numeric arguments of different types in these operators. You can add an int and a float (getting a float). You can compare a float and an int, etc. This is not the case in all computer languages, however, so be careful as you move on.

Not everything you can do has so little value, however. You can give a robot a method that will ask it to move any distance you like, rather than just one block. Here we use two additional features of Python, int valued parameters and int valued *local variables* within a method. Each of these has a lifetime only that of a single message execution. Fields (instance variables) on the other hand, live as long as the object does.

```
def moveMany(self, howMany):
    for corner in range(howMany):
        self.move()
```

Note that we need a different name, *moveMany*, so Python won't confuse it with the UrRobot *move* instruction. Here *howMany* is a parameter to the instruction and *count* is a local variable managed by the FOR statement and count is only visible within the FOR statement, not even throughout the method.

If *jonny* is a robot of this type, then `jonny.moveMany(8)` is like our earlier *moveMile* instruction. But be careful with such instructions. If you try to execute them when there are walls in front of the robot you are subject to error shutoff.

We can turn this idea around also. Suppose a robot named *paat* is facing west and we want to know how many steps paat is from the first wall it is facing, perhaps the boundary wall. Then patt can execute this functional method:

[1] Actually == and != can be used with any arguments of the same type, but we only focus on numeric uses here.

```
def howManySteps(self):
    result = 0
    while self.frontIsClear():
        self.move()
        result+=1
    return result
```

This sort of loop is called a counting loop. Note that since you have the count, it isn't hard to make the robot return to its original location if that is required as well. There is a flaw in the name of this method, however, since the name gives no indication that the robot moves. It is both a mutator and an accessor, though it only accesses local data. If you want a pure accessor, it is possible, in this case, to undo the robot moves, returning it to its initial situation:

```
def howManySteps(self):
    result = 0
    while self.frontIsClear():
        self.move()
        result+=1
    self.turnLeft() # undo the walk
    self.turnLeft()
    for count in range(result):
        self.move()
    self.turnLeft()
    self.turnLeft()
    return result
```

Here we use the value computed to get back to the original position.

## 9.6 A Program Using Numeric Data and Built by Composition

In this section we will see the core of an implementation of a simple calculator. The program will be both simple and sophisticated. It will, however, not involve robots at all, so this is our first attempt to build a program not in the robot world. It won't even be graphical. There is a reason for this that you should understand. When you build a sophisticated program it is important to divide it up into independent parts as much as possible. This lets you focus your attention at any time on a more limited number of concerns. In particular, programs that *are* graphical should have a clean separation between the graphical part and the underlying algorithms that do the work. You have been doing this all along, actually, since the authors provided the graphical parts of the robot world in the simulator without regard to the algorithms you would write, and you wrote algorithms for this world without concern about how the graphics is implemented. The underlying algorithmic part of an application is called the *model*, and the graphical part is the *view*. Another reason for the separation is that a given model can have multiple views. If you have ever used a spreadsheet program, be aware that the normal rows and columns view, is just that, a view. There is an underlying, but invisible, set of structures of data as well as algorithms. If you have seen a graph of a set of cells in a spreadsheet, then that is just another view, but the model isn't changed in any way to show this view.

Here we shall build just the model and shall do it in stages. The calculator will have only integer (int) data. It will have only a few keys, and will have a general algebraic structure, though we won't worry about the precedence of operators here. Such calculators used to be sold for a few dollars, but are now likely obsolete as more sophisticated ones can be manufactured for the same money as this simple model we shall build.

To get started, our goal is to make a sequence of key "presses" like "5 5 + 3 =" produce a 58 for the result at the end. Initially we will build only the four keys needed for this, but others can be added easily once we work out the details. In Chapter 12 we will see a set of steps that might have led to this design. It was not, however, developed in the order it is presented here.

### 9.6.1 A Calculator Model with a Display

The very first thing we want to do is: Create a Calculator that will give you its display. *A new calculator should have a display of 0.*

If we want to test this as we go we have some options. Here we will just build a main function somewhere that will exercise the calculator. So the above says that if we write the following main and execute it, we should see a 0.

```
if __name__ == '__main__' :
    calculator = CalculatorModel()
    print ("The display is: ", calculator.getDisplay())
```

Our basic framework then is a class called CalculatorModel and it needs at least a *getDisplay* method and an instance variable to remember the current display.

```
class CalculatorModel():
    def __init__(self):
        self._display = 0

    def getDisplay(self):
        return self._display
```

We don't need any imports here. We called the class *CalculatorModel* to emphasize that it is just the model. If we give it a graphical part later we can call that part the *Calculator*. The display field is an int and is (pseudo) private. We have a method to retrieve the value of this variable. A bit of explanation of this print method is in order.

The Python print function is very versatile. It can print some representation of just about anything, including some complex data structures. Technically, it prints strings, but it is clever enough to convert most things to some human readable string. (For user-defined classes this will require implementing a special method, though.) It will take multiple comma-separated arguments of different types and produce a string representation of them one after another.

In our getDisplay method

```
def getDisplay(self):
   return self._display
```

the returned value is the current value of _display, which is still 0 if nothing else has changed it.

We create instance variables for a class by defining them in the __init__ method of that class. Then, each CalculatorModel object we create will have its own *_display* variable.

Suppose our main is:

```
if __name__ == '__main__' :
    calculator = CalculatorModel()
    value = calculator.getDisplay()
    print ("The display is: ", value)
```

Then, when we run the program the output will be

```
The display is: 0
```

### 9.6.2 Numeric Keys

Next we want to achieve this: *Give the calculator keys like 5 and 3. When you hit a single key the value of the key should "show" in the display.*

So far what we have done has been extremely simple. There is only one class and one object. However, we said we wanted to do this using composition so now we will start to build some objects. Actually the display itself could have been an object rather than an int, but it seems a little simple for that. Objects have behavior and the display has none yet. Later, perhaps we will decide to change the code (*refactor* is the technical term) and make an object of it also. We are going to build parts of the calculator. These parts will be objects, therefore defined by classes. These parts will be internal to the calculator itself. Therefore the classes that define the parts will also be inside the CalculatorModel class. We discussed inner classes briefly in the exercises of Chapter 4 and here we need them extensively.

First let's note that we shall have several kinds of keys and the action we want to do to all of them is to press them. Therefore lets start out by building a unifying framework for keys using a concept called an *interface*. We will define this inside the CalculatorModel class as a private inner class. The name, beginning with two underscores indicates that this class is private to its containing class.

```
class __calculatorKey: # an interface
    def press(self):
        pass
```

Here the press method does nothing. We can make the "requirement" to implement much stronger if we raise an exception for such "abstract" methods:

```
def press(self):
    raise NotImplementedError("press not yet implemented.")
```

Making it private means that having a reference to a CalculatorModel instance gives us no direct outside access to this. Had it been public, say, calculatorKey, then the class CalculatorModel.calculatorKey would be visible throughout the program. This way it is just an implementation detail for building calculators, like the design of a piston in an automobile.

Next we need a class that we can use to define the number keys like 3 and 5. Here we can use one class and give its constructor a value saying which value we want the key to have. The key will remember this value.

However, objects of this class will need to actually modify fields like _display of the model they are attached to. This isn't automatic in Python, so we need to create each key with a reference to the CalculatorModel it will manipulate.

```
class __NumberKey(__calculatorKey):
    def __init__(self, value, model):
        self.__value = value
        self.__model = model

    def press(self):    #Temporary version
        self.__model._display = self.__value
```

As usual the fields of these objects (*__value*) are private. We implement the CalculatorKey interface here so we need to include the press method. The implementation we have given of this method is very naïve, however and will be updated as we proceed.

There is an important caveat here. "interfaces" are not a Python concept and they aren't actually needed here. If we hadn't written the __calculatorKey class and included it here as a superclass the program would still be fine and would operate just as with what we are going to do. It is purely a way for a programmer to make a formal notation of what is required in an implementation. We shall have several different kinds of keys for this calculator and __calculatorKey is just a unifying concept.

If we had defined the press method of the __calculatorModel class to throw an exception instead of just being empty (*pass*) then we would be forced to build a new implementation here or the exception would probably occur if we forgot.

If we create a five key and a three key as fields of the CalculatorModel in its constructor as usual:

```
def __init__(self):
    self._display = 0
    self._three = self.__NumberKey(3, self)
    self._five = self.__NumberKey(5, self)
```

Note that we also pass the new object a reference to self, the CalculatorModel object.

We are trying to build up a consistent metaphor here. We want the result to somehow "feel" like holding a physical calculator in your hands and using it. We want this to be true both of an eventual user of the program, but also to guide it's development, helping us keep our concepts clear.

Then pressing the five key (*five.press()*) will change the display to 5, but following this with a *three.press()* will change the display to 3, not 53. Still it is all the above "development story" called for, so let's delay the more sophisticated thing for a bit.

Note that the NumberKey objects have no methods to change their state. So, the key that produces 5 will always do so.

But, since the keys themselves are private, code that "sees" a calculator still needs to have some way to get these keys pressed. We can provide methods of the CalculatorModel itself for this:

```
    def pressThree(self):
        self._three.press()

    def pressFive(self):
        self._five.press()
```

Since we have developed this in pieces, perhaps it would be good to see it all together.

```
class CalculatorModel:

    def getDisplay(self):
        return self._display

    def pressThree(self):
        self._three.press()

    def pressFive(self):
        self._five.press()

    class __calculatorKey: # an interface
        def press(self):
            pass

    class __NumberKey(__calculatorKey):
        def __init__(self, value, model):
            self.__value = value
            self.__model = model

        def press(self):   #Temporary version
            self.__model._display = self.__value

    def __init__(self):
        self._display = 0
        self._three = self.__NumberKey(3, self)
        self._five = self.__NumberKey(5, self)
```

Now let's update main a bit:

```
if __name__ == '__main__' :
    calculator = CalculatorModel()
    print(calculator.getDisplay())
    calculator.pressThree()
    print(calculator.getDisplay())
    calculator.pressFive()
    print(calculator.getDisplay())
```

This will show 0, 3, and 5 on separate lines, of course.

We might even add Python assertions to the above main:

```
if __name__ == '__main__' :
    calculator = CalculatorModel()
    print(calculator.getDisplay())
    assert 0 == calculator.getDisplay()
etc.
```

#### 9.6.3 Accumulation

Next we want the numeric keys to behave better: If you press a sequence of number keys, the results should accumulate in the display. A 5 followed by a 3 should display 53.

When we enter digits into a calculator we enter them from the right end of the accumulating value. When we press the 5 key, 5 becomes the rightmost digit. When we then press 3, the 5 moves to the left and the 3 becomes rightmost. But shifting a value to the left, in numeric base 10, is the same as multiplying by 10. So if we multiply the current display by 10 it will shift left, permitting us to simply add the new digit, which is one of 0…9 and so only occupies one "space" in the value. Thus we can change (refactor) the press method for the NumberKey class, which now becomes:

```
    class __NumberKey(__calculatorKey):
        def __init__(self, value, model):
            self.__value = value
            self.__model = model
```

```
def press(self):    #Temporary version 2
    model._display = self.__model._display*10 + self.__value
```

The first statement in press defines a local variable (local to the method) that makes the second statement easier to read. The variable *model* here is a reference to the CalculatorModel and therefore to its _display field. It works because self.__model is an object. But the following version, simpler to read, wont work because _display isn't an object, just an int:

```
def press(self):    #won't work
    display = self.__model._display
    display = display * 10 + self.__value
```

So, it is only the local variable being updated, not the _display of the model.

Notice that in a numeric assignment like this, we evaluate the right side first, before we can do the actual assignment. So we take the current value of display, multiply it by 10, thereby shifting it to the left, and then adding the value of this key. If the display was previously 52 and this is the 3 key, the value should now be 523 = 52 * 10 + 3.

Let's back up a bit and think about our design. Note that we are capturing the numeric keys as objects and it is up to us to decide how many of them to create. We can therefore assure that we create keys for numbers 0…9, but no others. On the other hand, if we had instead just given the CalculatorModel a pressNumber method with an int parameter such as this:

```
def pressNumber(value):
    ...
```

then it would be more difficult to guarantee that the value is a legal digit, though we could certainly do this with an IF structure. But eventually someone would possibly try pressNumber(10) even though there is no 10 key on a calculator. We have made that impossible with this design, though at a cost of requiring many methods, one for each key to be pressed.

With the above change, the *main* of the previous sub-section will now produce, 0, 5, 53 on successive lines of the output since we show the display after each key press. Like counting, this process of accumulation is very common in computing. It simply means that a value is changed, usually repeatedly by somehow using its old value to help compute its new value. Counting is a special case of accumulation, of course as we just modify the old value by adding one each time we *accumulate*. Another common form of accumulation is to repeatedly add a series of numeric values to a current value as the new ones become available using some process, such as pressing keys in a graphical interface or reading in values from the keyboard (which we have not seen yet here). For example if we execute:

```
currentValue = 0
```

once and then repeatedly execute:

```
currentValue = currentValue + newValue
```

as the newValue values become available, then currentValue will hold the sum of all of the values that have been obtained. Perhaps this latter *accumulation* step appears in a WHILE structure.

#### 9.6.4 Operators

Next, let's add an operator key: *Give the calculator a + key that adds the results of two operands. Other operator keys will be added later (-, *, /). Sum isn't done till you hit equals, though.*

Note that when you press the + key there is only one value (operand), but addition is a binary operation. So we need to also accumulate the second operand and then perform the addition later, when we press the = key. This means that we will need to save the current value we have been accumulating, of course. Another small detail is that pressing + doesn't clear the display. You can still "see" the accumulated value. It isn't until you press another number key that the display seems to change its behavior. Therefore pressing a numeric key has two different possible behaviors, depending on what has recently happened. If we just hit a numeric key, keep accumulating. If we just pressed an operator, start over on a new value. This is a perfect place for strategies and pressing the = key is a perfect place to switch from one strategy, accumulating, to the other, saving. Before we write these strategies, however, it might be good to look at the transitions that can occur in the internal state of the calculator as the user presses keys. Figure 9.1 is a simplified *state transition diagram* that shows what we have discovered up to now.

The calculator starts out in the Accumulate "state," and as long as we keep seeing digit keys pressed, it stays in that state. The strategy in effect is also an instance of __AccumulateStrategy. However, once we see an operator key, such as + we go to the Save state and get a new Strategy. But if in that state another digit appears, we go back to accumulating, but for the second value. Later, when the "user" presses the = key we perform the operation of the operator key. Thus we need to save that operation somehow. We will have strategies to represent both the accumulate state and the save state, as we shall see.

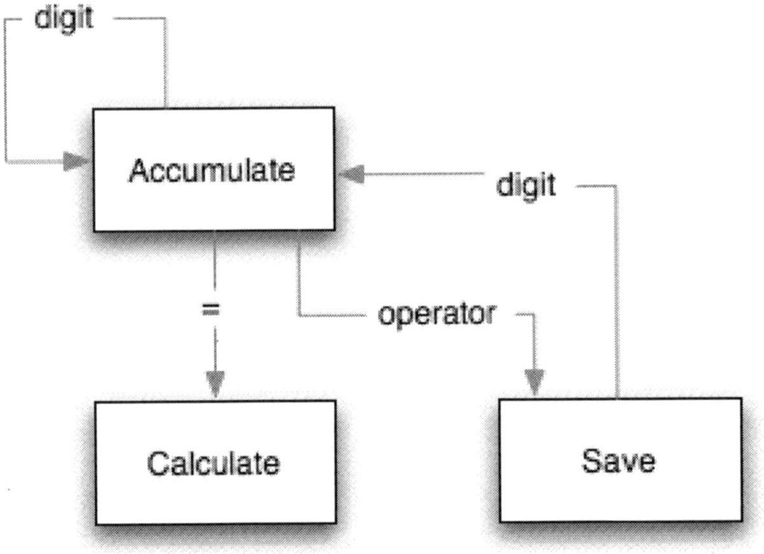


Figure 9.1. State Transition Diagram (simple version)

To get started building this we need to define the NumberStrategy "interface" that gives the framework of our strategies. The number keys will delegate the press method to one of these each time.

The actual transitions will follow a logic that we can show with a flowchart. We won't implement strictly according to the following design, but the pictures give a sense of the sorts of things that need to happen when each key is pushed.

First, pushing a number key like the five key has the following structure:

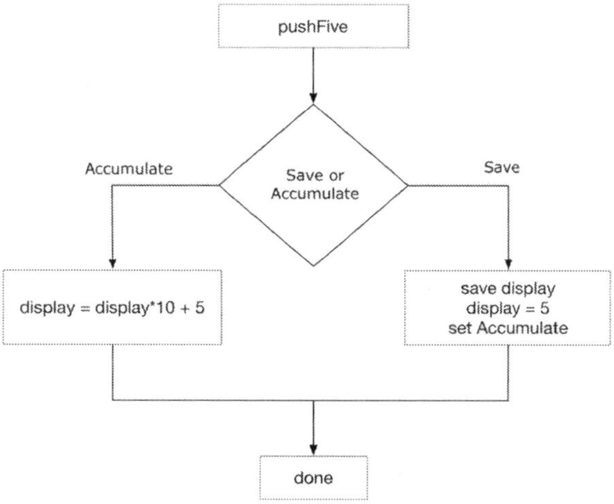


Figure 9.2

Depending on the state, as represented in the diamond, we do one of two things: accumulate into the display or save the display and start a new value. These "decision" points are often handled by IF statements, but we shall use strategies instead. In effect, the strategy objects, defined below capture the essence of the individual actions and rather than using bool values to decide which path to take, we will just execute the current strategy. In effect the strategy captures everything in the above diagram except the top and bottom boxes. The picture is just a description of what happens, not a design tool.

When we push the plus key or the equals key we get the associated behavior below.

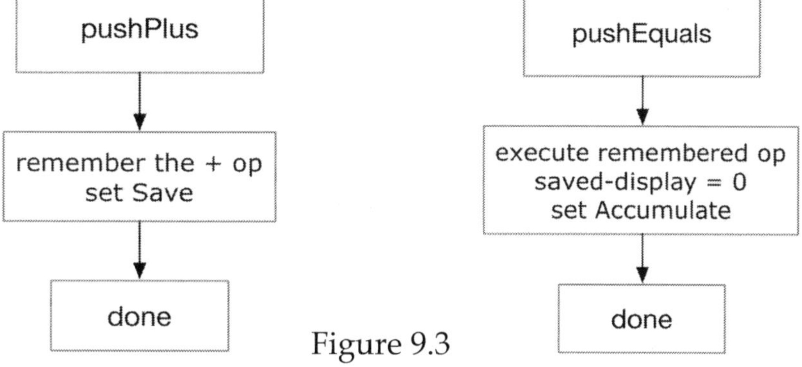


Figure 9.3

And, we set Save or set Accumulate by assigning an appropriate object to the current strategy.

We will, again, set protocols with a special interface class:

```
class __numberStrategy: # an interface
    def execute(self, value):
        raise NotImplementedError("execute not yet implemented.")
```

And here we do raise an exception to guarantee that subclasses implement it. The __AccumulateStrategy must implement this interface:

```
class __AccumulateStrategy(__numberStrategy):
    def __init__(self, model):
        self.__model = model

    def execute(self, value):
        model = self.__model
        model._display = model._display*10 + value
```

Next we need to create one of these and connect the NumberKeys to it. Note that this class defines objects without any state other than the model they are part of. There are no other fields and the only data they use is in a parameter to the execute method. Therefore we never need more than one of them. So we will let the CalculatorModel create one of these and we will use it as needed. On the other hand, we need to switch strategies as we discovered above. Therefore we also need a *current strategy* field in the CalculatorModel that knows which strategy the keys of the model are using at that instant. So, the __init__ method of CalculatorModel becomes:

```
def __init__(self):
    self._display = 0
    self._savedValue = 0 #see below for use
    self._accumulate = self.__AccumulateStrategy(self)
    self._currentNumberStrategy = self._accumulate
```

Then we need to change the press method of __NumberKey so that it delegates to the current strategy. We repeat the entire class definition, since it is short:

```
class __NumberKey(__calculatorKey):
    def __init__(self, value, model):
        self.__value = value
        self.__model = model

    def press(self):
        self.__model._currentNumberStrategy.execute(self.__value)
```

Note that so far we have changed no behavior, but just refactored the code: it has the same behavior, but a different structure. If you run it at this time it will produce exactly the same results as before as well as having the same limitations.

Now we need to see the operator keys, like + and the new strategy that will be substituted for the accumulate strategy when we push +.

Next, let's note, again, that the actual operation of the + key will be delayed until we later press the = key. Since we can't execute it immediately we need to capture the operation somehow. The operator key itself seems like the best place to capture this, since with different operators we can capture the explicit operation of each right there. Suppose, then, that we create a subclass of __calculatorKey to add another method. We won't modify the _calculatorKey class, since NumberKeys don't need the new operation but operator keys need both press and operate.

```
class __operatorKey(__calculatorKey): # partial implementation

    def operate(self):
        raise NotImplementedError("operate not yet implemented.")
```

Then the plus key can implement this interface. Note that an interface *extends* another, not *implements* in Python. The __PlusKey class will be used to implement just this one key here, though we might be able to generalize it later. Note that it needs both press and operate. Here we show just the structure and will fill in the method bodies after we examine the situation a bit more.

```
class __PlusKey(__operatorKey):
    def __init__(self, model):
        self.__model = model

    def press(self):
        # TODO

    def operate(self):
        # TODO
```

The calculator itself needs to remember some additional things. When the plus key is pressed we need to assure that the current display is saved somewhere so that we can start to accumulate the next value.

```
self._savedValue = 0  # field of CalculatorModel (seen above)
```

The display will be moved to this location with an assignment at the right moment.

The body of *PlusKey.operate* can then use this value and the display to update the display.

```
    def operate(self):
        model = self.__model
        model._display += model._savedValue
```

Note that in a MinusKey the only difference would be the subtract operation instead of the addition above.

Next, we need to remember the most recent operation so that we know what operator key was pressed as we accumulate the second value, so that we can apply its operate when the = key is pressed, so the __init__ method is now:

```
def __init__(self): #CalculatorModel
    self._display = 0
    self._savedValue = 0
    self._accumulate = self.__AccumulateStrategy(self)
    self._currentNumberStrategy = self._accumulate
    self._lastOperation = None
```

Note that we don't yet have a _lastOperation when the CalculatorModel is created, hence the assignment of None.

When we press any operator key like plus or equals, we need to remember that this was the last operation.

```
def press(self): # from __PlusKey
    model = self.__model
    model._lastOperation = self
    model._currentNumberStrategy = model._save #below
```

However, saving the current key as the _lastOperation needs to be done in every __operatorKey, so we refactor this and move the statement to that superclass. We update _operatorKey so that all subclasses can have access to that instruction:

```
class __operatorKey(__calculatorKey): # full implementation
    def press(self, model):
        model._lastOperation = self

    def operate(self):
        raise NotImplementedError("operate not yet implemented.")
```

We now have two "press" methods here, but they have different protocols. The one inherited from _calculatorKey has only *self* as a parameter, but this new one also takes a reference to the model, and updates _lastOperation. We will see the use in the next paragraph.

The press method of PlusKey looks like the following:

```
def press(self):
    model = self.__model
    super().press(model) # invoke the superclass version
    model._currentNumberStrategy = model._save #below
```

A *press* has the calculator remember that this key is the most recent operator and it changes the current strategy to one we have not yet developed or even discussed. But relating this to the state transition diagram is useful. When we press the plus key we want to move (in the diagram) to the Save state from the Accumulate state. When we do this we replace the *accumulate strategy* with a *save strategy*. Anticipating what we are about to see below, if we then press another number key we want to go back to the Accumulate state and put the accumulate strategy back in place. Think about what else needs to happen as we go from the Accumulate state to the Save state on pressing the plus key. It is the save strategy that will be responsible for these *state* changes.

The save strategy is also created by the CalculatorModel, so the new (and final) version of the __init__ is:

```
def __init__(self): #CalculatorModel
    self._display = 0
    self._savedValue = 0
    self._accumulate = self.__AccumulateStrategy(self)
    self._currentNumberStrategy = self._accumulate
    self._lastOperation = None
    self._save = self.__SaveStrategy(self)
    self._three = self.__NumberKey(3, self)
    self._five = self.__NumberKey(5, self)
    self._plus = self.__PlusKey(self)
    self._equals = self.__EqualsKey(self)
```

Recall that it is the number keys that actually send messages to the strategy objects: the execute message. The accumulate strategy makes that key accumulate its saved value into the display. The save strategy on the other hand has to copy the display to the saved value. It then has to put the current number key's value into the display because that key has just been pressed and we are starting a new accumulation. Finally it has to set the current strategy back to the accumulate strategy. Figure 9.4 shows a sequence diagram with the sequence of operations. Things farther down the diagram happen after things above. The arrow indicates which object sends a message to or otherwise operates on which other object.

Here is the code that carries this out:

```
class __SaveStrategy(__numberStrategy):
    def __init__(self, model):
        self.__model = model

    def execute(self, value):
        model = self.__model
        model._savedValue = model._display
        model._display = value
        model._currentNumberStrategy = model._accumulate
```

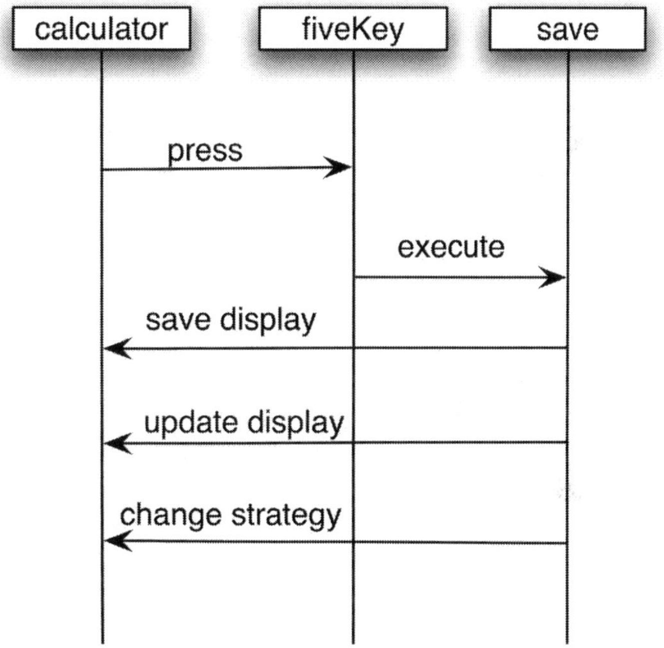


Figure 9.4 Sequence Diagram for a Number Key press.

Then, the calculator model must create one of these strategies and save it in the field *_save* since the PlusKey class refers to this object. See the __init__ method (above) for the creation statement.

We aren't done yet, but it is time to see everything together again. We now have a lot of interacting parts here, so be sure you can connect them all together in your mind. We have also added *pressPlus* to the model. It may help to go through the explanations above once more and find the code here that we refer to. Notice especially that the public interface of the calculator model is quite simple, that we have quite a lot of objects, and that we have both composition (to build the model) and delegation (to build the number keys) going on here. Also, it would be useful to step through pressing a few keys in a legal sequence watching what happens in the code and also in the state transition diagram.

```
class CalculatorModel():
    ''' Simple Calculator '''

    class __calculatorKey: # an interface
        def press(self):
            raise NotImplementedError(\
               "press not yet implemented.")

    class __numberStrategy: # an interface
        def execute(self, value):
            raise NotImplementedError( \
               "execute not yet implemented.")

    class __operatorKey(__calculatorKey): # partial
implementation
        def press(self, model):
            model._lastOperation = self

        def operate(self):
            raise NotImplementedError( \
               "operate not yet implemented.")

    class __NumberKey(__calculatorKey):
        def __init__(self, value, model):
            self.__value = value
            self.__model = model

        def press(self):
            self.__model._currentNumberStrategy.execute \
                  (self.__value)

    class __PlusKey(__operatorKey):
        def __init__(self,  model):
            self.__model = model
```

```
        def press(self):
            model = self.__model
            super().press(model)
            model._currentNumberStrategy = model._save

        def operate(self):
            model = self.__model
            model._display += model._savedValue

    class __AccumulateStrategy(__numberStrategy):
        def __init__(self, model):
            self.__model = model

        def execute(self, value):
            model = self.__model
            model._display = model._display*10 + value

    class __SaveStrategy(__numberStrategy):
        def __init__(self, model):
            self.__model = model

        def execute(self, value):
            model = self.__model
            model._savedValue = model._display
            model._display = value
            model._currentNumberStrategy = model._accumulate

    def __init__(self):
        self._display = 0
        self._savedValue = 0
        self._accumulate = self.__AccumulateStrategy(self)
        self._currentNumberStrategy = self._accumulate
        self._lastOperation = None
        self._save = self.__SaveStrategy(self)
        self._three = self.__NumberKey(3, self)
        self._five = self.__NumberKey(5, self)
        self._plus = self.__PlusKey(self)

    def getDisplay(self):
        return self._display
```

```
    def pressThree(self):
        self._three.press()

    def pressFive(self):
        self._five.press()

    def pressPlus(self):
        self._plus.press()
```

Now let's update main once more:

```
if __name__ == '__main__' :
    calculator = CalculatorModel()
    print('initial: ', calculator.getDisplay())
    calculator.pressFive()
    calculator.pressThree()
    print('after 53: ', calculator.getDisplay())
    calculator.pressPlus()
    print('after plus: ', calculator.getDisplay())
    calculator.pressThree()
    print('after 3: ', calculator.getDisplay())
```

The last line of this should just be a 3 and we expect that 53 is in the savedValue field, but have no way to test it here. But just before and just after pressing the plus key, the display prints as 53 at least.

What we have done here is simpler than you might think. We have added two strategies, one to capture each possible behavior of the number keys. We organized the switching between them using a state transition diagram. That is the core of what has happened in this section.

A few things might be subtle, though. Note that the strategies are properties of the calculator, not the number keys themselves. This is for a number of reasons, but primarily because we have ten number keys (only two created so far), and they must all behave alike and the changes in behavior are the same for all. Changing this in the number keys themselves, if that were necessary, would be a messy solution that we might like to avoid. Conceptually, the current strategy *of* the number keys is a property of the calculator as a whole, of course, so we don't do damage to our guiding metaphor here by doing this.

### 9.6.5 The Equals Key

It is the = key that actually gets the work done: *Give the calculator an = key that performs any outstanding operation and clears for a new calculation.*

After the previous section we will see that not much is left to be done. The equals key must perform the previously saved operation, stored in the operator key and make sure that we can use the calculator for a new calculation.

```
class __EqualsKey(__calculatorKey):
    def __init__(self, model):
        self.__model = model

    def press(self):
        model = self.__model
        model._lastOperation.operate();
        model._savedValue = 0
        model._currentNumberStrategy = model._accumulate
```

With this, the calculator works as far as it goes, but it has a couple of flaws. The main one is that adding three numbers is a bit awkward. This is because the calculator only performs any operation when you press =. So to add 5, 3, 5 you need the key sequence 5 + 3 = + 5 = and you will then see 13 properly. But the = in the middle is kind of superfluous and easy for a user to forget. We can correct for this quite easily, but also having the operator key perform the previous operation along with saving itself for future use. PlusKey.press then becomes:

```
def press(self):
    model = self.__model
    super().press(model)
    self.__model._lastOperation = self
    model._currentNumberStrategy = model._save
```

Alas, this breaks something else. If you now try to do two independent operations back to back, you find that the second just continues the first. The correction for this is also quite easy and corrects another flaw we haven't mentioned yet. Notice that the *_lastOperation* field of the calculator was not initialized when it was declared and didn't get any value until we press an operator key. But if the user presses the equal key before any operator key the program will fail (try it) with a null pointer exception (None) since the equals key tries to send a message through this reference. But what *is* the lastOperation when you start up the calculator? There isn't one, of course, but None will give us exactly the same difficulty. We could use an IF structure to check for None but once you let None fly around in your program you seem to have to check for it everywhere. Better if we avoid that by initializing the reference to an object that will "do the right thing" in this context, which is nothing. This suggests we create a NullKey operator class and object that has completely empty behavior for both of its methods. We can then initialize lastOperation to this nullKey object and set lastOperation to it at the end of EqualsKey.press as well.

```
class __NullKey(__operatorKey):
    def press(self):
        pass
    def operate(self):
        pass
```

Then add the following to the CalculatorModel __init__:

```
        self.nullKey = self.__NullKey()
        self._lastOperation = self.nullKey
```

and:

```
class __EqualsKey(__calculatorKey):
    def __init__(self,  model):
        self.__model = model

    def press(self):
        model = self.__model
        model._lastOperation.operate();
        model._savedValue = 0
        model._currentNumberStrategy = model._accumulate
        model.lastOperation = model.nullKey    # added
```

Note that if we press an operator immediately after = we continue a calculation, but pressing a number key instead starts a new one. This implies that there are additional state transitions here, and one more strategy type that we have not discussed yet. With these changes Figure 9.5 shows our state transitions.

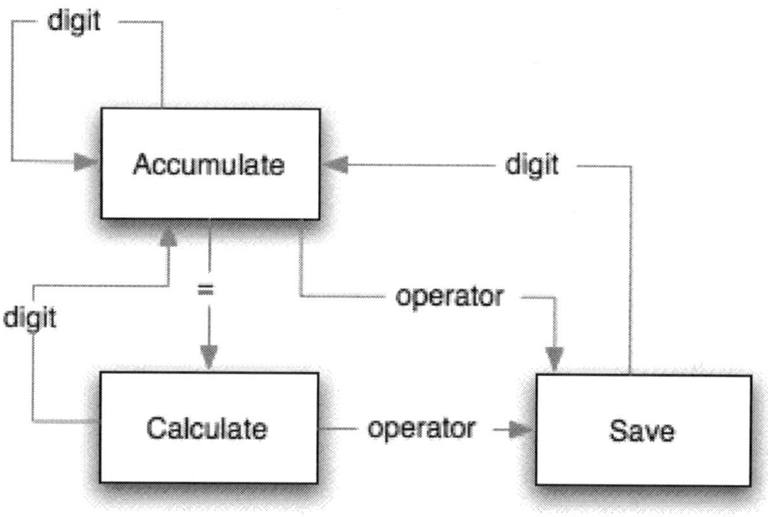


Figure 9.5. State Transition Diagram (complete)

## 9.7 Simple Functions

Until now, we have focused on object-oriented programming and so the methods of classes have been the means of providing actions in our programs and of obtaining the results of calculations. However, Python, like other languages, also has simpler functions, which are similar to methods but which aren't associated with any objects or classes. Like methods, they can be accessors, which is preferred, or mutators, which change the state of the computation.

If you sort of think of the overall program as an object, then you sort of have the right idea about the role of functions. But only *sort of.* Simple functions can also be defined within classes, often to do simple things. Here is a function that probably doesn't need to be defined.

```
def product(x, y):
    return x*y
```

Functions can have default arguments following any that don't:

```
def product(x, y=2):
    return x*y
```

will double x if no y is provided and only one argument is given: `product(3)`.

Functions can be recursive:

```
def factorial(x): #recursive
    if x <= 1: return x #Note - if statement all on one line
    return x * factorial(x-1)
```

An interesting recursive function is the solution to the Towers of Hanoi puzzle.

The problem is to move the disks from the original tower to the one at the middle one using the third tower as a temporary location. You can only move one disk at a time and never place a larger disk on a smaller one. While this is a modern puzzle (See Wikipedia), there is a myth that places it in a historical context. But if you have 64 such disks and move one per second, optimally, it will take longer than the current life of the universe: billions of years. There is a solution at the end of the chapter, but you are encouraged to write it yourself. Hint: It is highly recursive with two recursions needed. There is also an iterative solution possible as well.

Functions can access and modify global data. Suppose aValue is defined in a file (a Python module) and not nested within another structure:

```
aValue = 0
def increment(): #mutator
    global aValue # required for access to toplevel
    aValue += 1
```

Functions can be nested within other functions (an abstract example):

```
def top(x): #nesting example
    locx = x+2
    def nest(): #nested function
        nonlocal locx # required
        locx *= 3
    nest()
    return locx
```

Note that ordinary, simple, functions don't have a self parameter, since there is no containing object to refer to. Actually, though, the methods of classes are just specialized functions that have access to other elements of the class.

If a name is first introduced within a function, like *locx* above, it is visible only within that function and special notation (*nonlocal*) is needed for it to be seen even within nested functions. Parameters to a function are similar. Their visibility is limited to the text of that function. The function name, however, is different.

The global and nonlocal keywords will be discussed below in the section on Scope.

Functions themselves are actually assignable values. You can make the assignment `fac = factorial` and then call `fac(3)`. You can similarly pass one function to another. In an assignment, omit the parentheses: distinguish between the function itself, as an object, and calling the function.

While Python is dynamically typed, functions can give hints about the inputs expected and the output:

```
def factorial(x: int) -> int: #recursive
    if x <= 1: return x #Note - if statement all on one line
    return x * factorial(x-1)
```

However, the "hints" aren't enforced by the system. They are documentation.

If a function has several parameters they are usually passed in the order defined in the function def. However, that isn't necessary. For example, the call

```
product(y=2, x=5)
```

will properly associate the x and y arguments with the parameters. We have only seen positional arguments so far. There are other options that will be discussed below, once we examine *list* and *dict* types.

When you pass a value to a function as a parameter, the parameter name is treated inside the function just as if an assignment had been made to it. So, if you pass in a mutable object, such as a Robot or a Python *list*, changes made inside the function will be reflected outside. In particular, the function isn't working with a copy, but with the original.

It is possible to define a function in Python without giving it a name. These derive from earlier languages, primarily lisp (List Processing Language). The keyword *lambda* introduces such a function. That is followed by one or more argument variables, then a colon and finally an expression involving those variables: *lambda x, y: x+y* is a simple example. The expression will be returned when values of the arguments are supplied. A lambda is an expression itself, and it can be assigned to another variable. That variable can also be used as a function supplying the arguments:

```
f =  lambda x, y: x+y
print(f(3, 5))
print(f("Monty ", "Karel")
```

Note that the "+" operator is interpreted differently for numerics and for strings. So both of the above are valid. One big advantage of lambdas is that they can be passed to other functions and executed within that function. And, those expressions defining the return value can have arbitrary complexity.

Lambda can also be called directly if you enclose the expression in parentheses followed by any needed arguments, also in parentheses:

```
(lambda x, y: x+y)(99,1)
```

## 9.8 Other Primitive and Built-In Types in Python

The numeric types mentioned so far are called *discrete* since they model subsets of the integers of mathematics. The opposite of discrete is continuous and the *floating* (sometimes called *real*) types are an attempt to model the real numbers of mathematics. That is very difficult (though not impossible) since the digital nature of computers makes them discrete not continuous. There were once analog computers (even the slide rule is a simple example) that better model continuous mathematics. The floating point type of Python is *float* and it will probably use 64 bits. The encoding uses a binary fraction and an exponent, much like the scientific form of numbers, though in base 2 instead of 10.

Floating numbers trade range for precision. A 32 bit *int* type in many computer languages covers a range from about –2 billion to + 2 billion. Its values are all of the integer values in between, represented precisely. But it isn't possible to represent 2.7 with an int other than very approximately as either 2 or 3. Floating values do a little better with this.

A 64 bit float value in Python represents a value somewhere in the range beyond $-2^{308}$ to $+2^{308}$ . That is beyond 5 x $10^{92}$ which is vastly bigger than $2^{64}$ which is about 2 x $10^{19}$. Float values are also good for representing values between the integers, but only approximately. 2.7 can be represented approximately and 2.7 is a valid float value. However, it is not precisely represented. Think about it for a minute. If we are covering a much wider range, we must not be covering it as well as the integers. And since we can represent many values between integer values, it must also be true that successive floating values at some point of the range must be a lot farther apart than the integers are.

One of the most disconcerting things for novices about float values is that arithmetic is not precise. If you add up 0.1 a thousand times you don't get 100. You get something approximating 100, but that is because the float value 0.1 only approximates the real number one-tenth. There are some programs that do so much floating arithmetic in a naïve way that the answers are completely meaningless. It is even true that if you add up a long string of float values from smallest to largest and again from largest to smallest you are extremely likely to get different results. So even though we can represent values with decimal points using float values, they aren't very good for representing things like money. In fact money is a very sophisticated concept since the money value of a number depends on where you are. 100 (dollars) is very different from 100 (yen). Conversely two different numbers can therefore represent the same *money*. By the way, calendar dates are similarly sophisticated, since people use different calendars around the world and calendar systems have changed over time.

We won't try to give all the rules here (there are a *lot* of rules), but it is possible to translate from one type to another. Sometimes it is seamless and invisible, and other times you need to specify better what you might mean. For example, something like

```
x = float(7)
```

is permitted, even though 7 is an int. This is considered a *widening* conversion and it is the closest float to 7 that will be stored in x. The above statement actually uses the *constructor* from the float class to construct a *float* from its input. Some inputs will fail. You can't create a float from a string, for example, unless the string actually contains literal numeric. And there is one disconcerting thing about int values in Python version 2. If you use zero as the leftmost character, the value will be treated as if you want octal (base 8) encoding, not the normal base 10, so 0377 is really the same as 255. In version three you now specify that you want octal with 0o377, and the version 2 format become illegal.

If you want to make a *narrowing* conversion, where information might be lost, you need to specify it with a *cast*. For example the following results in 7:

```
y = int(7.2)
```

and

```
y = int(7.8)
```

will round up to 8.

Here for simplicity of example we have used constant values, but the same will be true if you try to assign a variable of one numeric type but require the target to have a different type.

y = int(z)

stores an int in y even if z is a float.

Also int(False) results in 0 and int(True) is one. Likewise float(True) is 1.0. In fact any non-zero numeric value is True.

Finally, if you put a sequence of characters in single or double quotes, like "Python" or 'Python', it is a String, but *str* is the formal name of the String type. You can use one form inside the other: print("We're 'fine' here").

Strings in Python are more sophisticated than you might think. They are a kind of immutable sequence. They can be indexed like lists.

A string enclosed in three single quotes can extend over several lines:

```
value =  '''Monty
Python'''
```

You can do substitutions into a string, producing a different string, not a modification (strings are immutable):

```
words = 'first %s second %s done'
print(words %('one', 'two'))
print(words) #unchanged
```

produces:

```
first one second two done
first %s second %s done
```

You can split a string into its words where the split happens at whitespace characters like space, tab and newline.

```
print('These are the times...'.split())
```

yields the list: `['These', 'are', 'the', 'times...']`

You can split on other characters. To split a multi-line string into lines, use split with a parameter: ...split('\n').

You can iterate over the characters in a string:

```
for x in 'python':
    print(x)
```

produces the characters on separate lines.

You can index into a string, forwards and backwards

```
print('python'[0], 'python'[-1])
```

gives

```
p n
```

The len function (length) can be applied to a string, or any sequence: `len('mumble')` yields 5.

You can capitalize the letters in a string with the *upper* method: `'karel'.upper()` gives `KAREL`

If you want to capitalize only the first character of the first word in a string use the *capitalize* method instead of *upper*.

This is only a portion of what is available in Python strings. Much of it is also available for lists and other sequences as well.

If you are sure that a string contains an arithmetic expression you can evaluate it with *eval*: eval('3+4') gives 7. If the string doesn't contain just an expression you will get a SyntaxError, which can be caught in a try block, as discussed in Chapter 10.

Python has a large number of built-in non-numeric types. We will explore some of them below. Some are very sophisticated.

## 9.9 Modules, Scope of Variables, and More on Naming

How and where you create a variable determines what part of the program it is associated with. This is related to, but slightly different from visibility, which also affects where the variable can be used.

In general, variables need to be defined before (generally above, in the text) it can be used. This is normally done in an assignment, though naming a variable as the parameter to a function gives its "definition". Functions and methods, however can be defined after they are first called.

There are some naming conventions that Python programmers use that aren't actually enforced, but embody important concepts. One is that a variable whose name is all capitals is intended to be a constant and never changed by the program:

```
SIZE = 20
WIDTH = 3
NAME = 'Maria'
```

The use of underscore prefixes in names is also a convention.
A Python m*odule* is a file with name suffixed by ".py". We usually put classes and such into modules, often one class per module, but that isn't necessary. If you want to use things defined in one module in a different one, you *import* the one with the required elements. So, if you create a set of mathematical functions in a file called math.py, then you can use them in another module by including

```
import math
```

in the new module. If the math module has the function *fibonacci*, then in the new module it is *math.fibonacci*. (The import statement has other options.)

A module doesn't need to define classes. It can define simple variables and functions, and much of Python is used this way.

Suppose you define a simple variable in a module and it isn't defined within a function or class. You can *access* it within functions defined below. However, if you need to change it from within a function you need to be explicit that you are using a global variable, rather than one locally defined, since names defined in a function are local to it. Suppose we want to keep track of the maximum argument used with the factorial function. The following will fail, since a local reference to maxArg in the first comparison is assumed and no local with that name has been defined locally.

```
def factorial(x): #recursive
    if x > maxArg: maxArg = x
    if x <= 1: return x
    return x * factorial(x-1)
```

`The solution is to mark maxArg as` *`global`* `within the function, indicating we are referencing a global value.`

```
def factorial(x): #recursive
    global maxArg
    if x > maxArg: maxArg = x
    if x <= 1: return x
    return x * factorial(x-1)
```

We have defined fields in our classes in this Chapter and earlier. Ordinary fields belong to the objects that we create. If we create two CalculatorModels, for example, we have two _five keys as well, one for each.

Variables associated with each object (instance variables) are defined within the class constructor, __init__, as we have seen. Those with underscore prefixes (one or two) are considered private by convention: `_counter = 0`.

It is also possible to create variables that are not part of the objects of the class, but part of the class itself. These variables are defined within the class, just as fields are, but outside the constructor. These are sometimes called *shared* variables because all of the objects in the class have access to the same variable, and if any one changes it, it is changed for all to see.

If it is public then other places in the program can see and alter it as well. However, class variables are referenced using a qualified name, with the qualification being the name of the class. Here is an example in the spirit of robots, but not part of the actual implementation in Monty Karel:

```
class Direction:

    NORTH = 0
    WEST = 1
    SOUTH = 2
    EAST = 3

    def __init__(self):
        self.names = ('NORTH', 'WEST', 'SOUTH', 'EAST')
         #see below

    def turnLeft(self, fromDirection):
        return (fromDirection + 1)%4

    def nameOf(self, direction):
        return self.names[direction]


    def allNames(self):
        print(self.names)

if __name__ == '__main__':
    direct = Direction()
    print(direct.turnLeft(Direction.EAST))
```

Note how the *toplevel* name *EAST* is referred to. Usage would be the same in methods of the Direction class. And, yes, *NORTH* etc. are all capitals, since they are intended as constants.

You can also define ordinary functions within a class, often to access or manipulate shared variables. So, we could include the following in Direction.

```
@staticmethod
def directionLeftOf(direction):
    if direction == Direction.NORTH:return Direction.WEST
    elif direction == Direction.WEST:return Direction.SOUTH
    elif direction == Direction.SOUTH:return Direction.EAST
    else: return Direction.NORTH
```

All objects defined in the class will share this function: self.`directionLeftOf`. You can invoke a static method using an instance reference or the class name.

Another possibility is a class method. It can also be invoked via an instance or the class name either inside or outside the class:

```
@classmethod
def valueOfNorth(cls):
    return cls.NORTH
```

(The above illustration isn't meant to be very useful in practice.)

```
if __name__ == '__main__':
    direct = Direction()
    print(direct.turnLeft(Direction.EAST))
    print(direct.nameOf(3))
    direct.allNames()

    print(direct.valueOfNorth())
    print(Direction.valueOfNorth())

    print(direct.directionLeftOf(Direction.WEST))
    print(Direction.directionLeftOf(Direction.WEST))
```

One possible use for a shared counter variable in a robot program might occur if you had a lot of robots of a given class wandering around the world putting down beepers. You might want to know the total number of beepers placed by all the robots. You could have a shared variable *totalBeepers*, initially 0, to keep track of this. The *putBeeper* method could be overridden to increment this variable. You would also probably provide a shared (classmethod) method in the class to get the current value of it.

We can also define variables within methods. The scope of the variable is that method itself and the variable is visible nowhere else as is true for other functions. You can, for example, declare and create a helper robot within a single method and it can be used only there.

In general, it is a good idea to define variables with the smallest scope that makes sense: class, object, method. This limits the places at which the variable can be modified and that helps you with your thinking process since it means there is a smaller part of the program over which you need to keep track of it mentally.

When one class is a subclass of another, the instance variables of the superclass are visible within the methods of subclass just as if they were local. So if *_size* is defined in the superclass, then *self._size* can be used in subclasses. There is a mechanism for conflict resolution for multiple inheritance, but it is beyond our scope here.

## 9.10 Introduction to Tuples, and Lists

Often a program will need to manipulate more information than we can conveniently provide individual names for. With three or four robots it is not a problem, but if the program needed to manipulate 3000 robots it would be a big problem. While we could incorporate numbers into the names (karel_1, karel_2,…) it would still be difficult to make all of them move, for example. We therefore need a more flexible way to handle large amounts of data. For this we need some sort of *data structure*. Data structures are various ways of organizing data with associated operations for manipulating the data or the structure itself. Python provides a very large number of built in structures and its libraries provide more.

One of the oldest mechanisms for this, and still supported by most programming languages, is the *array*. An array is a linear (one after the other) structure that is compactly and efficiently stored in computer memory. An array consists of a fixed number of cells, each of which can hold one item, perhaps an int, perhaps a reference to an object. Arrays are *indexed*, meaning that you retrieve items by knowing their relative locations in the array. In Python, indexing starts at zero, so the first item is in cell 0, the second in cell 1, etc. The reason-to-be for arrays, is that it is very efficient for the computer to retrieve an item knowing its index. If we have an array of Harvester robots named *crew*, then crew[5] is a reference to the sixth Harvester, provided that the array has at least six *elements*. In fact, crew[5] is a variable, so we can assign a new value to it as well as retrieve the reference it holds.

However, Python doesn't have direct support for arrays, though it has alternatives. There is a library (NumPy) that you can import to get arrays, however. But we will discuss the Python solutions here: Tuples and Lists. The usage of NumPy is very similar to what we do here. The difference is in the somewhat more efficient implementation, which is important for some programs.

Tuples and Lists, like Strings are types of *sequences*. As such they partly share a user interface, though "sequence" is a concept in Python, not an actual type. The big difference between lists and tuples is that tuples, informally, "lists of values", are enclosed in parentheses and are immutable. They have a fixed length and the entries can't be changed, though if they are objects they can still receive messages.

```
names = ('NORTH', 'WEST', 'SOUTH', 'EAST')
```

has four elements: names[0]...names[3]. You can't add names and you can't change the names through assignment. Strings are also immutable sequences.

Contrast this with a python *list*, enclosed in square brackets:

```
names = ['NORTH', 'WEST', 'SOUTH', 'EAST']
```

We could append a name to this list or change a name:

```
names.append('Elsewhere')
names[0] = 'NorthPole'
```

Then names would have five elements, with the last being *Elsewhere* and the first being *NorthPole*. This is possible for lists, but not tuples.

List, Tuples, and Strings and other sequences are all example of iterable types. User defined classes can also define iterable values. We shall see this later. And iterables have other uses than in the *For* statements we use just below.

You can index over any sequence, or other iterable, in a *For* statement:

```
def showAll(self):
    names = ('NORTH', 'WEST', 'SOUTH', 'EAST')
    for name in names:
        print(name)
```

To create a list of 1000 Harvester robots you would start by writing:

```
crew = [None]*1000
```

There are two things to note here. The first is that a list is an object with fields and methods, there are also built in functions that work with lists (and generally with sequences) as arguments. One of these functions is *len* and it works with lists and tuples just as it does with strings. Once we create a list its length can change so we need discipline. So len(crew) will be 1000, but it doesn't contain any robots. The important fact is that the above creates the list, but not the robots. It is really an empty list of 1000 None references, so not yet very useful.

One of the simplest of iterables is the *range,* seen below.

We create the robots with a for loop.

```
for street in range(1000):
   crew[street] = Harvester(street + 1, 1, East, 0)
```

We would then have 1000 Harvester robots "arrayed" along first avenue. And note that the list cell numbers start at zero, but our streets in the world begin at 1, so we needed to make an adjustment in our delivery specifications here: the robot referenced in cell k is standing on street k + 1. It is easy to make errors, of course, when you need to do this kind of adjustment. It is just one more thing you need to keep track of as you program. In fact, using the name *street* in the above might be misleading, as there is no street 0.

Note that in the assignment within the For loop above, we are giving a new value to each element in the list. What was None, will now be a reference to a new robot. So the syntax aList*[cellNumber]* is valid in any context in which a variable of the same type could be used. In particular, since our array crew holds references to robots, we can send messages to them as we see next.

Now with a thousand robot crew, we could harvest a huge field of beepers, by having each one harvest one row. To do this, however, we would want to use another For loop (or perhaps a While loop). For loops and sequences are sort of made for each other, of course.

```
for street in range(1000):
   crew[street].harvestOneRow()
```

Recall, that crew[k] is a reference to the k+1$^{st}$ cell, which is a reference to a Harvester, so the above works, though it might be clearer to write:

```
for street in range(1000):
   harvester = crew[street]
   harvester.harvestOneRow()
```

But these are really the same thing, and there is no need for the intermediate local variable named *harvester*.

It is easy to make errors in your sequence indexing, especially when you notice that the index, also called the *subscript*, can be any integer expression. We could make every other robot harvest one row with this For loop:

```
for street in range(0, 1000, 2):
   crew[street].harvestOneRow();
```

The following also works, but is a bit chancier

```
for street in range(500):
   crew[2*street].harvestOneRow();
```

Trying this with every seventh robot will require a bit of care that you get the last one and don't go outside the current range.

If you index a list cell outside the range 0..len-1 you will get an `IndexError` and will need to fix your error.

There are more complex versions of *range*. Note that the simplest form as used above produces values from zero up to one less than the "terminator" value named: `for i in range(30)` produces values from 0 through 29. However, you can define a range with a given start, termination, and increment as, for example `range(5, 20, 3)`, which will produce 5, 8, 11, 14, 17, but not 20. The increment defaults to 1 and the terminator is never included.

If the size (length) of the list isn't too large, and especially if the values stored in it won't change, there is a nice way to create and initialize the sequence. For example, back in Chapter 4, the Choreographer had two helper robots named lisa and tony. There was really no need for them to have individual names, however. We could have done this instead, using a list or tuple to hold the two helpers:

```
class Choreographer(UrRobot):

   helpers = (
      UrRobot(4,2,East,0),
      UrRobot(6,2,East,0)
   )

   def move(self):
      UrRobot.move(self)
      for helper in helpers:
         helper.move()
```

We replace the declarations of lisa and tony with the declaration of a tuple of UrRobots (references to UrRobots, of course) and immediately initialize it with two values creating the robots immediately. The list of values is enclosed in parentheses here (indicating a tuple) separated by commas. The move instruction then just sends move to each helper, but using a for loop indexed by the tuple itself. If we add another robot to the helpers declaration, this for loop will still send the move message to each helper, since we didn't assume here that there would be just two. Had we *hard coded* the 2 into the loop bound (range(2)), an update would have been more error prone. A list (rather than a tuple) initialized this way is just like any other and its elements can be changed as usual, though this is most often used for fixed sequences - even quite large ones.

In Chapter 11 we shall see other, slightly less efficient, but much more flexible, collections of data. In old computer languages, such as Fortran, arrays were the only collections provided, so programmers got very good at manipulating them. We shall see an application of tuples and lists in the next chapter and will use them extensively in the Primo Intermezzo.

There is a way to use functions and tuples together. Many functions have a fixed number of arguments, but some require more. (The following illustrates this, though Python has tricks to do it more simply.) If you precede the name of an argument to a function with an asterisk, *, you can have an arbitrary number of arguments. They will be collected into a tuple with the name of that argument. For example:

```
def sumAll(*args):
    print(args)
    x = 0
    for y in args:
        x += y
    return x
```

The name “args” is often used for this, but it can be anything valid. Note that *args must follow any positional arguments. There is another type of argument (**kwargs) that will be discussed later when we have seen dictionaries.

If we call sumAll(1, 2, 3) we get 6, though the arguments will also be printed as a tuple.

## 9.11 Introduction to Sorting

Often it is necessary to produce a collection that has its data values sorted by some measure, say, smaller integers before larger ones. This is a large field of study and will be explored in a course on Algorithms. Here we will look at one example, *quickSort*, of a recursive algorithm to sort lists of integers. While there is little specific need for this in Python, since it already knows how to sort a list, it is an important skill for a programmer.

The algorithm has two parts. First, in the *partition* step, it moves items around within the list so that smaller items, generally speaking, come first, with larger elements later. Then it repeats the same process, recursively, on those two parts so that the list becomes more and more sorted as it proceeds. Note that parameters lo and hi are inclusive here and represent valid list subscripts.

```
def quickSort(aList, lo, hi):
    if 0 <= lo < hi:
        lastLow = partition(aList, lo, hi)
        quickSort(aList, lo, lastLow-1)
        quickSort(aList, lastLow+1, hi)
```

Also note that the recursions omit one element, which as been moved by partition into that slot. It will be between the small-ish elements and the larger ones in size as well as position. The hard work is in the partition step: which uses swapping of elements to move things about.

A swap of the elements in cells i and j of an array is simply:

```
aList[i], aList[j] = aList[j] = aList[i]
```

While it can be carried out in a single assignment, note that behind the scenes such a swap requires three steps. The value in aList[i] must be saved "somewhere" before it is overwritten with aList[j] so that the value can then be used to set aList[j]:

```
temp = aList[i]
aList[i] = aList[j]
aList[j] = temp
```

As with many Python shortcuts, some things are hidden from view to make programming easier.

With that, partition becomes:

```
def partition(aList, lo, hi):
    pivot = aList[hi]
    lastLow = lo - 1
    for j in range(lo, hi):
        if aList[j] <= pivot:
            lastLow+=1
            aList[lastLow], aList[j] = aList[j], aList[lastLow]
    lastLow += 1
    print(lastLow, hi)
    aList[hi], aList[lastLow] = aList[lastLow], aList[hi]
    return lastLow
```

To help understand the above and what it does, examine the following graphical picture of the algorithm in action, with j having some intermediate value:

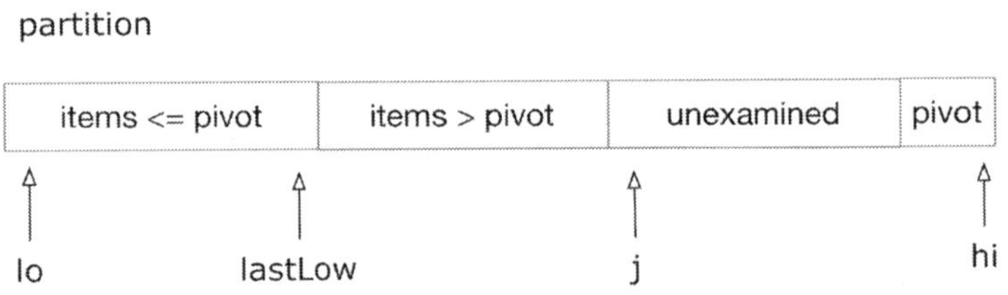


Figure 9.6.

If we find, examining the entry at j, that it is a small value, smaller than the pivot value, we first increment lastLow and then swap the entries at j and lastLow. When j reaches the end, we swap the pivot entry with the first of the larger elements. Note that we can make this more general, and sort things that can't be compared with < and = if we supply a compare operation to replace <= in the above.

The figure describes an *invariant* of the algorithm. Its truth is maintained as it proceeds. Initially both the small and large item sections are empty, explaining the initial setting of lastLow. If a change in j would make the invariant false, the truth is re-established by the swap. Invariants are an important feature of many such algorithms.

An interesting project is to instrument the algorithm to let you know how many swaps it does. It is easy to count and print the number of swaps on a single execution of partition, but harder to accumulate the total count over the full run of quickSort, since partition is executed repeatedly. For an instrumented version, it could, instead, return a pair of values with the count as a second element, since the lastLow is required for the algorithm to proceed.

## 9.12 A Few Python Tricks and Shortcuts

Python has a few features to make programming simpler. For example, you can set several variables to have the same value in one assignment.

```
x = y = z = 5.4
```

You can also give several variables distinct values in one assignment.

```
x, y = 3, 4
```

You can bundle up a tuple with an assignment with its values on the right:

```
x = 1, 2, 3, 4
```

produces (1, 2, 3, 4) assigned to x.

You can also unpack a tuple (or other sequence) with an assignment:

```
first, second, *rest = “Karel”
```

will leave *first* referring to "K", *second* referring to "a" and *rest* referring to "rel". The * is a special operator preceding a name. Add ", last" to the left side of the above after **rest* and see what happens.

You can put several Python statements on the same line if you separate them with semicolons.

```
x = 5; y = 2
```

You can pass a function to another, and have the receiving function execute it.

```
def maybe(x, func = None):
    if func == None:
        return x
    return func(x)
```

You can learn if some expression has a definite type.

```
print(isinstance('hello', int)) # should give False
```

You can learn the type of a function.

```
print(type('hello')) # should give str.
```

A function can return more than one value. Just put a comma separated list of values in the return statement. Catch the returned values in an assignment with an equal number of variables on the left side of the assignment.

Python actually has many, many tricks.

## 9.13 Important Ideas From This Chapter

implicit state
program counter
explicit state
instance variable (field)
local variable
shared variable
inner (nested) class
invariant
variable
primitive
int
float
list
tuple
counter
counting loop
off by one error
accumulator
String (str)
accessor
mutator
encapsulation
module
import
composition
delegation
refactor
numeric types (float, int)

## 9.14 Problem Set

1. What changes to the state occur when:
    a. A robot moves?
    b. A robot turnsLeft?
    c. A robot putsBeeper?
    d. A robot is created with the new operator?
    e. The simulator for the robot world executes World.readWorld(...)?
    f. An int variable is incremented?
    g. The program executes any statement?

2. Build a simple Robot class in which a robot keeps count of how many moves it has made and will report return that value (as an int) from the method distanceTraveled. Would there be any reason to use a long for this?

3. Build a Robot class in which the robot keeps track of the number of beepers in its beeper bag and can report it if asked.

4. Write a robot program in which a robot has a method to count and return the number of beepers on its current corner.

5. Build a Robot class in which the robots can keep track of their current street and avenue and return the int value when asked. To do a good job of this, you must consider error shutoff situations as well. Return the street and avenue as a tuple.

6. Exercise 5 normally requires a lot of IF statements. Can you think of a way to employ strategies instead? A North facing strategy, for example. How (when) will you switch between strategies? This has a simple state change diagram that you might explore.

7. Extend the CalculatorModel class with one more feature. Make it possible to toggle between two states. The first is the normal state in which it does just exactly the same as above. The other state is such that whenever the display changes, it is automatically printed to the console. This is easy to do with an IF statement and a simple boolean flag. It might be more interesting if you employ two more simple strategies. In either case, it will be helpful to find

all of the places in the program in which the display changes and replace them all with an invocation of a simple message: setDisplay(value).

8. Suppose a robot needed to employ a different strategy depending on which street it was on. Suppose that we could also be sure that it would never go north of 12th street. Would a list be a good way to store the strategies? Why or why not? What else might we need in order for this to work? Write a program to test your ideas.

9. The distance from a robot to the origin is simply the sum of its street number and its avenue number minus two, but only in a world without walls other than the boundary walls. Write a class with a method to compute this.

10. If the world has walls, the distance to the origin is harder to compute. It might not even be possible to do so, as the robot might not be able to reach the origin at all. Write a class with a method to find the length of the shortest path to the origin if one exists and to signal that it can't reach the origin if that is the nature of the world. This is a hard problem. One solution involves recursive backtracking, which you would need to explore. Problem 2 of Chapter 7 actually gives some insight into this problem. If the robot starts out with an infinite number of beepers and is willing to put down a lot of beepers, another solution might be devised.

11. When we have given delivery specifications for robots we have so far always used constants for all arguments in the constructor, but that isn't necessary. Here is an idea to explore. Suppose that a Choreographer-like robot doesn't know how many dancers it will need, but there is a pile of beepers at the origin that holds the right number - one dancer per beeper. The dancers should be arrayed out along first avenue starting with 2nd avenue. The Choreographer picks up the beepers in the pile, and for each one creates a dancer one block farther north, with the first on 2nd street, the second beeper causing creation of a dancer on 3rd, etc. After all of the robots are created all should move one block to the East. Implement this. We note that any of the parameters of creation of robots can be set with variables. You might want to explore this creatively.

12. A robot named karel is going to go for a stroll round and round a square four blocks on a side. Karel won't know how many steps to take until sent the meander message which has this prototype

```
public void meander(int steps)
```

Karel should move exactly steps times while walking around the square. But karel needs to turn after every fourth step, of course. At the end, we would like to know how many steps karel took along the final side, which may be 0 to 3 steps. This number should be printed to the standard output.

Hint, you many want separate counters for steps on a side and total steps. Can you do this with local variables in the meander method or do you need fields?

13. A robot named countula is in a completely enclosed rectangular room that contains zero or more beepers. Give countula a method that will return the number of beepers in the room. Suppose the room isn't rectangular?

14. Give countula another method that will return true if and only if the number of beepers in the room is an even number. Can you use the method of problem 13 to help you do this?

15. There is an associate of countula named reportula that is outside the room. (See the two previous exercises.) Devise a way for coutula to tell reportula how many beepers are in the room. The robot named reportula will then put that many beepers on its current corner. The two robots may be in different classes, of course, since they have different behaviors. Test this thoroughly.

16. Modify the robot of Problem 5 so that it keeps a list of all of the corners visited (a list of tuples) and can return it when asked.

17. In the Choreographer class, write a function (not a method) that will report the total number of moves taken by any of dancers. Have the dancers update a value whenever they move.

18. Give the calculator a "." key to implement float calculations. When this key is pressed, the number strategy changes so that further numeric key presses continue a decimal number.

19. How many single disk moves are required to move n disks in the Towers of Hanoi scenario? After you figure that out, modify the move instruction to count them. You can also print the current count with each move.

20. Examine mergeSort in the literature and implement it.

21. Note that if you apply the above quickSort to an already sorted list, that it still does swaps. You can improve the performance of the algorithm a bit by figuring out when a swap isn't needed and skipping it in those cases. Update partition with this idea.

22. Provide an instrumented version of partition, along with updating quickSort so that you can have the total swapCount returned as suggested in the text. This version isn't valuable for the actual process, but will teach you something about such algorithms.

## 9.15 Solution to Towers of Hanoi

```
def move(a, b):
    print('move', a, 'to', b)

def hanoi(n, a, b, c): # a to b using c
    if n == 0: return
    hanoi(n-1, a, c, b)
    move(a,b)
    hanoi(n-1, c, b, a)
```

The structure of this function has other uses as we shall see.

# 10 Input, Output, and Exception Handling

In this Chapter we discuss getting information into and out of the computer. Input and output in Python is handled by classes in the Python libraries. Nothing needs to be added or imported for simple file usage. For some things you need to import the *os module* since it knows about the file structure on your system.

```
import os
```

For some things you may also need the *struct* module.

There are separate classes for input and for output and separate classes for producing and reading human readable files (text files) and machine-only readable files (binary files). We will focus here on only text input and output.

## 10.1 File Output

To write text to a file to a file, you first need to *open* it. Then you can write strings to the file with the *write* function. The open command has a 'wt' argument that indicates the file is open for writing text. Actually, the 't' is assumed. The write function takes one argument and writes it to the file. Be sure to supply appropriate spacing if you construct a string for output, including '\n' to generate end-lines for multiple line output.

```
def example(filename, streets:int = 10, avenues:int = 10):
    outFile =  open(filename, 'w')
    outFile.write('KarelWorld\n')
    outFile.write('streets ' + str(streets) + '\n')
    outFile.write('avenues ' + str(avenues) + '\n')
    outFile.write('beepers 5 4 7\n')
    outFile.write('beepers 3 4 4\n')
    outFile.close()
```

This will produce a not very interesting Karel world description suitable for input. Note the end-lines and the spaces, including in '*streets* '. The filename needs to be in a format suitable for your system. It is just a string that may include a path to the appropriate directory. This is too specific to be useful, of course. A loop in which the beeper specifications is gathered before writing each line would be more useful. The file is closed when you are done with it.

The variable *outFile* is a reference to a *file* object created by the *open* statement.

The file created above could then be read (see below) using a file opened for reading.

In a useful application, a Python class might provide functions to correctly format and output important files. An example will follow.

## 10.2 Exceptions

Errors occur in Python programs as in most human activity. When an error occurs in a Python program we say than an exception (small e) has occurred. When this happens an Exception object (capital e) is created and "raised". This can be caught or not, depending on the kind of Exception it is and on the program. Here is the result of an uncaught exception that occurred when a robot tried to walk through a wall. It has been reformatted since the lines it produces are long. The first two lines are boilerplate indicating that something went wrong. The rest should probably be read from the bottom up. Each "section" tells where the error occurred tracing the execution back to the original "self.run()" statement. The following has removed some personal information with ellipses.

```
Exception in thread Thread-1:
Traceback (most recent call last):

  File_
"/Library/Frameworks/Python.framework/Versions/3.1/lib/python3.1/th
reading.py", line 509, in _bootstrap_inner
    self.run()

  File_
"/Library/Frameworks/Python.framework/Versions/3.1/lib/python3.1/th
reading.py", line 462, in run
    self._target(*self._args, **self._kwargs)

  File "/Users/jbergin/.../milemoverch2.py", line 32, in task
    lisa.move()
```

```
    File "/Users/jbergin/.../milemoverch2.py", line 17, in move
      UrRobot.move(self)

    File "/Users/jbergin/.../karel/robota.py", line 155, in move
      self.__direction(self, world)

    File "/Users/jbergin/.../karel/basicdefinitions.py", line 95, in
     West" facing west")

  karel.basicdefinitions.FrontIsBlocked: at (1, 1) facing west
```

The code that was executing when this was thrown was the move method of a class called *MileMover* on line 32 of the "task" method of the file that was running. That move instruction was invoked most recently from a class called MileMover, in its moveMile method on line 17 of the file. Depending on your environment (mine is Eclipse), clicking on one of those lines will take you to the code that caused the error. Many of those lines point to code in the Monty Karel implementation, not the user written code.

It is easy to generate an exception. Simply declare a new Robot variable and send it a message without actually creating any robot.

```
john = None
john.move()
```

This will generate an *AttributeError* which will be raised, but not caught. The program will terminate and we will get a message informing us of the fact, perhaps even telling us which line in our program contained the error. An informal alternate terminology for "raise" an exception is to "throw" it.

```
Traceback (most recent call last):
  File
"/Users/jbergin/Documents/eclipse/PythonWorkspaceV3/KarelPythonWRobots/
src/default/milemoverch2.py", line 39, in <module>
    john.move()
AttributeError: 'NoneType' object has no attribute 'move'
```

We can *catch* this exception and therefore prevent the program from terminating. To catch an exception if it arises you include the statements that might raise the exception in a try block. Here is a program fragment with no purpose but to demonstrate the idea.

```
try:
    john = None
    john.move()
except Exception as e:
    print(e)
```

Running this will produce: `'NoneType' object has no attribute 'move'`, `but the program will continue running rather than halting if the exception isn't caught.`

When we catch an exception we name the class of the exception we are interested in and give a variable that will have that type. Within the body of the except clause we can print it out as here. You can do anything you like in the except clause, including trying to recover from the error.

When an exception is thrown in a try block, the execution of the try is abandoned immediately and the system searches for a handler (an except clause) of the type of the exception that was thrown. But the program as a whole can continue.

If the code can raise more than one kind of exception, then you can have several except clauses with a single try. These are written one after the other following the try clause. The most specific ones should be listed first, and the more general ones later. Exceptions are objects from classes. Here, more general means a super class, and more specific means a sub class.

```
try:
    x = b + 1
    x = x/a
except TypeError as e:
    print(e)
except ZeroDivisionError as e:
    print(e)
```

Depending on the values of x and a this can be fine, or not. If x is 'a' then you will see a TypeError since you can't add a string and an int. The try clause would then terminate. But if x is an int, but b is zero you get a ZeroDivisionError instead.

Alternatively, a tuple of exception types can be listed in a single except clause:

```
try:
    x = b + 1
    x = 10
    x = x/a
except (TypeError, ZeroDivisionError) as e:
    print(e)
```

Some sorts of exceptions can occur even in a correct program. For example, when we try to create a file, the operating system may not permit it, perhaps because the disk is locked, or there is no space available, or you try to read a non-existent file. These kinds of problems are beyond the control of the programmer. Therefore, even a correct program can generate them. For this reason such exceptions must be caught by the programmer. The IOError discussed in Section 10.1 are like this so all the code there must be taught to handle exceptions. They must be caught or passed on for handling elsewhere.

```
try:
    inFile = open('mumble.t')
except IOError as e:
    print(e)
```

This might produce: `No such file or directory: 'mumble.t'`

One question arises as to how big a try block should be. This depends on whether you can recover from the exception or not. If you can't create a file, for example, then you can't write to it, and perhaps your program can't continue. In this case, any statement that writes to the file should also be in the same try block, though you can make the program terminate. If the statement writing the file were outside the try block, then we might be trying to write to a file that we haven't created.

Another possibility, not applicable here, is to provide some default value for the information that was being created when the exception was thrown. If this can be reasonably done, then the program can continue, and the try block can be relatively short. This might be possible if `ZeroDivisionError` is thrown because we divide by zero.

Exception objects have quite a lot of state themselves. In particular, when a program fails, the exception object that is raised captures information about all the methods that have begun execution but not yet finished execution in that thread. If a method sends a message, some other method starts but the current one suspends until the new one completes. This is the runtime stack structure that the Python runtime uses to manage the execution. If you don't catch the exception, the standard procedure is for the system to print a stacktrace for this exception object. Usually this stacktrace (most recent message at the bottom) includes the program line number at which the program failed. This is very useful in finding program errors during development.

It is possible for the programmer to create new Exception classes using inheritance. It is often useful to do this to indicate special program specific errors that might occur. When the program finds that the error has occurred it throws an exception by creating a new object and "raising" it:

```
class ExplodingRobotException(Exception):
    def __init_(self, message):
        super().__init__(message)
```

Later you can raise the exception with:

```
raise ExplodingRobotException('karel has exploded')
```

And you can also include code that might raise it in a try-except block.

The exception can be caught or not in the usual way. The typical superclass of your own exception classes is *Exception*. With this superclass the programmer is forced to catch the exception or propagate it, or the runtime will complain.

## 10.3 File Input For Text

Input is the opposite of output. We are trying to obtain information from somewhere for the program. The principles of use are the same as for output, but more exceptions may be thrown. In fact, nearly every input statement might throw an exception since the source of the data might have become unavailable.

Text files are typically broken into lines, separated by the end-line character: '\n'. We can read a file a line at a time or grab it all at once. Once we have a line or the entire file we can break it up into smaller chunks with *split,* which normally assumes space separations between "words" but other separators will do.

Suppose we want to read one line at a time or to read the file as individual lines all at once. The readline method will read one line:

```
file = open('simpleWorld.kwld ')
line = file.readline()
print(line)
line = file.readline()
print(line)
```

produces

```
KarelWorld
streets 10
```

If we follow the above with a simple *file.read()* it will read the rest of the program as above, since the "file pointer" has been advanced by the two *readline* invocations. The `read()` method is described below.

We also have the opportunity to read the whole file and get the line split done automatically. The *readlines* method reads the file into a *list* of lines.

```
file = open('simpleWorld.kwld ')
lines = file.readlines() #note the spelling: readlines.
print(lines)
```

This gives:

```
['KarelWorld\n', 'streets 5\n', 'avenues 5\n', 'beepers 5 4 7\n',
'beepers 3 4 4\n']
```

And, note that the end-line indicators are preserved. However, we might not find the file and an exception would be thrown instead. We can check for the existence of a file with something like the following:

```
    import os
  ...
    filename = input("Name of the input file: ")
    if not os.path.exists(filename):
        print("There is no file named: " + filename)
        print("Exiting.")
        exit(1)
```

One could also include the open statement in a try-except block.

```
try:
    inFile = open('mumble.t')
except IOError as e:
    print(e)
```

If you try to read past the end of a program, these methods simply return the empty string: ''.

## 10.4 File At A Time Input

In some ways the most efficient way to read a file, assuming that it isn't absolutely HUGE, is to read it all at once into a list. We read a file all at once with the *read* method of a file. It returns the entire file as a single string with lines separated by the end-lines as they appear in the file itself.

Suppose we want to read the file written by the first example in Section 10.1, above, supposing the file exists in the current directory:

```
file = open('simpleWorld.kwld')
wholeFile = file.read();
wholeFile.close()
print(wholeFile)
```

We will get:

```
KarelWorld
streets 10
avenues 10
beepers 5 4 7
beepers 3 4 4
```

We might, however, want to process the file as individual "words", where the "words" are separated by whitespace: spaces, tabs, and new-lines:

```
file = open('simpleWorld.kwld')
wholeFile = file.read();
words = wholeFile.split()
print(words)
```

We could process *wholeFile* as we can any list.

```
['KarelWorld', 'streets', '5', 'avenues', '5', 'beepers', '5', '4', '7',
'beepers', '3', '4', '4']
```

Note that we don't have the line structure preserved in this listing. That may be an important consideration. If you want individual lines, use *split* with an argument: `wholeFile.split('\n')`:

```
['KarelWorld', 'streets 5', 'avenues 5', 'beepers 5 4 7', 'beepers 3 4
4', '']
```

Note that each string in this list is now one of the lines of the file, each of which could, itself be split as needed.

If you want individual characters instead of lines or words, you can simply apply the *list* function to *wholeFile*: `print(list(wholeFile))`.

```
['K', 'a', 'r', 'e', 'l', 'W', 'o', 'r', 'l', 'd', '\n', 's', 't', 'r',
'e', 'e', 't', 's', ' ', '5', '\n', 'a', 'v', 'e', 'n', 'u', 'e', 's', '
', '5', '\n', 'b', 'e', 'e', 'p', 'e', 'r', 's', ' ', '5', ' ', '4', ' ',
'7', '\n', 'b', 'e', 'e', 'p', 'e', 'r', 's', ' ', '3', ' ', '4', ' ',
'4', '\n']
```

And note, here, that we do get the line break characters as well as the spaces. Of course, we are just using ordinary string methods to do this.

The following uses what we have learned so far:

```
import os

    def countBeepers(filename):
    # format of a beepers line is: 'beepers' street avenue
    # numberOfBeepers
        if not os.path.exists(filename):
            print("There is no file named: " + filename)
            print("Exiting.")
            exit(1)
        file = open(filename)
        result = 0
        wholeFile = file.read();
        lines = wholeFile.split('\n')
        for line in lines:
            words = (line.split())
            if not len(words) == 0 and words[0].lower() == 'beepers':
                result += int(words[len(words) - 1])
        return result
```

We simply look for lines that begin with the word "beepers", spelled in any case and then only look at the last token on the line, which is the number of beepers. We accumulate this into the *result* local variable, which we eventually return. The tokens are String objects, however, so we need to translate the final token to extract the int encoding that it contains. The string "1" and the int 1 are not nearly the same thing in Python or most languages.

## 10.5 Character At a Time Input

Sometimes you really do need to process a file one character at a time. There are a couple of standard tricks for doing this.

The first is described above, where we just push an input string into a list and then process the list one element at a time. You don't really even need to do that, since strings, themselves can be indexed: 'Karel'[0] is the character "K".

But when you really need to read it one character at a time, you can just give the read method of the file an argument telling it how many characters to read, here 1: `file.read(1)` will read a single character. Doing this in a loop will process as much of the file as you desire. Note, however, that whitespace characters including end-line will be returned like any other.

```
file = open('simpleWorld.kwld')
some = file.read(12);
print(some)
```

We will get:

```
KarelWorld
s
```

If you read past the end of the file the returned values will be the empty string.

## 10.6 Reading From the Console

Some programs want to take information from the user typing into a command window. Graphical windows for input are actually much more common today, but in the past command entry from the console was just about the only way a program could take data from a user.

The function *input* takes a string typed by the user at the console. Its argument is the prompt typed by the system to indicate than input is desired:

```
def echo():
    x  = input('>>')
    print(x)
    return x
```

Something more meaningful than '>>' is often needed:

```
def echo(prompt = '>>'):
    x  = input(prompt)
    print(x)
    return x
```

Note that the value returned is a string that can be processed as usual.

A program can't predict what a user will type, of course. If a program really needs an int value to be entered, something like the following is useful:

```
def getValue():
    x = None
    while x == None:
        try:
            x = int(input( 'Type an int:  '))
            return x
        except Exception:
            print('try again')
```

If the conversion of the input to int fails, x will get the value None, continuing the loop.

## 10.7 A Simple I/O Illustration

Here we will illustrate a few ideas about input and output in a simple program. It might be the very beginning of the development of a program to manage your growing library. It will be overly simplified, since all we want to do here is to show how to put the I/O classes together to do some simple work.

First we want a simple class to represent a Book object, though we won't really do anything with these here. This class will be expanded later:

```
class Book:

    def __init__(self, title, author):
        self._title = title
        self._author = author

    def title(self):
        return self._title

    def author(self):
        return self._author

    def __repr__(self):
        return("Title: "+self._title+": Author: "+self._author)
```

We haven't seen the __repr__ method previously. It should produce a string suitable for use by the print method to represent objects of the class

```
book = Book('Beyond', 'J Bergin')
print(book)
```

should produce:

```
Title: Beyond: Author: J Bergin
```

Books have a title and an author, and can report these values when asked. A more realistic class would include publisher, etc, and perhaps the date we purchased it, and our cost.

Somehow or other, though, we would need to find a way to start to build up the information in our "library" and to save it in files. Here for example is a simple example of a file of books, with just two books. The title and author are on separate lines and a blank line separates books. This is a simple format, though not very robust.

```
Tom Sawyer
Twain

Huckleberry Finn
Twain
```

Let's see how this file might have been created by reading information from a user at a keyboard, creating objects for each book and saving the results in the file we see here. The file happens to be called books.txt on the disk drive of my computer system.

Before we get started, though we need to think about how the user will interact with this program. It is a difficult and error-prone task to enter data into a computer. At a minimum, the computer needs to prompt the user for what is needed at each stage. Here is the minimum needed and it is what we shall build here. This is the output of the program we will build.

```
Name of the output file: books.txt
Input books. Answer no to end.
More? [YES/no]
Title:  Tom Sawyer
Author: Twain
More? [YES/no] y
Title:  Huckleberry Finn
Author: Twain
More? [YES/no] no
```

The first line of the above is the a *prompt* and it was output by the program up to the space following the colon. The user then typed *books.txt* followed by the return/enter key. The next line is another prompt giving a simple instruction about how to proceed.

The third line is another prompt also showing the options [YES/no]. The intent of capitalizing the YES is to indicate that this is the default response and that unless you type no it will assume yes, more books. The user has responded with just the enter/return key so you don't see anything but the computer will assume there is to be another book because of this.

The computer then prints another prompt "Title: " and the user has responded with Tom Sawyer and a return. Then the computer asks for the author. The user responds Twain. The computer then asks again if there is more input and this time the user responded *y* and a return. And so it goes until the user specifically types *no*.

This is really inadequate for a real program, since it gives the user no chance to correct errors or even confirm that what was entered is correct. People make typing mistakes all the time doing this, so it is critical to make this as safe as possible. But it is enough to illustrate input and output processing. The first program we will see manages this dialog with the user and captures (reads) the users responses. Note that it goes back and forth between output (prompting) and input (user's response captured). When the program has a title and author it creates a book object and also writes a notation about the book to the output file that the user specified after the first prompt.

We will just show a simple program all done in a simple function, though in a more realistic example we would capture this instead in a class method. This might, more realistically be a staticmethod of the Book class. If this function is in a different module, however, it would need to import Book from the Book module.

```
def main():
    try:
        filename = input("Name of the output file: ")
        with open(filename, 'w') as outFile:
            print("Input books. Answer no to end.")
            response = ""
            while response.lower() != "no":
                bookTitle = input("Title: ")
                if bookTitle == None: break
                bookAuthor = input("Author: ")
                book = Book(bookTitle, bookAuthor)
                book.write(outFile)
                response = input("More? [YES/no] ")
    except IOError:
        print("File error, cannot proceed.")
```

To make this work, however, requires that the Book class have a write method that can write to a previously opened file.

So, the Book class is now:

```
class Book:

    def __init__(self, title, author):
        self._title = title
        self._author = author

    def title(self):
        return self._title

    def author(self):
        return self._author

    def __repr__(self):
        return("Title: " + self._title + " Author: " + self._author)

    def write(self, outFile):
        outFile.write(self.title())                    # more...
```

```
        outFile.write('\n')
        outFile.write(self.author())
        outFile.write('\n\n')
```

The *with* block in the *main* function above introduces the name `outFile` for use in the statements of the block.

As *main* runs, it first prints a prompt. The system waits (forever if necessary) for the user to type in something. The program then reads a line from the input file and stores the result in a string called *filename*. All of this is wrapped in a try block because this input(...) might fail. There might not be a console, for example. If an IOError is thrown here or by any other statement, it will be caught and we will see a message and the program will halt. Let's assume this doesn't happen and continue.

Function *main* then creates an output file so that we can write strings to the file.

Next, two more prompts are printed out and the program reads a response string from the user. The response is compared with "no" but ignoring any case changes, so that "NO" is the same as "no", etc. If the response is anything else the program enters the loop in which it gets a title and author, again prompting for each. The "more" prompt is output again at the bottom of the loop so that the program knows whether to loop again or quit.

For each title-author pair, the program creates a Book object (which isn't actually used here in any way, though it could be; see Chapter 11), and writes two lines into followed by a blank line to the output file by asking the just-created book to write itself to the file.

## 10.8 Introduction to Graphical User Interface Programming: Dialogs

The other way to get information from the user (as well as to display limited amounts of information) is to use a Dialog box. This is a window that you pop up onto the screen that has controls that the user can manipulate. The typical controls are labels, buttons, and fields. Labels simply present simple information. Fields permit user input, and buttons let the user control the dialog. Here we shall build a simple dialog controller, a Prompter, that will accept either an integer, a float, or a string from the user, depending on the needs of the program.

The WorldMaker dialog of the Karel Python simulator is an example of such a dialog. It has fields in which to enter the number of streets and avenues, Buttons so that you can "pick up" the various tools, such as the beeper tool. More buttons so that you can read or save a world, etc.

> **break and continue**: When a loop is executing it occasionally happens that you learn either that the loop should exit prematurely or that this pass around the loop is done and the remaining statements in the body need not be executed. We see a case of the former in the above. If the book's title is None there is nothing more to do in this read loop, so we execute a *break* statement. This takes us out of the closest containing loop, though there are other forms.
>
> If you still need to stay in the loop, but are finished with this one iteration, you can execute the *continue* statement instead. It too has more complex forms.
>
> These statements are fairly rare, but occasionally they represent the clearest way to code a solution to the problem at hand.

Once we have created the Prompter class, using it is very simple. Here is an example:

```
prompt = Prompter()
val = prompt.getInteger("How old is it?")
print('Age: ', val)
val = prompt.getFloat("What is its width?")
print('Width:', val)
```

The dialog will be shown twice. In Figure 10.1 we see it the first time after we send the getInteger message. It is waiting for the user to enter an integer value into the reply field and then press the OK button. This is being run on a Macintosh, by the way. On another computer it will look more like your own system dialog boxes. If you enter a value that can't be interpreted as an integer, the dialog won't disappear. That "verification" of data is much more difficult in the command window version above. It usually requires testing the input value and then looping until the program gets a value it will accept. The same thing happens here, but it is easier to program, though other things are more detailed.

Figure 10.1 A Dialog Input

If you press the cancel button, however, or the upper left "close" button the default value of 0 is returned.

These dialogs are standard in the tkinter graphics package that you may need to install separately. I use Eclipse on a Macintosh with PyDev and tkinter is included automatically with PyDev.

The getInteger method of a Prompter is also not difficult. But note that it runs a separate tk program when executed:

```
import tkinter as tk
from tkinter.simpledialog import askinteger, askfloat, askstring

      class Prompter:
          '''Manage simple dialogs for data value entry'''
          def getInteger(self, message, initial = 0):
              ''' Get an integer from a simple dialog'''
              root = tk.Tk()
              root.withdraw() #root.deiconify()
              result = askinteger( "Integer", message, \
                     initialvalue=str(initial))
              root.destroy()
              if result == None: result = 0
              return int(result)
```

First we create the dialog itself giving it the code "Integer" that will become the label in dialog box to indicate what kind of data is desired. Once we make it visible with askinteger() the user is in control until he or she hits either the OK or Cancel button. The value entered into the reply field needs to be saved in a Prompter field called *result* so that the *getInteger* method can pick it up to return it forced to int type. There is a similar method, *askFloat*, that will do about the same thing, using exactly the same tk system for its display. It's look will be a bit different, as the heading will say Float instead and it will get a float value, of course.

The invocation of tk.Tk() creates a graphics program with its own window. We immediately hide (withdraw) that window since it isn't used, but deiconify() will make it visible again if we like. We then ask that application for a value with askInteger(). This is what creates and displays the dialog and catches the input. Then we destroy the application (root) and return the value entered by the user.

Note that tkinter is a very rich library. The Monty Karel graphical system was built with this. It has a steep learning curve, however. There are alternative Python libraries with similar functionality. There are ways to change the size and location of the dialog and askInteger also has optional arguments for specifying min and max values that can be accepted.

The Prompter class has the advantage that it isolates the use of tkinter into a single module so that other parts of the program don't need to be concerned with it.

We shall use another level of indirection, in fact. A Prompter isn't a dialog, but it knows how to create them: a dialog *factory*. A Prompter creates dialogs as required. When we ask the prompter for an integer value, it will show us a new dialog tailored for int values. After the dialog is successfully dismissed, the prompter gives us the value. If we cancel the dialog, either by pressing the Cancel button or closing the window, the value returned will be 0. And the Prompter isolates the tkinter materials in one place.

The Prompter class here is just a mediator between the users's code and the simpleDialog class of tkinter. That class provides many capabilities, including the askInteger, askFloat, and askString dialogs. So we have almost nothing to do here other than to invoke methods of that class. This simple Prompter class is useful form many things, but, suppose we want a dialog that will produce two values instead of just one. We need a simple class for two values: a TwoValueDialog that can label its two input fields. Here is an example dialog that we shall see soon:

Figure 10.2 Police Dialog

In the FMGame that we will explore in the next chapter, this dialog could be used to get the "move" for a human player who represents a game role The Police. The user is indicating that they want to move a game piece from cell 0 to cell 2. This dialog can be created by using the TwoValueDialog directly.

We will build two things. The class itself and a helper function to manage it and its return values. The helper function is invoked from the main program and will return a tuple of two strings, giving the results entered by the user or a default value if the user presses Cancel. If you writer.

```
result = dialogResult('Police','From', 'To', (0, 0))
```

then the dialog will show with both fields initialized to zero as per the last argument of the invocation. If the user enters 2 in the "To" field, then the result will contain ('0', '2'). Note that these are strings, not ints and the caller will need to deal with that. In fact, there is no requirement in this class that the user must enter integers and can enter any strings. We will see later how to overcome that and require certain types for the dialog to be dismissed returning properly typed values. This will require modifying (no, no) or subclassing this one (yes). The helper function looks like this:

```
def dialogResult(title, first, second, default=('', '')):
    root = Tk()
    root.withdraw()
    TwoValueDialog(root, title, first, second, default)
    root.destroy()
    return TwoValueDialog.get()
```

It is useful because TwoValueDialog has some quirks. The parameters are in order, the title of the dialog (here we used 'Police'), the label for the first input box, the label for the second, and, finally, the default value to be returned if the user cancels. Here the default is a tuple of two empty strings.
The first statement of the body creates a Tk application window and runs an application to manage it. We don't want to see this window so the second statement (*withdraw*) hides it. To show it again, if needed, *root.deiconify()* will do the job. Then we invoke the constructor of the class, giving required arguments. The call to destroy kills the root window and its execution. The actual result after the user exits the dialog is obtained (and returned) by the last statement. Notice that it is a class method being called. The reason for that complication is that after a dialog is dismissed the object is no longer available to query so we need to move results elsewhere – a class level variable in this case.

The helper function is really just hiding the details of tkinter and the class method means of getting the result. This isn't the only possible solution.

The class itself is short, but needs explanation as it uses tkinter features:

```
class TwoValueDialog(simpledialog.Dialog):

    def __init__(self, root, title:str, first:str, second:str, default =\
            ('', '')):
        self._firstLabel = str(first)
        self._secondLabel = str(second)
        self._title = title
        TwoValueDialog.__result = default
        super().__init__(root)

    __result = None

    @classmethod
    def get(cls):
        return cls.__result

    def getResult(self):
        return ((self._first.get()), (self._second.get()))
```

```
    def body(self, master):
        self.title(self._title)

        Label(master, text=self._firstLabel).grid(row=0)
        self._first = Entry(master)
        self._first.insert(0, TwoValueDialog.__result[0])
        self._first.grid(row=0, column=1)

        Label(master, text=self._secondLabel).grid(row=0, column=2)
        self._second = Entry(master)
        self._second.insert(0, TwoValueDialog.__result[1])
        self._second.grid(row=0, column=3)

        return self._first # initial focus

    def apply(self):
        TwoValueDialog.__result = self.getResult()
```

The constructor takes the user's labels, and such and saves them into private instance variables. It then invokes the superclass version of the constructor, from the Dialog class. This is the statement that actually creates the dialog and shows it. Without that, nothing would show.

We then have a private class variable __result where the dialog will put the results (a tuple) and a classmethod *get* to obtain it. This is the function called by the helper.

The getResult method is just a helper that packages up the results in a tuple for convenience elsewhere (below). The object self._first is one of the entry fields of the dialog and its *get* method of that object retrieves the value at the time it is called. Likewise for self._second.get(). Notice the "extra" parentheses, which create a tuple to be returned.

The other two methods, *body* and *apply* are part of the Dialog infrastructure, so we are overriding superclass methods. The do nothing at all in Dialog, so there is no need to invoke the superclass versions here. This is where you build the dialog (body) and where you capture what it contains just before it is destroyed (apply). The *master* argument is the overall dialog box to which we will be adding visual elements.

The *apply* method here is simplest to explain. It just uses the getResult helper method to push the results into the class variable so that it is available.
It is the *body* method that creates the dialog.

The title method of a Dialog sets its title ('Police' in the example).

The next two groups of four lines each will create the labeled fields for display.

The last line the body method says that the initial focus of the dialog will be the first of the input fields: *self._first*. You might see a blinking cursor in that field when you run the program.

To create a labeled field we use four statements. The first creates the label and places it in a grid. The first "line" is line 0 and we want it in column 0, the first column. The second label (in the other grouping) will be at row=1 and column=0. Note that the grid method has default arguments (0). The *Label* statement is a constructor invocation and we don't capture the result in a variable since we don't need to refer to it, but we immediately send the *grid* message to that object.

The next three statements create the *Entry* box as part of *master*, then give it a default value, using the *__result* class variable, and, finally placing it in the grid. We haven't actually seen invoking a method by naming its arguments up to now, but it is a general Python feature. They are keyword arguments and can be given in either order.

The tkinter libraries of Python have many classes and many options. Some are more complex than this, but in general, the ideas are about the same throughout the libraries. Layouts in particular are messy and it takes some experimentation to get used to them. The Monty Karel Python simulator, by the way, consists in large part of a Canvas object within a frame. The program can draw on the canvas and does so to make the walls, beepers, and robots visible to the programmer. It also has a few dialogs, such as the World Builder dialog. The Karel Universe editing system (Java) is much more sophisticated. Not counting the simulator that it is integrated with, the editor has about 140 classes spread over about 60 files. Some of these are for presentation, similar to what we see here, and some are for managing the flow of information as the user manipulates the interface.

## 10.9 Important Ideas From This Chapter

Exception
Try ... except
GUI
File input
File output
Reading characters
Console

## 10.10 Problem Set

1. Write and test a subclass of Robot that will print a trace of all robot actions to a file that the user can name when he or she creates the robot to be traced. The trace should consist of lines with commands like the following:

```
move
turnLeft
turnLeft
move
turnOff
```

2. Write a method in an appropriate class to count the number of books in a library read from a file. Add the cost of the individual books to the structure and provide a method to find the total cost of the books in the library.

3. Give the Book class a method to list all of the books by a particular author.

4. Build a GUI dialog that will prompt the user for the street and avenue number on which to create a robot and creates a North-facing robot there with no beepers. Note that the street and avenue numbers must be positive for this to be sensible, but you can ignore that for an initial version and then add the checking.

5. A robot named wcfields is going to take a random walk of 100 steps. At each step, wc will roll a four sided die (with faces 0, 1, 2, and 3) and will then make that many left turns. Wc will take the step and roll again, repeating this 100 times. At each step, wc will put down a beeper. Random walks introduce interesting properties of random numbers. If you run the program a large number of times, recording your results in a file, do you notice anything about the paths taken? The Die class is shown below.

6. Our robot wcfields is going to go on a random walk in a room that is completely enclosed and 10 blocks on a side. If wc finds its front is blocked it will roll again (and again...) until it can actually move in the direction indicated by the die roll. Wc still needs to take 100 steps, not just 100 tries. If you run this program 100 times, what is the average number of different squares visited by wc per walk? Note that you can automate the counting of the squares with a beeper counting robot. Record your results in a file.

```
from random import randint

class Die():
    ''' A die with a given number of faces numbered from 1. A
          variation could give lower and upper bounds.
    '''

    def __init__(self,faces):
        self._faces = faces

    def roll(self):
        return randint(1, self._faces)

    def faces(self):
        return self._faces
```

# Primo Intermezzo – The French Military Game

Let's take time out from the main topic sequence to consolidate some of the things we have learned. We will develop an interesting game using object decomposition and (especially) lists using array-like methodology, with a bit of input and output, both from the console and from files. Overall, it will require about 400 lines of Python code. We will return to the structure later in the book.

## 1 The Game

The French Military Game (FMG) is a moderately small game, bigger than Tic-Tac-Toe, but smaller than Checkers. It is small enough that a complete analysis of it is possible. The person will play one side and the computer the other. Initially the computer plays badly, but it will learn from its mistakes. This is possible since there are not too many possibilities, so it can record everything about every game it has ever played. It can also save these results in a file, so that when it returns to a game it "remembers" what it learned when run previously. It represents the simplest kind of *artificial intelligence* by having and improving its memory.

The version we will work on will only use the console for input, output, and display, but a graphical version might look like this:

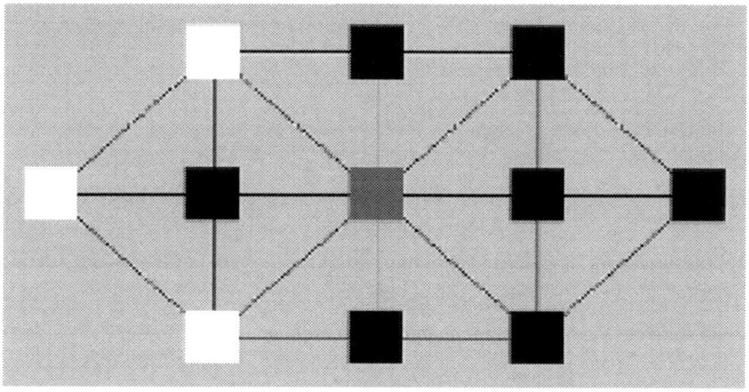

Figure 1. A Graphic Interface for FMG

There are eleven cells, connected by pathways. The white player, called The Police, has three pieces and the red player (shown here in medium grey), called The Fox, has one. The person plays the Police and tries to trap the Fox so that it has no legal move. Moves are along the pathways and the police can only move vertically and to the right. The fox moves in any direction and has the goal of reaching the leftmost cell. If the fox can evade the police for twenty moves it also wins the game. The board looks like this:

```
      1--4--7
     /|\ | /|\
    / | \|/ | \
   0--2--F--8--10
    \ | /|\ | /
     \|/ | \|/
      3--6--9
  Police at 0, 1, 3
  Fox at 5
```

In this form, the fox starts at 5, the police at 0, 1, and 3 and the fox wants to get to cell 0. The police can perhaps trap the fox at 6 if they occupy cells 3, 5, and 9.

The player will make a move by typing the *from* and *to* squares for one of his or her police pieces, separated by a space. If you want to move the piece at 0 to cell 2, type "0 2" (without the quotes). A dialog might be used to capture the move. A graphical version might play by using mouse clicks or drags. Here is a transcript of the beginning of a game:

```
      1--4--7
     /|\ | /|\
    / | \|/ | \
   0--2--F--8--10
    \ | /|\ | /
     \|/ | \|/
      3--6--9
  Police at 0, 1, 3
  Fox at 5
  Your move: from to  ( 0 0 to resign)
  0 2
  Police at 2, 1, 3
  Fox at 4
```

```
     1--F--7
    /|\ | /|\
   / | \|/ | \
  0--2--5--8--10
   \ | /|\ | /
    \|/ | \|/
     3--6--9
Police at 2, 1, 3
Fox at 4
Your move: from to  ( 0 0 to resign)
2 5
Police at 5, 1, 3
Fox at 7
     1--4--F
    /|\ | /|\
   / | \|/ | \
  0--2--5--8--10
   \ | /|\ | /
    \|/ | \|/
     3--6--9
Police at 5, 1, 3
Fox at 7
Your move: from to  ( 0 0 to resign)
```

The computer program has control of the fox and will try to make the best move it can. After it has played for a while it becomes very difficult to beat it. The graphic we have used here is an example of something often called *ASCII graphics*, named for a character encoding (American Standard Code for Information Interchange) that was standard in the early days of computing. We now use a more sophisticated code called UNICODE that permits the representation of all of the world's languages, but in only simplified form for Chinese, which has so many symbols. It was once quite common for students to create sophisticated artwork with just ASCII graphics. Some email signatures still use this, and "smileys" are another example ;-). Something like ASCII is a subset of UNICODE, by the way, but it is called Latin-1 there.

We will build a number of classes and they are dependent on each other. Here is a class diagram to show the structure. An arrow from A to B says that class A needs to know something about class B.

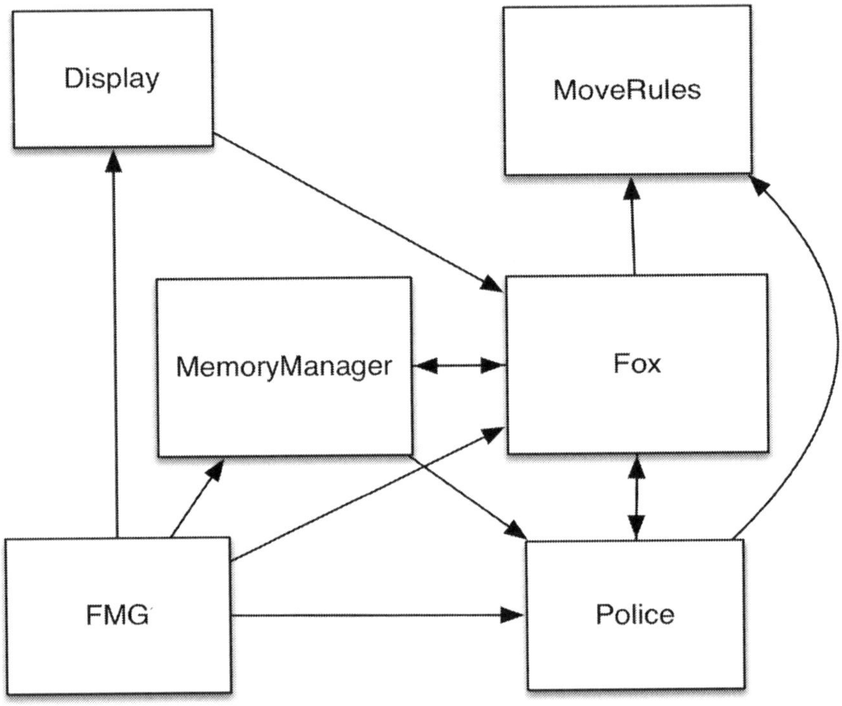


Figure 2. The Class Diagram

## 2 Move Rules

The *MoveRules* class keeps track of legal moves for all players. The *Fox* and *Police* classes manage information about each player, such as the current position. *Display* is just the ASCII graphic figure we've shown above, but encapsulated so as to make it easy to use and less error prone. The *MemoryManager* keeps track of everything having to do with the game remembering an individual game, a sequence of games, and the file that stores the information between plays. The *FMG* class is the game itself and carries on a dialog with the user, via the console.

As is usually the case, the classes that don't depend on others are the easiest to understand, so we start with the *MoveRules* class. We need a way to indicate the board and what constitutes a legal move upon it for both the fox and for the police. Since there are only 11 board positions, a square table or *matrix* (array of arrays) can be used for this, with a non zero entry at row x and column y could indicate a legal move from cell x (say 5) to cell y (say 3). We have two players, so we could use two such matrices, or we could encode the moves in a single one. Here is the definition of such a matrix. Note that it is a two-dimensional tuple or a tuple of tuples. This can never change, so we use tuples rather than lists.

```
# tuple of tuples: 11 by 11, rectangular - immutable Class variable
LAYOUT = (
         ( 0, 2, 2, 2, 0, 0, 0, 0, 0, 0, 0 ),
         ( 1, 0, 2, 0, 2, 2, 0, 0, 0, 0, 0 ),
         ( 1, 2, 0, 2, 0, 2, 0, 0, 0, 0, 0 ),
         ( 1, 0, 2, 0, 0, 2, 2, 0, 0, 0, 0 ),
         ( 0, 1, 0, 0, 0, 2, 0, 2, 0, 0, 0 ),
         ( 0, 1, 1, 1, 2, 0, 2, 2, 2, 2, 0 ),
         ( 0, 0, 0, 1, 0, 2, 0, 0, 0, 2, 0 ),
         ( 0, 0, 0, 0, 1, 1, 0, 0, 2, 0, 2 ),
         ( 0, 0, 0, 0, 0, 1, 0, 2, 0, 2, 2 ),
         ( 0, 0, 0, 0, 0, 1, 1, 0, 2, 0, 2 ),
         ( 0, 0, 0, 0, 0, 0, 0, 1, 1, 1, 0 )
         )
```

This is a field of the MoveRules class. It will never be changed. We have capitalized LAYOUT to indicate it is a constant. The rows of this, from 0 to 10 indicate the "from" part of a move, and the column is the "to". The zeros in the matrix indicate, among other things, where there are no connections between cells.

Here a 2 represents a legal move for the police, say from cell 1 to cell 2, and any non-zero entry is legal for the fox: 3 to 0, say. Recall that the police can only move to the right. There isn't much else to the MoveRules class so here it is, entire:

```
class MoveRules(object): # static class, no objects
    ''' A static class that represents the rules of the game
    '''
    # tuple of tuples: 11 by 11, rectangular - immutable Class
    # variable
    LAYOUT = (
            ( 0, 2, 2, 2, 0, 0, 0, 0, 0, 0, 0 ),
            ( 1, 0, 2, 0, 2, 2, 0, 0, 0, 0, 0 ),
            ( 1, 2, 0, 2, 0, 2, 0, 0, 0, 0, 0 ),
            ( 1, 0, 2, 0, 0, 2, 2, 0, 0, 0, 0 ),
            ( 0, 1, 0, 0, 0, 2, 0, 2, 0, 0, 0 ),
            ( 0, 1, 1, 1, 2, 0, 2, 2, 2, 2, 0 ),
            ( 0, 0, 0, 1, 0, 2, 0, 0, 0, 2, 0 ),     #more...
```

```
            ( 0, 0, 0, 0, 1, 1, 0, 0, 2, 0, 2 ),
            ( 0, 0, 0, 0, 0, 1, 0, 2, 0, 2, 2 ),
            ( 0, 0, 0, 0, 0, 1, 1, 0, 2, 0, 2 ),
            ( 0, 0, 0, 0, 0, 0, 0, 1, 1, 1, 0 )
            )
    #  fixed tuple of tuples: 11 by 11, rectangular immutable

    @classmethod
    def legalPoliceMove(cls, from_, to):
        return cls.LAYOUT[from_][to] == 2

    @classmethod
    def legalFoxMove(cls, from_, to):
        return cls.LAYOUT[from_][to] > 0
```

Note, however, that a two dimensional tuple isn't necessarily rectangular. It is just a tuple of tuples, and the inner tuples can have different lengths. This makes it important to keep track of things to avoid a IndexError.

Since MoveRules is immutable and is only queried for the basic game rules, it is encoded with static methods. No object of *MoveRules* is ever created. The classmethods here are just class level functions, invoked via the class name: `MoveRules.legalPoliceMove(f, t)`, for example.

## 3 The Display

The *Display* class is conceptually simple, but very messy. It also uses a two dimensional "array[2]" to do the graphics, but in this case it isn't rectangular. We need to change it to display the fox position as the game proceeds so this one is a tuple of lists. The tuple has seven "rows" but each row is a list whose elements (strings) can be updated. Notice that the lines in the board display are all of different lengths. We also want to be able to display an F at the position of the fox, so *Display* needs to know about the fox, though only as a parameter to a method. The display won't send any messages to the fox other than to ask it for its location.

---

[2]We use "array" here informally to indicate some general Python sequence, such as a tuple or a list. There is a non-standard Array type that we won't discuss here.

The structure itself took a long time to get exactly right so we want to encapsulate it to make sure that we can perform only legal operations on it. It is a field of the Display class.

```
self._display = ( # a tuple of lists. Entries will be modified
        # during a game to show the Fox. Warning: NOT rectangular
        [ "     ","1","--", "4", "--", "7"],
        [ "    /|\\ | /|\\"],
        [ "   / | \\|/ | \\"],
        [ "  ", "0", "--", "2", "--", "5", "--", "8", "--", "10" ],
        [ "   \\ | /|\\ | /" ],
        [ "    \\|/ | \\|/" ],
        [ "     ", "3", "--", "6", "--", "9"]
        )
```

This is what it looks like if we print out each internal list on a single line:

```
   1--4--7
  /|\ | /|\
 / | \|/ | \
0--2--5--8--10
 \ | /|\ | /
  \|/ | \|/
   3--6--9
```

We need to be careful in doing this, of course, since each row has a different length. The fact that any list knows its own length helps us here. The method to show this is like this:

```
def _unwind(self):
    line = ''
    for entry in self._display:
        for string in entry:
            line += string
        line += '\n'
    return line

def show(self):
    print(self._unwind())
```

It uses a helper method (_unwind) to create a single string to be printed. Note that the lines are terminated with \n characters. Here we use nested loops, first looping over the elements of the tuple and then individually over the elements of the lists it contains.

There are seven rows in display and len(display[i]) is the length of row i. If we had to keep track of this ourselves it would be very painful.

The double backslashes in some cells is just a way to show a single backslash. The \ character has a special use in Strings. It is used to *escape* or *quote* other characters to get special effects. For example '\n' represents a newline character and '\t' is a tab. This means to get backslash itself we need to also escape it, so '\\' is a single backslash.

However, when we actually display this during a game, we want to overlay the fox position on it. We will do so, by changing the cell in the array that represents the fox position to the character 'F'. The rest of the game knows the fox's position just by a game cell number, so we want a mapping that will translate that into an array cell in this display. For example, the fox is initially at cell 5, but that is on row 3 in column 5 of the display tuple. We use an array to do this mapping and initialize it as follows:

```
MAPPER = ( # tuple of pairs - immutable, classVariable
        (3, 1), # 0
        (0, 1), # 1
        (3, 3), # 2
        (6, 1), # 3
        (0, 3), # 4
        (3, 5), # 5
        (6, 3), # 6
        (0, 5), # 7
        (3, 7), # 8
        (6, 5), # 9
        (3, 9), # 10 Maps game cell numbers to _display locations
        )
```

This is again a tuple of tuples since it is immutable. We have used comments in the above to show the mapping. Cell 5 of array MAPPER contains a reference to a point with x = 3 (row 3 for us) and y = 5 (column 5).

The Display object remembers the old position of the fox (in variable *_theFox*), so to change it to a new position we can use the following method:

```
def moveFox(self, fox):
    where = Display.MAPPER[self._theFox]
    self._display[where[0]][where[1]] = str(self._theFox)
    self._theFox = fox.position()
    where = Display.MAPPER[self._theFox]
    self._display[where[0]][where[1]] = "F"
```

Suppose the fox is currently at cell 5. The display object remembers that in its *_theFox* field. The cell to move to is held in the Fox object passed as a parameter. Perhaps the *position* method of this object will return 7. We first use the mapper array to get a point that represents a row and column that needs to be restored to its previous numeric value (here 5). The display at that location is then reset to its numeric value, which is the remembered location of theFox. We then remember the new position for the future and again use the mapper to find the new cell to be changed and put the 'F' there. We have seen everything in the Display class except the field declarations, but here it is in its entirety.

```
class Display():
    ''' The visual _display in ASCII art for the French Military Game.
            It shows the game board with the fox's current location
            marked.

        Create a _display for the French Military Game with an initial
        position for the fox
            •  @param theFox the initial position of the fox player.
            •  Usually 5.
    '''

    MAPPER = ( # tuple of pairs - immutable, classVariable
            (3, 1), # 0
            (0, 1), # 1
            (3, 3), # 2
            (6, 1), # 3
            (0, 3), # 4
            (3, 5), # 5
            (6, 3), # 6                 more...
```

```
        (0, 5), # 7
        (3, 7), # 8
        (6, 5), # 9
        (3, 9), # 10 Maps the game cell numbers to _display array
                #    locations
        )

    def __init__(self, theFox):
        self._theFox = theFox
        where = Display.MAPPER[theFox]
        self._display = ( # a tuple of lists. Entries will be modified
            # during a game to show the Fox. Warning: NOT rectangular
            [ "     ","1","--", "4", "--", "7"],
            [ "    /|\\ | /|\\"],
            [ "   / | \\|/ | \\"],
            [ "  ", "0", "--", "2", "--", "5", "--", "8", "--", "10" ],
            [ "   \\ | /|\\ | /" ],
            [ "    \\|/ | \\|/" ],
            [ "     ", "3", "--", "6", "--", "9"]
            )
        self._display [where[0]][where[1]] = "F"

    def _unwind(self):
        line = ''
        for entry in self._display:
            for string in entry:
                line += string
            line += '\n'
        return line

    def show(self):
        print(self._unwind())

    def moveFox(self, fox):
        where = Display.MAPPER[self._theFox]
        self._display[where[0]][where[1]] = str(self._theFox)
        self._theFox = fox.position()
        where = Display.MAPPER[self._theFox]
        self._display[where[0]][where[1]] = "F"
```

Let's step back a moment and consider the larger picture. It would be possible to put all of the game into a single class. Dividing it up like this, however, lets us put distinct concerns in different places: What are the rules of the game; How shall we show it, etc. This makes it easier to develop and to understand, easier to find errors, and easier to bring a team of programmers together in its solution. All of these are valuable, but you need to do the division sensibly. You want minimal interactions between the parts if possible. So the *Display* class doesn't know much about the *Fox*, other than that the fox can tell it its own location on the grid. As you program, you should continuously ask yourself "Which object should be responsible for that?". So the fox should know its own location and how to compute its next move, etc.

## 4 The Police

Let's look at the *Police* class next as it is fundamental in understanding how this program can be "smart." There are exactly 165 different positions for the Police pieces. That is, there are 11 cells for the first piece. For each of those, 10 for the second, since they can't occupy the same location. And for each of those 110 combinations, 9 for the third. But that 990 must be divided by 6 = 3 * 2, since which piece is "first" doesn't matter and so, imagining them colored, the green one on 0 and the blue one on 2 is the same as the opposite. But since there are 6 ways to order the three pieces before assignment, we get 990/6 = 165 possible positions. We want a way to encode these so that we can record them. We could use a three dimension array (or several other possibilities, but we shall use a bit of a trick. First an excursion into binary numbers.

Binary numbers are just like decimal numbers, only the base is two, rather than 10. There are two symbols (0, and 1) rather than 10 (0 through 9) and the position of a symbol in a multi *bit* (= binary digit) number represents multiples of powers of 2 not multiples of 10. For example in base 10, 132 represents 1 times ten squared plus 3 times ten (to the first) + 2 times 1 (ten to the 0). Likewise in base 2, 1101 represents 1 times 2 to the $3^{rd}$, plus 1 times 2 to the $2^{nd}$ + 1 times 2 to the 0. This is the number 13, of course, back in good ol' decimal.

Our board has 11 positions, so let us consider 11 bit binary numbers. If the police have a piece on square x let's put a 1 in the x'th bit position, counting from 0 and from the right. So the initial position of the police (0, 1, and 3) is represented in 11 bits as 00000001011. Back in decimal, this is number 11. The smallest such value is

7 = 00000000111 and the largest is 1792 = 11100000000. And, of course, there are exactly 165 such values, but these are not all of the 11 bit values of which there are 2048 = 2 to the $11^{th}$. The actual values of these are: 7, 11, 13, 14, 19, 21, 22, …1568, 1600, 1664, and 1792. If the police occupy squares 3, 5, and 9, then we can encode it as 2 to the $3^{rd}$ plus 2 to the $5^{th}$ plus 2 to the $9^{th}$ = 8 + 32 + 512 = 552.

The game wants to remember the outcome of every game. More than that, it wants to weight each position held in the game more or less, depending on how many times the game was in that position and the fox turned out to be the winner in the end. Being conservative about it there are 165 police positions and for each of these the fox could be in any of 11 positions. Well, not exactly, because the fox can't hold a square held by the police, but it will be easiest if we just assume all of these are possible. That means 165 times 11 positions. We could conceivably hold these in a two dimension array structure with 165 rows and 11 columns where each row represents a police position and each column one for the fox, so the intersection is a full game position. If this cell holds a large positive number it means the fox was in this position often and later won. If it is a large negative number it lost from this position often.

The problem with this analysis, however, is that we only have 165 values from 2048 possible values, since the police "values" aren't the numbers from 0 to 164, but *some* of the numbers from 7 to 1792. What to do? Here is the trick we will use, but there are many others. Some of the others will become easy after we have seen the next chapter, in fact. Suppose that we store the 165 possible police values in a tuple (`self._ALLMOVES`), ignoring their order. We will store them, in fact, in an order in which it is easy to generate them using nested *For* loops. Then, to find a "value" for the police, we will compute the sum of powers of two as above for the locations of the three pieces and then search for this number in the array. We have to find it, since we store all such three bit numbers. If we find it in cell k then we shall use k as the value instead of the sum of powers. The disadvantage of this is that we have to do the search, but the advantage is that the resulting value k is a number in the range of 0..164 and so serves as a subscript into the 165 by 11 array of total game positions. We can call this trick *reverse lookup* since we are using the value in an array to give us a subscript, rather than the other way about which is the usual usage. If we sort the array we could make this search go faster, but we won't since there are *only* 165 values. Instead we shall use a feature of Python sequences. If you have a value that might occur in a sequence (zero or more times) you can use the method *index* to get an index at which the value occurs, or a ValueError if it doesn't occur at all. So `(1, 2, 3).index(1)` will return 0 since 1 is in that position. After studying Chapter 11 you might want to consider a HashMap for this, as well.

The Police class has a field

self._ALLMOVES = []

to hold all of these moves. It is created in the constructor of the Police class. When we create a Police object it is initialized, as well as initializing the three pieces. There will be only one object of this class used in a game so we create it when we create that object. This would be inefficient if there were several such objects, in which case we would do it otherwise, perhaps only initializing it if its len (length) were zero.

```
def init(self):
    # for a new game
    self._policePositions = [0, 1, 3]

@staticmethod
def whereValue(L, M, R):
    return int(2**L + 2**M + 2**R)

def __init__(self):
    self._policePositions = []
    self.init()
    self._ALLMOVES = [] #all legal police values as binary numbers
    for L in range(9):
        for M in range(L+1, 10):
            for R in range(M+1, 11):
                self._ALLMOVES.append(self.whereValue(L, M, R))
```

We factored out the init method from __init__ because we want to be able to reset the position for a new game, but don't need to re compute the array again. The three pieces for the police are held in a list with three cells.

The loop control limits in the constructor are chosen as follows. L represents the police piece with the lowest game cell number. It can only be 0 through 8 (that is, in `range(9)`) if the others have to be higher. The middle loop then only starts at L + 1 but goes to 9. The final piece must have a cell number higher yet, so that loop starts at M + 1 but runs to 10. Again, there are 165 ways to do this. Each computes a value stored in the *next available* cell of allMoves.

Once allMoves is initialized, we can compute a *value location* (i.e. the subscript discussed above), like this using reverse lookup:

```
def computeValueLocation(self): #get a computed position in ALLMOVES
    position = self._policePositions
    a = self.whereValue(position[0], position[1], position[2])
    try:
        return self._ALLMOVES.index(a)
    except Exception as ignored:
        return 0
```

We are guaranteed to find the item in the list, actually, unless we have made an error somewhere. So the Exception shouldn't be raised. That isn't always the case.

The other interesting method of the Police class is its *moveIfLegal* method. Actually this does two things. It makes a legal move if possible from values supplied by the human player, and signals the client program (an instance of FMG) as to whether it was able to move successfully. Of course a person can give incorrect inputs, so we need to check the legality. The user has said to move the piece at location *from* to square *to*. If that is legal we shall do it, other wise do nothing but print a warning message and signal False.

```
def warn(self):
    print("Illegal: try again")

def moveIfLegal(self, from_, to, fox):
    if not MoveRules.legalPoliceMove(from_, to):
        self.warn()
        return False
    if fox.position() == to:
        self.warn()
        return False
    here = -1
    i = 0
    for i in range(len(self._policePositions)):
        if self._policePositions[i] == from_:
            here = i
```

```
            break
        if here < 0:
            self.warn()
            return False
        for i in range(len(self._policePositions)):
            if self._policePositions[i] == to:
                self.warn()
                return False
        self._policePositions[here] = to
        return True
```

(Note that *from* is a Python keyword, so we use *from_* as a parameter name here.)

The logic of the above is this. First we ask MoveRules if this is ok. Next we ask if the fox is already on the *to* square. If either is a problem, we can't do the move. Next we look to see if the Police actually have a piece on the *from* square and if so which one. If not, we signal. false again. Finally we need to be sure that the Police doesn't already have another piece on the *to* square. If we pass all the tests we make the move and signal True.

The game will also want to know if the Police hold a given square so the final method of Police provides this information:

```
    def holdingPosition(self, position):
        for i in range(len(self._policePositions)):
            if position == self._policePositions[i]:
                return True
        return False
```

Aside from a simple method to print the positions of the three pieces, there is nothing else in the class. Note, however, that whenever we wrote a for loop to process an array structure, we used the length of the array as the upper bound, rather than a hard-coded constant like 3 or 165. It is much harder to make a mistake this way, and much easier to correct them when you do. Assuming you want them to *stay* corrected, of course, as the program might change.

The Police class is actually primarily an information manager. It doesn't interact directly with the human user. That task is handled by game play. It will react to a request to move, however, updating information.

## 5 The Fox

In many ways the Fox class is simpler, but it does have the interesting feature that it computes an optimal move, based on past experience. It maintains its own piece position, of course, and can return and display it. It also provides an *init* to reset the piece for a new game, but the only interesting method of this class follows. This is invoked just after the police have moved, so we need to know the new position of the police. The memory manager object keeps the history of the game and will give us information about relative value of potential moves. Note when we start that there may not be any legal move at all. The police may have just trapped the fox. That will be signaled by setting the position to -1. Otherwise it will be a new "best" square on the board. Below is the entire class. The `self._position` is actually first defined in the simple *init* method, not the constructor, but the constructor invokes this method to assure its creation.

```
class Fox(object):
    '''Play the Fox, controlled by this program
    '''

    def init(self, start):
        self._position = start

    def __init__(self, start):
        self.init(start)

    def position(self):
        return self._position

    def optimalMove(self, police:Police, memory):
        policeEntry = police.computeValueLocation()
        best = -1
        for trial in range(11):
            if MoveRules.legalFoxMove(self._position, trial) and \
                    not police.holdingPosition(trial):
                if best < 0:
                    best = trial
                else:
                    if memory.smaller(policeEntry, best, trial):
                        best = trial
        self._position = best
```

```
    def showPosition(self):
        print ("Fox at " + str(self._position))
```

The class is declared with a superclass *object*, which is part of Python and assumed if no superclass is specified. But you may see this in code you read. Here the init method specifies the start location for the Fox, which is usually 5, though it doesn't check that this is legal, given the positions of the Police at the start of a game. That is a (minor?) flaw in this code.

We examine the *optimalMove* method. The parameter *police* is the Police object, which knows its own positions and the *memory* is the current remembered history of plays.

The for loop checks every possible square, first looking for some square that it is legal to move to. If it can't find any, it is trapped. Otherwise, it sets the first one found as its current best and looks for more. From that point, every time it finds a legal move it asks the memory to compare the new trial move with its current best. If the trial is bigger (better) the best becomes trial. We haven't seen yet, how the memory manager maintains the information and updates it, but we soon shall. It is similar to the analysis we did on the police positions. Notice here that our nesting of logic structures is pretty deep. Too deep? Can you understand it without the explanatory material? Without the comments? Perhaps this should be refactored so that helper methods handle some of the inner structures.

## 6 Playing the Game

Let's look at the game itself next and then look at how information is remembered. The game is managed by the FMG class.

The *play* method will interact with the user, playing several games as desired. Each game is managed by the *oneGame* method. It also interacts with the user through the console. In *play* the user just needs to respond yes or no when asked if a new game is wanted. Note that *play* uses an infinite loop, with break statements to end the loop. If break is executed it will exit the closest containing loop. The program prints a prompt and then awaits input. If the loop ever exits, the execution of the program terminates, but not until the memory object saves the game information for all games played in this session.

```
    def play(self):
        while True:
            self.oneGame()
            print("Play again? - Y or N[N]")
            raw = input().strip() # could use just lstrip()
            if not raw:
                break
            reply = raw[0]
            if reply != 'y' and reply != 'Y':
                break
        if self._smart:
            self._memory.saveMemory()
        else:
            print('Overwrite existing history? - Y or N[N]')
            raw = input()
            if not raw:
                return
            reply = raw[0]
            if reply != 'y' and reply != 'Y':
                return
            print('Writing')
            self._memory.saveMemory()
```

The raw input has its first character extracted as the basis of making the decision. Any answer to the prompt that begins with 'y' or 'Y' after stripping whitespace is interpreted as a desire for a new game, but anything else will result in termination. This is not very *robust*. In a more important situation you would need to do more to make sure the game correctly understood the user's intention.

The game can be played in two modes: smart = True or smart = False, when False, the game doesn't use past memory, so the Fox needs to relearn. So, when smart is False, it asks whether it should overwrite any existing memory file, completely erasing the memory of the past runs.

The getMove method wants two integers from the user and will loop until it gets them. When it is happy, it returns a tuple with the two values. It shows the game board as a prompt.

```
    def getMove(self):
        move = []
        while len(move) < 2:
            try:
                self.showPositions()
                print("Your move: from to  ( 0 0 to resign)")
                move = input().split()
                if len(move) < 2:
                    print("Two Integers needed. Try again:")
                if len(move) >= 2:
                    x = int(move[0])
                    y = int(move[1])
            except Exception as e:
                print("Integers needed. Try again:")
                move = []
        return (x, y)
```

We put everything inside the loop in a try – except block so that if the input fails to be two ints, we get to try again after some explanation to the user. The assignments to x and y will fail if the user enters things that can't be cast to ints. They will also fail if fewer than two inputs are typed. We will later see a dialog to capture the move, and it actually simplifies this as the dialog will do the validation of the inputs.

The actual play of a game is managed by the *oneGame* method. It is also an infinite loop with breaks. Each time around the loop we handle one play by both players. First the police, then the response from the fox. As soon as we know the game result we break. The outcome variable records +1 (WON) or -1 (LOST) depending on whether the fox wins or not. And recall that the fox wins if we go 20 moves. Note that if the person gives an illegal move we just ignore it and go around the loop again. Once more, not very robust, but this is a simple game. Perhaps you want to improve it.

```
    def oneGame(self):
        self.init()
        moves = 0
        print("Playing")
        outcome = 0
        while True:
            if moves > FMG.MAX_MOVES:
```

```
            print("Fox wins = timeout")
            outcome = FMG.WON
            break
        self._display.show()
        move = self.getMove()
        from_ = move[0]
        to = move[1]
        print('You moved from',from_, 'to', to)
        if from_ == 0 and to == 0:
            print("Fox wins = resign")
            outcome = FMG.WON
            break
        if self._police.moveIfLegal(from_, to, self._fox):
            self._fox.optimalMove(self._police, self._memory)
            position = self._fox.position()
            self._memory.record(self._fox, self._police)
            moves += 1
            if position == 0:
                print("Fox wins - home")
                outcome = FMG.WON
                break
            elif position < 0:
                print("Fox loses - trapped")
                outcome = FMG.LOST
                break
            self._display.moveFox(self._fox)
            self.showPositions()
    self._memory.summarize(moves - 1, outcome)
```

## 7 The Memory Manager

So that is everything except how the game learns. All of that is encapsulated in the MemoryManager class. But note that in the above, we ask the memory to record each successful move by the fox, and we ask it again to summarize the game at the end when we know the outcome. The task of managing the game's memory has three parts. It must remember each move in a single game. It must transfer the game information to an overall history data structure and it must be able to read such a structure at the beginning of play and save it again at the end. We will look at these in turn. There are two main data structures used by the MemoryManager and we will use a two dimensional rectangular tuple of lists here for the history and a list of tuples to record a single game. Both *thisGame* and *history* are initialized in the constructor. Initially the *history* is a structure with 165 rows of 11 columns, all entries are zero. The *filename* is the name of the history file:

```
def _buildHistory(self):
    history = []
    for outer in range(165):
        line = []
        for inner in range(11):
            line.append(0)
            history.append(line)
    return tuple(history)

def __init__(self, filename, maxMoves):
    self._filename = filename
    self._history = self._buildHistory()
    self._thisGame = []
```

The *thisGame* will have up to maximumMoves rows and two columns, one for the police and one for the fox. Each time a successful move is made *record* is invoked. We can see the method invocation above in *oneGame*. here is the method itself in MemoryManager:

```
def record(self, fox, police):
    self._thisGame.append((police.computeValueLocation(), \
        fox.position()))
```

A tuple is simply appended to the *thisGame* list. So, when the game ends we have the complete record of that game in the thisGame array. Column 0 holds the police positions as the "magic" array subscripts defined by the *allMoves* structure we discussed above. Column 1 holds the corresponding fox location at that point in the game.

At the end of the game, the *oneGame* managing method sends the message `memory.summarize(...)`, which transfers the game information into the history array. That array has a row for each possible police position and a column for each fox position. It's contents are integers that are incremented if a position (row, column) results in a fox win, and are decremented if the fox loses:

```
def summarize(self, moves, outcome): #public
    for i in range(moves):
        police = self._thisGame[i][0];
        fox = self._thisGame[i][1];
        self._history[police][fox] += outcome
```

Recall that the outcome can be either +1 or -1 and the last statement uses the += operator to add the right hand side value (outcome) to the left side variable. a += b is a shorthand for a = a + b. There are similar operators for all of the usual arithmetic operators; +=, -=, *=, /=, %=. There are even more, in fact, but those you can look for yourself.

One possible flaw in our design is this. The MemoryManager doesn't encapsulate the *moves* variable. It depends on the client (oneGame) to send consistent values of moves when it invokes both record and summarize. The information should be held in one place, not two, and here it is also needed in *oneMove* to determine whether a game should end, but we could have held it in MemoryManager instead with an accessor. You can explore a refactoring that implements it that way and then analyze the two for (a) ease of use, and (b) maintainability and safety.

Recall that the fox uses the MemoryManager object as a service to help it find an optimal move. The memory knows the history so it can tell us which trial move is better:

```
def smaller(self, row, current, trial):
    return self._history[row][current] < self._history[row][trial]
```

The question asked here is whether on row "row", which represents a police position, the *current* fox position is smaller than some trial (but legal) move. If so, the *trial* is a better choice so the fox will remember it as its current best choice. This is the basis of "intelligence" of the fox; nothing more. Really, it just remembers not to make the same mistakes repeatedly, but to repeat its successes. Not a bad strategy for most life situations, actually.

All that remains is the file processing methods. When the MemoryManager is created it is given a filename of the memory file, as well as the maximum moves in a game. This file is initially read and is later written. Things can go wrong, of course. The filename might not point to a file when it is read, or some other IOException might occur. Writing is a bit more definite, but it is possible that the disk we want to write to is locked or offline. So, as is typical, in i/o we need to deal with any possible Exception, either by handling it or by propagating it. We will see both here. First, let's look at how we save the history array into a file at the end of play.

```
def saveMemory(self):
    allvalues = ""
    for i in range(len(self._history)):
        for j in range(len(self._history[i])):
            allvalues +=  str(self._history[i][j]) + " "
    try:
        out = open(self._filename, 'w')
        out.write(allvalues)
        out.close()
    except Exception as e:
        print("Could not write the memory file.")
```

We wrote earlier about making i/o more efficient by doing less of it. Here we employ that idea. The first thing that this method does is stream the entire history array into a String with spaces separating the numbers. The array is read by rows; the outer for loop runs 165 times and the inner one 11, We don't hard-code those numbers, of course, but use the array lengths to control the loops. Note that we can use the += operator here, but this time it represents string catenation, since that is the meaning of + for String objects. Note, however, that we create a large number of Strings here, since catenation always produces a new String, rather than modifying an old one. The innermost statement runs 165 times 11 times. However, we hope to get back the time this takes, by doing only one write to the file. We only need to write the String named *all* to the file as one chunk.

We do the write in a try block so that we can catch the *Exception* if it should occur. First we open a file for writing pointed at the filename given earlier (in the constructor) so that we can write a String. We must also remember to close the file when done writing so that it is preserved by the operating system. But if something goes wrong we will wind up in the catch block instead. Here we just write out a message as well as the system's usual stack trace, and exit. We don't try to actually recover from this. In a more important application it might be essential to do a recovery as valuable information could be lost. It might be possible to arrange a re-try, perhaps with a different filename. The coding for this can be quite complex and we won't attempt it here.

At the beginning of play we need to read the file back in. The MemoryManager uses two methods for this. The *getMemory* method is the one the client (FMG) calls. The *smart* parameter determines whether we want the file read at all. If it is false (or if the file can't be found), the history will be initialized to all zeros. If smart is true we invoke readFile to try and load the history array from the file. Note that the MemoryManager already knows the filename, from its constructor, so we don't need to pass it here. We need to catch Exception here, since readFile might throw it via propagation.

```
def getMemory(self, smart): #public
    try:
        self._readFile(smart)
    except Exception as ignored: # wipe out the history if no file
        for i in range(len(self._history)):
            for j in range(len(self._history[i])):
                self._history[i][j] = 0
```

Finally, the method to actually attempt to read the file uses the smart parameter to determine whether to initialize the history from the file or simply to set zeros. If opening or reading the file throws an exception, we simply propagate it back to the client (getMemory). We again use a simple Scanner object pointed at a File with the given filename.

```
def _readFile(self, smart):
memoryFile = None
if smart:
    memoryFile = open(self._filename)
    text = memoryFile.read()
    strings = text.split()
    values = list(map(int, strings))
    memoryFile.close()
k = 0
for i in range(len(self._history)):
    for j in range(len(self._history[i])):
        if smart:
            self._history[i][j] = values[k]
            k += 1
        else:
            self._history[i][j] = 0
```

There is the possibility for another exception here, of course. If the memory file gets corrupted and there isn't an int where it is expected then an Exception will be thrown. Also, if the file gets truncated somehow, then we also get an Exception. We could guard against all of these by simply propagating Exception instead, and also catching that in *getMemory*. In this situation, that would probably be an improvement.

That is it; an interesting game that is quite challenging for the human player. More important, it exercises your knowledge of sequence structures (lists and tuples) quite thoroughly.

Before we end, however, you, the reader, must understand that this program was not developed in the order in which it was presented here. It is very valuable to read and understand such programs, but the development order and the presentation order are utterly different. The development did not start with the class diagram we showed at the beginning. It began, in fact, with a few ideas that were tried out, with some successful and some failing. The ideas had to do mostly with *features* that someone thought the program should have, and the features were added one at a time. Adding a feature takes "a little of this (data structure development, say) and a little of that (writing methods or classes)." Along with frequent testing as the program emerges. The first thing done (most likely - it was done by others, not this author, and has been in the literature for a long time) was to get the actual program flow right. Interacting with the computer, printing prompts and getting inputs. The ASCII art likely came much later and the saving to files among the last things to be done. The current form was refactored into the classes we present from a more monolithic version that the author once found in the language BASIC. In Chapter 12 we will look at a way that such a program might be developed from scratch.

## 8 A Dialog for User Inputs

Suppose we would rather have the user enter the police moves into a dialog instead of typing them into the program flow. The dialog can also do input validation. We will need a class, PoliceMove, as well as two simple changes to the *oneGame* method. To permit both sorts of inputs we will provide an alternative to *getMove* called *getMoveFromDialog(self)* and this will need to be invoked instead of *getMove*.

```
    def getMoveFromDialog(self):
        move = []
        while len(move) < 2:
            self.showPositions()
            print("Your move: from to  ( 0 0 to resign)")
            move = policeMove() # create the dialog
            if len(move) < 2:
                print("Try again:")
        return (int(move[0]), int(move[1]))
```

Note that like getMove it returns a tuple of ints.

The new dialog module, which will need to be imported, looks like this:

```
from tkinter import simpledialog, Label, Entry, Tk

class PoliceMove(simpledialog.Dialog):

    def __init__(self, root):
        super().__init__(root)

    __move = (0,0)

    @classmethod
    def get(cls):
        return PoliceMove.__move

    def getResult(self):
        return (int(self._from.get()), int(self._to.get()))

    def body(self, master):
        self.title('Police')
        Label(master, text="From:").grid(row=0)
        self._from = Entry(master)
        self._from.grid(row=0, column=1)
        Label(master, text="To:").grid(row=0, column=2)
        self._to = Entry(master)
        self._to.grid(row=0, column=3)
        return self._from # initial focus
```

```
    def validate(self):
        try:
            int(self._from.get())
            int(self._to.get())
        except Exception as e:
            print('invalid data - try again')
            return False
        return True

    def apply(self):
        PoliceMove.__move = self.getResult()

def policeMove():
    root = Tk()
    root.withdraw()
    PoliceMove(root)
    root.destroy()
    return PoliceMove.get()
```

This is an adaptation of the *TwoValueDialog* shown earlier and we present the adaption to emphasize the *validate* method of a simpleDialog. If *validate* returns false, then the dialog won't try to return values, but will wait for proper inputs. A more graphical (overall) application would put up a message box rather then print out the error, but we only have a simple application here.

If the cast of the results of the two Enter boxes both succeed we return True, otherwise the except clause will return False. That is all that is required. TwoValueDialog didn't seem to *validate* because it was happy to return anything the user entered. So, the inherited *validate* method it uses always returns True. The *validate* method is called by the *simpleDialog* infrastructure, so we don't see its invocation.

We will examine some alternate data structures that might be used to organize this game in the next chapter and you will get a chance to refactor it again.

## 9 Important Ideas From This Intermezzo

two dimensional structures
artificial intelligence
ASCII
reverse lookup
linear search
binary numbers
bit (binary digit)
array structure initialization
dialog
program composition

Note that the data structure we use here is the Python list, but we have treated it like other languages use arrays and have indexed through the structures with integer indices. There are better solutions that we will discuss in Chapter 11, but the techniques here translate easily to other languages that may have fewer and less flexible storage structures.

## 10 Problem Set

1. Consider a dialog for asking the user if they want to play another game. Consider another for asking if they want the history saved.

2. Find a better name for the first parameter of the *smaller* method of the MemoryManager. Names of variables should be in terms of the problem itself, not the way we choose to solve the problem. The name *row* refers to a row in the array, not anything in the problem. Hint. How does the client code use this?

3. Investigate the & (bitwise and) operator of Python. Suppose you have the 11 bit integer representing the Police and the integer representing theFox. What is the result of the following when theFox represents one of the police positions and what if it does not:

```
police & theFox
```

Try interpreting that as a bool. Can we use this computation in the FMG game?

4. Investigate writing a Tic-Tac-Toe game in exactly the same way. The person can play first and the computer tries to move as well as it can, knowing its own history. The game is also called Noughts and Crosses. The game can result in a *draw*, with no winner.

5. Investigate a winning strategy for the police. If you can find one, try to program it either to play the game so that the Police always win or as a separate program you run to cheat. If you do the former, look at the history after a few hundred runs.

6. Consider sorting the allMoves array when it is created. Look in the Python sequence methods for the sort method. An online search with Python, and perhaps tkinter in the search string is often productive. Also look into the possibility of generating it in sorted order.

7. Notice that the ASCII visual presentation of the game shows the Fox position, but not the Police. Modify it so that 'P' appears for each of the three police positions.

# 11 Collections

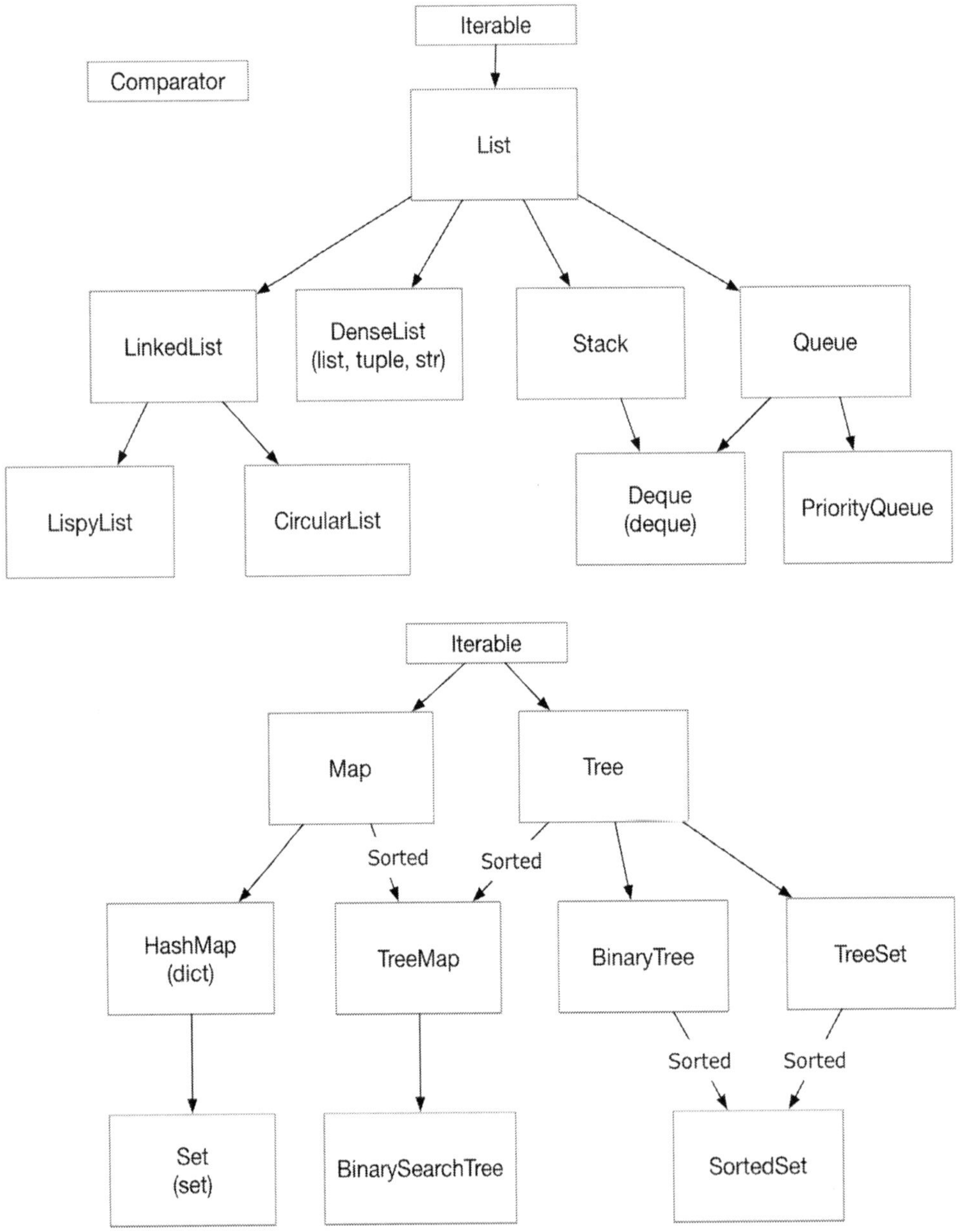


Figure 11.1. Conceptual Collections Framework

## 11.1 Collections Framework Overview

A collection is a type of object that can contain values, including other objects. The stored objects are *data*. Python lists, strings, and tuples are examples, but there are others. Collections differ in their implementations and those implementation structures give them different properties. Some collections, for example, are sorted, others not. Conceptually a Robot holds a collection of Beepers, for example, and a World has a collection of Walls. Some collections are *sequences*, which is a Python concept, but not a type. Lists, tuples, and strings are sequences. Sequences are index by integers, usually starting from zero. You can ask for the fifth element, for example.

Many collections can contain data of any type, but a few are specialized. A Python string (str type) always contains only characters. A list can contain anything, including other lists, as we have seen. Many collections are heterogeneous, meaning they aren't restricted to holding a single type of object and it might take discipline if you really require homogeneity. Other languages may favor homogeneous collections, the element type of which might need to be specified.

The classic collection type, implemented in most languages is the *array*. Python, however, favors lists over arrays, though there is a library (NumPy) that you can import for arrays. Arrays favor efficiency over flexibility and lists (in Python) favor flexibility. An array is normally a homogeneous, densely stored, fixed size, structure indexed by integers, usually (not always) starting at zero. The advantage of these properties is that lookup in an array is very fast. Homogeneity assures that each cell of the array has the same size. So, entry k can be found by multiplying that size by k (assuming zero-based indexing). We will have a few things to say about arrays as we go along, but won't discuss them in detail.

In this chapter we will examine many of the built-in Python collections as well as implementation strategies for these and others. The image on the preceding page is only a conceptual framework, thought he Python types are mentioned where they occur. The arrows are conceptual also, with no implication about inheritance or implementation. We will save some of them for Chapter 13. Some of them you will need to explore in the literature, though a course in *Data Structures and Algorithms* should give a complete picture of the area. We will also revisit some of the data structures used in the Intermezzo and provide some alternatives.

One of the most important concepts with collections is that many (actually most, in Python) of them are *iterable*. This means that, for example, that you can easily get the stored data as a list and you can also use *For* statements to process all of the data contained in them. Lists, for example, are the sort of prototype of an iterable collection. For example, the *moveIfLegal* method of the Police class iterated over the police positions (twice) to determine the legality of a move. The Python built-in collection types (str, list, tuple, dict, set, deque) are all iterable and it is possible to provide this in user defined collection classes as well. This isn't the case in other languages – at least not in the consistent and flexible way that Python provides.

Python has a large number of functions that work with any iterable. For example, you can capture the elements of an iterable collection, say *tree*, with list(tree). The print function will also work with any iterable. You might want to investigate the *enumerate* function.

Moreover, many Python tricks make use of iterable collections. For example, if you have a tuple and treat it strictly like other languages treat arrays, and you want access to the contents you write something like the following:

```
for i in range(len(options):
   print(options[i])
```

In other words you get access to the contents through its indices. But the Python way of programming with an iterable would be to grab direct access to those contents with:

```
for val in options:
   print(val)
```

The variable options, as an iterable, works directly in *For* statements, avoiding the intermediate steps of using the index, but also when an iterable isn't indexed at all. The Python way is both efficient, and, importantly, expressive of intent. We saw the first usage in the Intermezzo, and will see more of the second, below.

Collections can be *indexable* or not. When a collection is indexible you can access elements of it with subscripting notation. For example if you have a list, _policePositions with three elements, then _policePositions[i] gives one of the positions for i between 0 and 3. Strings are indexible, as are are lists and tuples, starting with index 0. You can do the same with a dict (dictionary) or binary search tree, though the "subscript" will be one of the key values, which isn't likely an integer.

Collections can also be *mutable* or not. Strings (str) and tuples are not mutable. Once created they can't be extended or changed, though you can create new values from old. The other Python collections are all mutable, so you can add values to a Python set or list.

Collections can be *ordered* or not and they can be *sorted* or not. These aren't the same concept. A list is ordered (first element, second, etc) but a tree is not. On the other hand sorting implies some ordering based on the data, not just the position in the structure. Lists can be sorted or not, but sorting requires some work to achieve. BinarySearchTrees, on the other hand, are naturally sorted (but not ordered). So, when you extract the values from a BinarySearchTree you get them in the order of the data. But sorting requires that you be able to compare values. Some things can be compared with the natural operations of a language such as < and >=, but other types of data may not be. Is one Robot greater or less than another? However, in a well designed collection class it may be possible to provide a comparator, often a lambda function to provide a comparison.

Suppose, for example, that we could ask a robot for its beeperCount, getting an int. Then

```
compareLess = lambda r1, r2: r1.beeperCount() < r2.beeperCount()
```

would let us know which of two robots was "less" on that measure. And lambdas are often passed as function parameters to provide flexibility in sorting a collection. We could then make decisions based on invoking such functions:

```
if compareLess(monty, morgan):
    ...
```

### Specifics of Some Built-in Collection Types

Type *str* (string) is immutable, iterable and ordered. Strings can be single or double quoted and you can use one kind within the other.

```
list('These are the times')
```

will produce a list of the characters in the string. You can also easily split a string into words with the split method.

```
'These are the times'.split()
```

produces a list of four words as strings. The default is to split using whitespace, but you can specify the character(s) on which to split and the maximum number of splits that will occur. The split character won't be included in the strings of the list.

```
'aardvark activism'.split('a')
```

will produce: `['', '', 'rdv', 'rk ', 'ctivism']`

Type *list* and *tuple* are similar except that tuples are immutable. They are ordered, iterable. Both are indexed by integers starting with zero and ending one less than the length.

*List comprehension* is a technique that is a bit misnamed as it isn't restricted to lists. For example:

```
    x = tuple(v for v in range(5))
    print(x)
    y = [v*2 for v in x]
    print(y)
```

defines a tuple and then a list (the specific tuple constructor is required so that this doesn't just seem like a parenthesized expression. It produces:

```
(0, 1, 2, 3, 4)
[0, 2, 4, 6, 8]
```

The structure of a comprehension is first an expression (as in the second example) followed by a *For* expansion giving values to the variables used in the expression. It looks like, making a list for example: `[expr for variable in iterable]`, and will produce a list of the results of evaluating the expression for each element of the iterable. More complex forms are also possible. But it is really a shorthand for something like, using the second example above:

```
result = []
for v in x:
   result.append(v*2)
```

Type *set* in Python is a specialization of type dict, but it is simpler to explain. It is something like a mathematical set. It is mutable, iterable, heterogeneous, and enforces the rule that an item can appear only once. A literal set is a pair of curly braces enclosing a sequence of values separated by commas: *band = { 3, 'dog', 'night'}*. It is unordered, so printing it might show a different ordering than what you wrote originally.

Like many collections, sets support the "in" operator. So:

```
if 'dog' in band:
   ...
```

should result in True for the test.

A dictionary (type *dict*} is a set of key:value pairs, with an explicit syntax for creating it. The purpose is to associate some set of keys with a set of values. The keys are unique, but don't need to be of the same type. The keys are used to get the associated values:

```
simpleDict = {3:'jonny', 'foo':'bar'}
```

associates the key 3 (an integer) with the value 'jonny' and the key 'foo' with the value 'bar'.

```
simpleDict['foo']
```

results in 'bar'.

A given key can appear only once, but the association can be changed:

```
simpleDict['foo'] = 'bas'
```

will replace the association in the mapping.

Typical usage has the keys all of one type and the values all of one type, but that isn't a requirement. If you iterate over a dictionary, you get the keys in some order. Once you have a key you can get the associated value with subscripting:

```
for key in simpleDict:
   print(key, simpleDict[key])
```

You can insert a new value into a dictionary using subscript notation, though it will change the current value associate with that key if it already exists:

```
simpleDict['alpha'] = 'beta'
```

will insert 'alpha': 'beta' into the dictionary, but

```
simpleDict[3] = 'mary'
```

will change the value already associated with key 3.

Dictionaries, by the way, are implemented as hashmaps, sometimes called hashsets. They are optimized for fast lookups. We will look at something similar below.

Note that the various updating and accessing techniques of values of these types are enabled by a set of special functions that are implemented by collections. We shall see some of these later in the chapter.

The order in which an iterator returns the values depends on the collection. For a set there is no implied order at all as it is much like a mathematical set. For a list, it will be in the position order within the list, much like an array in other languages, with positions 0 through size()–1 as the legal positions. A TreeSet, on the other hand, keeps the values in an order dependent on the values themselves as we shall see and the iterator returns them in this order. If the TreeSet or BinarySearchTree contains key objects in order of their comparator, though not in a linear manner.

```
robotList = []
robotSet = set({}) # so that it isn't considered a dict
robotDict = {}
karel = Robot(1, 1, North, 0)
robotList.append(karel) # insert karel into the end of the list
```

```
    robotSet.add(karel)
    robotDict['leader'] = karel
# later in the program
    worker = robotList[-1] # extract the last item
```

The above shows insertion into various collection types.

We will make use of this shortly.

## 11.2 Collections Exploration – Part 1, Variations

Let's see what we can do with some of the collections and maps in the framework. We shall transform the FMG game of the Intermezzo into a more modern form, replacing many of the array-like concepts we used with objects from the framework. There are many ways to do this, so some of it will be exploratory, looking at tradeoffs: costs and benefits.

First, we shall not touch the MoveRules class as it seems like the best solution we can think of. It is an ideal application of a two dimensional tuple. It is rectangular; it has fixed values; it is well matched to its problem of determining the legality of a matching (move) between two values. So we leave it be. The Fox and FMG classes will have few changes, none structural. We shall change these only to react to changes elsewhere. We will also be careful not to require gratuitous changes in these. The reason for leaving them is that there are really no collections of data within them and our purpose here is to explore collections.

Recall that we need the MAPPER in FMGame so that we can indicate where the fox is in the display when we draw it. If the fox is at logical game cell 7, then we want to place the "F" string at cell `display(0,5)` and the MAPPER holds these subscripts in a tuple object. While there is nothing wrong with using a tuple for the mapper we can, at least, look at some alternatives.

First, though, we should note that a tuple is itself a mapping. It maps a contiguous set of integers starting at 0 to the elements that are contained in the tuple. The map for a tuple named *values* is: x -> values[x]. In fact, then a tuple (or list) is a finite mathematical function from a *domain* of integers starting at 0 to a *range* consisting of the values stored. In the above, the mapping is from {0, . . . , 10} to a set of tuple objects, actually pairs. Lists do the same thing, so we could also represent MAPPER with a list. We prefer the immutability of tuples here, however.

There is another way we could do this with a tuple, however, which makes the mapping more apparent.

```
class Display():

    MAPPER = (
            (0, (3, 1)), # 0
            (1, (0, 1)), # 1
            (2, (3, 3)), # 2
            (3, (6, 1)), # 3
            (4, (0, 3)), # 4
            (5, (3, 5)), # 5
            (6, (6, 3)), # 6
            (7, (0, 5)), # 7
            (8, (3, 7)), # 8
            (9, (6, 5)), # 9
            (10,(3, 9)), # 10
            )
```

This explicit version is probably less error prone, so we prefer it. However, it requires a few changes to the code, since this is now a two dimensional structure where the original was one. The changes are all in the same class, one of the advantages of using this class structure in the first place.

While we could easily switch to a LinkedList (below) for this with almost no changes (except the original declaration) we should not do so in this case. This is due to the nature of the dense lists like tuples and LinkedLists and how they match (or not) with our use. The fox starts at cell 5 of the game board. Its first move could take it to any of a number of cells (depending on what the other player does, of course). This means that we can go directly from the 6$^{th}$ entry in the mapper list to any other but the first and last in the next move of the game. Array-like things (dense storage) are well suited to randomly accessing cells, but linked structures are not.

Lists and tuples, like arrays in most languages, utilize a densely packed storage mechanism in which it is possible to compute the location of any cell from its index with a simple computation. This is due to the fact that all of the things in the array have the same size, so knowing that you want cell 7 (the eighth cell) says that you can find it at a location 7*sizeOfCell memory locations from the beginning of the structure in the computer's internal memory. This is because 7 cells (0 through 6) precede cell 7 and all have the same size. This is fast for a computer to do since it knows the beginning and the size of the cells.

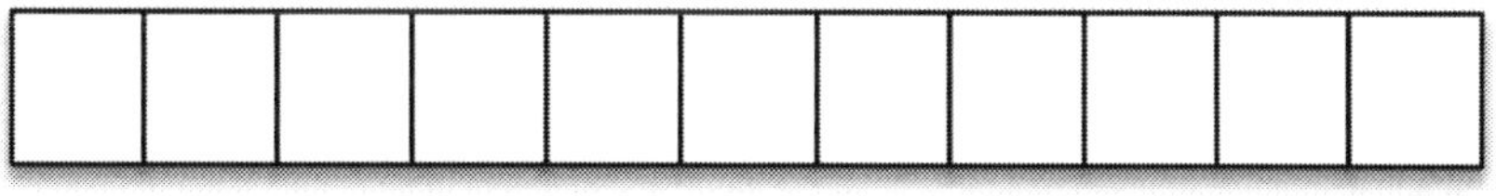

Figure 11.2. Dense Storage

While it is possible to *add* data into a dense structure, between two existing items, it is relatively expensive (time consuming) to do so, as the elements to the right of the new location need to be moved farther right to make room and we need to assure a cell exists at the farthest right. Adding at the end (right) of such a structure is normally quite fast, as the structure maintains some extra space to permit this to happen fast, though if you exceed the capacity for that, it will take a while to create new capacity. The time for it will be proportional to the number of cells currently in use since the old data will need to all be copied into a new structure. While this sounds very bad, it doesn't happen very often, so on the average it works out. If a cell in a list already exists, we can modify its contents with by referencing the index on the left side of an assignment (assuming mutability: `aList[3] = 42`.

Linked structures, on the other hand, are stored completely differently. A linked structure contains a small amount of data (one value) along with a reference to the location of the next such cell. This makes it possible to easily expand such a structure, since we don't need a contiguous block of memory cells to hold it, but can put the next cell anywhere that is free in the memory. But the cost is that to find cell 7 you need to start at cell 0 and follow its link to cell 1 and from there to cell 2, etc, until you count to the 8$^{th}$ such cell. This is slow by comparison. So the tradeoff is memory flexibility against operational speed and if you need to access cells in arbitrary (often called random) order you want something that uses dense, not linked storage. On the other hand, if we were only processing mapper in the order of the cells, then linked might be preferable.

Figure 11.3 shows linked storage with a single link from each cell to the next. The program keeps track of the first cell (at the upper left) separately. The linked structures we will see below will show examples of single linking, like the above, and also double linking with a reference in both directions, so that it is possible to move either direction in the list, but only from cell to cell. So, to go from the 6th to the 10th you have to move through all of the intervening cells, one step at a time.

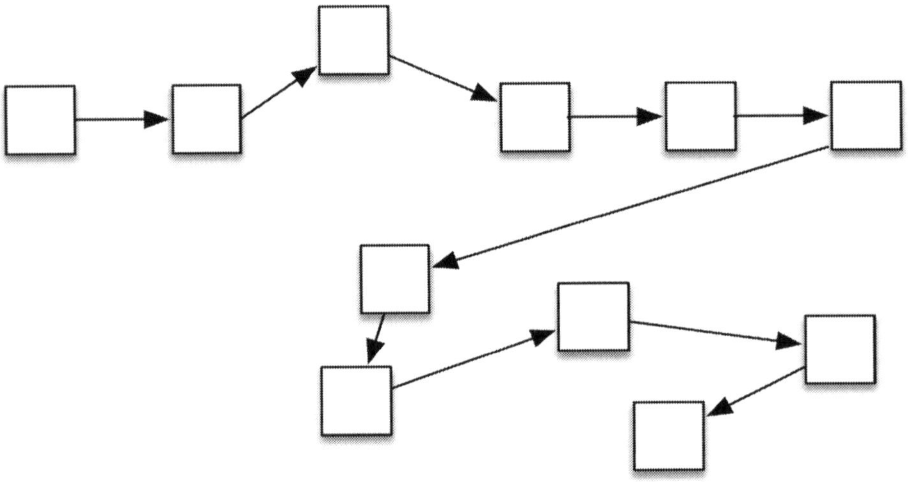

Figure 11.3. Linked Storage

Linked structures are nothing new to you, in fact. Any object that holds a reference to another is linked. That other may be linked to a third, etc. What makes linked lists special, if at all, is that the items in the list are data with some purpose in the program. Back in Chapter 4 we actually built a linked list of decorators of a strategy. The last item in the list was a simple strategy and terminated a chain of decorators that form the bulk of the list. Problem 21 in Chapter 4 is the clearest example of this. A *node* in a list holds some data, perhaps, but also a link to the next node. Many implementations of lists terminate them with the *None* value.

Terminating a list with a special object that has no next link is a superior way, however. This is called the Null Object Pattern and in our decorator chain, the innermost Strategy took the role of the Null Object. The problem with the None value is that it can't be polymorphic, so you need to explicitly check for it with an *If* at every step. With a Null Object the innermost (last) item just handles the message in a different way, but, being an object, it CAN handle a message whereas None cannot.

However, if you need to find a given element in a linked structure you need to start at the beginning and search one node at a time. This the time it takes you to find your data requires time proportional to the number of nodes. This *linear* time behavior (since the graph of time vs. number of nodes is a straight line) is much worse than the *constant* time required to access an item in a dense structure such as a list or tuple.

While we have seen options for the Display class mapper structure, none of this has yet had any real benefit for our program, other than in learning about these options. It is hard to justify either of these as better in this situation. The number of cells on the game board is fixed, so the size of the structure we use need not be adaptable. There is a bit more overhead in the list actions than in the array actions. The only real benefit is that we are sending messages when we use objects and so the usual message "dot" syntax that serves for everything else we have done works here also. And, of necessary we open the possibility of using polymorphism too, though it is very unlikely to be of benefit here.

The final variation we will look at for Display is to replace the mapper tuple with a mapping, In Python, a dict is a mapping, actually. The keys will be the integers 0 through 10 and the values will be the location pairs.

```
MAPPER = {
          0: (3, 1), # 0
          1: (0, 1), # 1
          2: (3, 3), # 2
          3: (6, 1), # 3
          4: (0, 3), # 4
          5: (3, 5), # 5
          6: (6, 3), # 6
          7: (0, 5), # 7
          8: (3, 7), # 8
          9: (6, 5), # 9
          10:(3, 9)  # 10
          }
```

The order of insert here is immaterial, unlike the list version, since a map has no sequential structure. Subscripting with a key in a dict returns the value, assuming the key is actually stored, or None if the key can't be found. So MAPPER[3] gives (6, 1). Note, however, that dictionaries in Python are mutable.

Documentation says that a Python dictionary is implemented as a HashMap, but it could be changed to a TreeMap with no difference in effect other than (possibly) different efficiency of operations. A TreeMap keeps the information in key order. There is no reason to do so here, since a TreeMap is a bit less efficient for this purpose and keeping the elements in key order internally is not needed here, so there is no benefit to the tree.

Hash and tree structures are quite different from each other, as well as being different from list structures we saw earlier. A hash structure works by doing a computation on the key to determine where in the structure to store the value. Actually both the key and value are stored together as we shall see. The computation is quite different from the one done in dense structures, however, since the keys don't need to be integers and we don't need to store in key order. Instead, the *hash* method that is possessed by every object is used to start the computation process. Figure 11.4 has a schematic of one kind of hash map, though there are others as well.

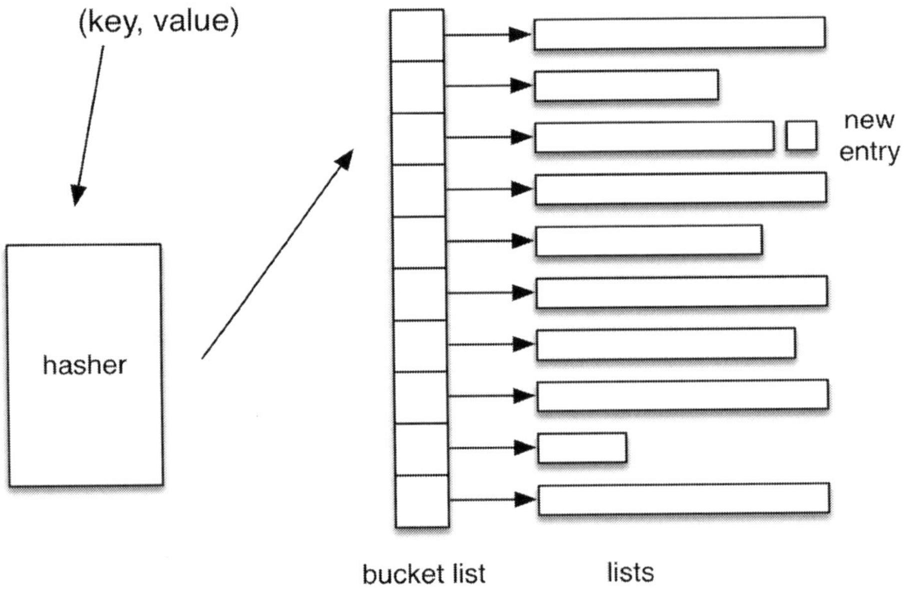


Figure 11.4. HashMap (schematic)

In this structure the key is sent to the hasher, which is just a computation method. It computes an array index by taking the hashCode of the key and then computing a remainder upon division by the length of the so called *bucket* list. The bucket list holds references to lists (either linked or dense) called buckets. The computation provides an entry in the bucket list that will point to one of the buckets. The key-value pair will then be inserted into that bucket, replacing any entry with the same key. (Note that it is possible for HashMaps to behave differently from this description).

When two different keys compute the same bucket number it is called a *collision* and we don't like a lot of collisions, since then the lists get long and the searching gets slow. For this reason, the number of buckets is kept to a more or less constant fraction of the number of entries stored (the load factor) by expanding the size of the bucket list periodically. While this reorganization takes time, it guarantees fast look up. And in fact the *reason to be* of a HashMap is to minimize the *access* time.

There is some caveats here however. While the search operation is going on within a bucket, an equality method is employed to see if the key being stored is already there. For each stored key we ask is it equals to the one being stored. An implication of this is that within the logic of your program, if two distinct objects should be considered equal, then they had better return the same hash value. If not, then lookup might fail, since the program will be searching the wrong bucket. But it is a concern if you use your own class objects (say Robots) as keys in a HashMap.

The second caveat is that if you define your own hash method, it has to always return the same value for a given object. If it is based on mutable values of the object, and those change, then hash won't be consistent and you might "lose" things. And, don't use a randomizer in a hash.

And you want, as much as reasonable, different objects to return different hashCodes. This is so that the hasher will spread the data more or less evenly among the buckets. If your hash function always returns 0 for example then all of your data will end up in the first bucket and you can do no better than linear search of this bucket to find it again. This will defeat the entire purpose of a hashMap: fast lookup. So, our dict version of the mapper in Display is pretty good, but still, not likely to be as good as an array index lookup.

Finally, note that the built in hash function of Python will be consistent for a given execution of a program, but not for another run of the program. So, if you dump a hashed structure into a file and then read it again, you need to take precautions.

But a hash map with a decent hasher and an adaptive method for modifying its structure as we add new items will achieve approximately constant time retrieval on the average, though not necessarily for each lookup (get). Inserts are also quite fast on average, though if an insert (put) forces a reorganization, that insert will take longer.

The TreeMap implementation is built on a completely different concept. Integer data have a size, of course: the value of the integer. Other objects can be given a size as well. A circle has a radius, for example, and a person has a height. In fact, some objects have different "sizes" for different purposes. People also have weight and income, etc. The idea of a TreeMap is to keep key-value pairs in order of the "size" of their keys.

A *binary tree* is, conceptually at least, a linked structure in which each node has two links, called the left and right child nodes. Either or both of the children can be None, or a special "leaf" node. A general node typically holds some data as well as the links. In a TreeMap, the node will hold a key-value pair. A TreeSet holds only the keys. It is also possible, as we shall see, to keep the contents of a tree in key-order, assuming they can be compared. Thus we can have a SortedMap or SortedSet.

A *binary search tree* is a binary tree in which the data are associated with a key and the nodes of the tree have an ordering dependent on the key. The ordering of the nodes is such that for any node, the left child holds data that has a *smaller* key than this node and the right child has a larger key. We need to be able to compere keys with something like a < operation, however. This may be natural or not, depending on the objects you want to store. Integers have this natural "size", of course, but other things may need to have a way to compare them for use as keys.

In general, a tree structure can contain duplicate keys, but we need to prevent that if we want to implement a dictionary or a set.

When values are the same they are resolved in a uniform way, depending on what is needed. For a tree map the keys can only be present once and so if we try to insert a pair with a key already held, the new data can either replace the old with the older value lost, or the new insertion can just be ignored. So there are decisions to make when you build such a tree determined by its usage. It is also possible to build trees in a flexible way so that different uses are possible.

Figure 11.5 shows a simple binary search tree showing only keys. If we wanted to insert key 72 into this tree we would do the following: Starting at the top node (the *root*), we see that 72 is larger, so we go down to the right child and examine that (93). 72 is smaller so we go left. It is also smaller than 78 and when we go left again we find the None value (an empty space in the drawing) and so we create a new node to hold the new data and link it as the left child of the "78" node.

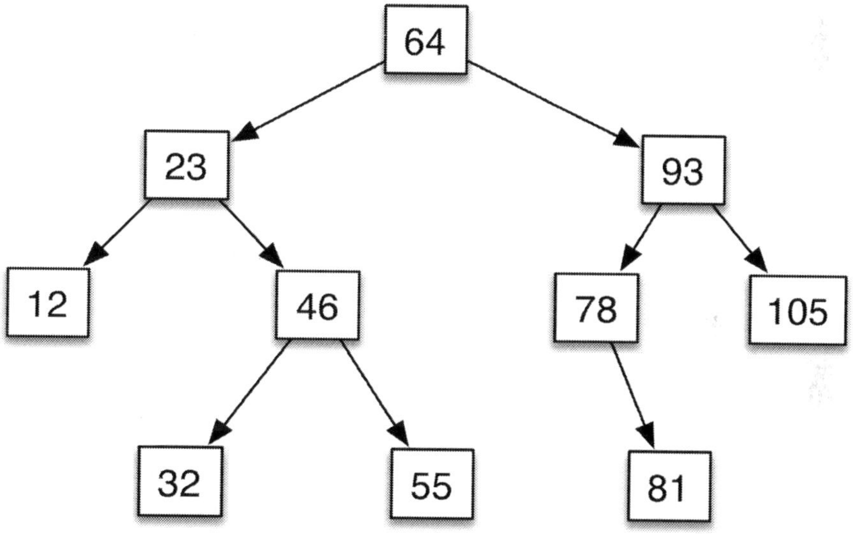


Figure 11.5. A Simple Binary Search Tree

Actually, though, the above simple tree isn't good enough as it can wind up wildly unbalanced. If you start with a small value and repeatedly insert larger and larger values the process described above will always move to the right. The tree will then degenerate to a linked list. On the other hand, if we can keep the tree *balanced*, meaning that each path from the root to a *leaf* (a node with no children) has "about" the same length, then the number of nodes in the tree is exponentially related to the length of such a path. The *height* of a tree is the length of the longest path from root to leaf, counting links, not nodes. Our example tree has height 3. But it is possible to store as many as 15 nodes in this tree without changing the height if we either (a) enter them in correct order (hard) or (b) adjust the shape of the tree so that it stays balanced as we go (also hard). The former method is usually infeasible as we don't often get the data in an appropriate order. The other is possible to do, though the algorithms are complex. In general, it is possible to store as many as $2^{n+1}- 1$ nodes in a tree of height n. Therefore a tree of height 20 can store over a million nodes. Looking at the reverse of this, it is possible to search a tree with a million nodes and take no more than 20 steps to do it. This *logarithmic* behavior is what makes a TreeMap attractive, though it requires the tree be kept balanced as inserts are done. The algorithms to balance on insert need to move the nodes around a bit, but they move only a logarithmic number of nodes, so their performance is also quite good. Not as good as a HashMap, but if you want the data kept in order, very good. The iterator for the keySet of such a tree will yield the keys in order, and given the keys, we can get the associated values *in key order*. One good implementation is a *Red-Black Tree*, in case you want to investigate further.

Not everything can be put into a TreeMap as a key since the structure needs to be able to compare the keys for what we have called "size". In fact, there are two ways to make it possible for objects of a class to serve as keys in a TreeMap (or elements in a TreeSet, which we shall see shortly).

The first way is for the potential key type to be able to respond correctly if we use the normal comparison operators; <, <=, etc. Python provides a way for arbitrary objects to implement these, using special functions (__lt__, __le__ , etc.). We will also see how some of these functions can be built into your own classes. If we want to be able to compare Robots, by how many beepers they hold we could provide the following function in the Robot class, which makes some assumptions about other things. It would be a bad idea to do this for using Robots as keys, since the number of beepers is mutable.

```
def __lt__(self, robot):
    return self.beeperCount() < robot.beeperCount()
```

Then, if karel and martha are robots, karel < martha, will return True or False, depending on the number of beepers each carries.

Therefore we would need to implement this one method. The *contract* for such a comparator is this: If the object executing the method (i.e. self) should be considered smaller than the argument, then < should return True. If self should be considered larger or the same, then < should return False.

In a class that implements such comparison operators, the __lt__ method imposes an order on the elements called their *natural order*. TreeMaps use the natural order, if available, in the absence of the second solution.

The other way to create a TreeMap for elements that, perhaps, have no natural order or for which we want the ordering to be other than the natural order is to use a special kind of object called a comparator.

In essence a Comparator provides a function of two variables that gives back how to specify the "size" of a key object. Comparators can be as simple as a lambda:

```
compare = lambda r1, r2: r1.beeperCount() < r2.beeperCount()
```

If you want to use a comparator in a TreeMap you create one before creating the map and then pass the comparator as an argument to the constructor of the TreeMap. A Comparator could also be an instance of a class providing several different comparison methods.

Before we look again at the FMGame, let's examine a few user built collection structures and how some are related to the Python standard types.

## 11.3 List Structures

There are two sorts of lists: linked and dense. The Python *list* is dense and implemented (usually in C++) with arrays. But linked lists are also common structures in programming so we will examine these first, along with some variations:

### Linked Lists

A linked list is a recursive structure. One of the early and important versions comes from the Lisp language, which has many successors and is an example of a Functional Programming Language. A list in lisp is made up of "cons cells", named for an implementation detail from the first version on an IBM 704 computer. A memory unit on the computer had two parts: the address register part and the data register part. This led to naming conventions that have persisted to some extent: *car* = contents of the address part and *cdr* = contents of the data part. In Lisp, the car was used to hold data, perhaps a link to something, but the cdr was used to point to another cell. The name *cons* comes from construct and is how you built up a list.

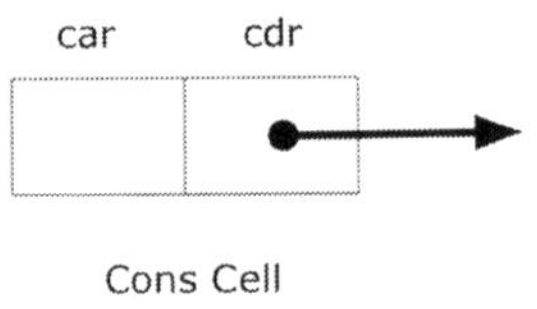


Figure 11.6

We will first build something in the spirit of lisp; a LispyList to show basic linking techniques.

First, a list might be empty. We will use None as an empty list but refer to it with the name nil by defining that value to be None. A variable representing a LispyList either refers to nil or to a cons cell. A cons cell has a car and a cdr, but nil has neither and it is an error to ask nil for either. Lisp lists are normally manipulated using three functions. The definitions follow, but they all need to be backed up with a class defining the structure.

```
nil = None

def cons(value, aList):
    return Lisp(value, aList)

def car(aList):
    return aList.car()

def cdr(aList):
    return aList.cdr()
```

The car is the head of a list and the cdr is its tail. It is, perhaps useful to use those names if you aren't an IBM 704 programmer and that is easy in Python:

```
head = car
tail = cdr
new = make = cons
```

Functions are like any other object and can be assigned so car(aList) and head(aList) are the same.

The class that backs up these functions is actually very simple:

```
class Lisp:
    def __init__(self, data, tail:Lisp):
        self._tail = tail
        self._data = data

    def car(self): #head, a value
        return self._data   #(self._top._data

    def cdr(self): #tail, a Lisp
        return self._tail

    def cons(self, data)-> Lisp: #newList
        return Lisp(data, self)
```

You create a list, starting with nil and calling cons repeatedly:

```
bList = nil
bList = bList.cons(3)
aList = bList.cons(5)
bList = bList.cons('Monty')
bList = bList.cons(7)
bList = bList.cons(9)
```

Here we keep reassigning new lists to the same variable, but note that cons doesn't actually modify a list. It just creates a new one from an old one. At the end of the above, aList will still hold just 3 and 5 with 5 at the head. Note that this sort of list is recursive on Lists. A List points to a List. The cdr of aList would be a List containing just 3.

As built above, a list isn't iterable, though we could make it so by giving the class a few more functions. Nor will it fit well with other Python collections; again, a solvable problem.

There are a number of important data structures used in computing. One of them, the Stack, is fundamental to the internal operation of most programming languages, especially in calling functions. A stack can be empty or it can contain values. You insert into a stack with "push" which inserts a value at the "top", like placing a plate on a stack of plates. You remove (and modify) a stack with "pop" which gives you a reference to the top value (most recently pushed) but also removes it from the stack. It is easy to build a stack structure from a LispyList, since all we need to handle is the removal operation.

```
from LispyList import car
from LispyList import cdr
from LispyList import cons

class LispyStack:
    def __init__(self):
        self._elements = None

    def push(self, value):
        self._elements = cons(value, self._elements)

    def pop(self):
        value = car(self._elements)
        self._elements = cdr(self._elements)
        return value

    def top(self):
        return car(self._elements)

    def isEmpty(self):
        return self._elements is None

    def clear(self):
        self._elements = None
```

Here push is just cons, top is just car, but pop needs to use the cdr as its collection of elements.

To make this a bit more Pythonic, we will add an iterator to it. This requires two additional methods; __iter__ and __next__ which are all that is needed to make it iterable. The first is an initialization method and must return an object, usually self. The second updates things set by the initialization and returns the "next" value, depending on the meaning of "next" for the structure. For a stack, it seems like top to bottom is the proper ordering.

```
def __iter__(self):
    self._temp = self._elements
    return self
```

Note that it introduces a new instance variable (outside the __init__ method of the class. This _temp will be manipulated by __next__.

```
def __next__(self):
    if self._temp is not None:
        val = car(self._temp)
        self._temp = cdr(self._temp)
        return val
    raise StopIteration
```

This will return the car of the temp list and will replace the temp with its own cdr. The *stopIteration* exception needs to be raised here and in every such method to prevent infinite iteration and a crash of your program. Note two things. This doesn't affect the list itself, and if the list itself is modified in some ways the iteration could go wrong. Many iterables have this restriction.

Now the following will work since *for* and *in* know about iterables:

```
stack = LispyStack()
stack.push(4)
stack.push(5)
stack.push(6)
for i in stack:
    print(i, ' val ')
if 7 in stack:
    print('yep')
```

It will produce:

```
6 val
5 val
4 val
```

With such an iterator, we could also transfer the values in the stack to a tuple with the method:

```
def values(self): #as tuple
    result = []
    for i in self:
        result.append(i)
    return tuple(result)
```

It would also be easy to add a "size" method to such a structure.

One more Pythonic refinement; the __str__ method, which should return a string appropriate for the structure. With the above method this is also easy:

```
def __str__(self):
    return str(self.values())
```

It depends on the fact that the str function (constructor actually) looks for this method. The print function uses the __str__ method when available, so if we extend the above example with *print(stack)* we will get the tuple printed: (6, 5, 4).

There is another way to interpret cells such as cons cells. Instead of the recursion being direct (a list is made up of lists), it is indirect. A list points to a node and the nodes point to other nodes. Thus the recursion is among the nodes, not directly the lists. So, in this interpretation, a list *has* nodes, rather than *is a* node. The following picture should suffice, though the pointer into the node is normally captured as an instance variable of some class.

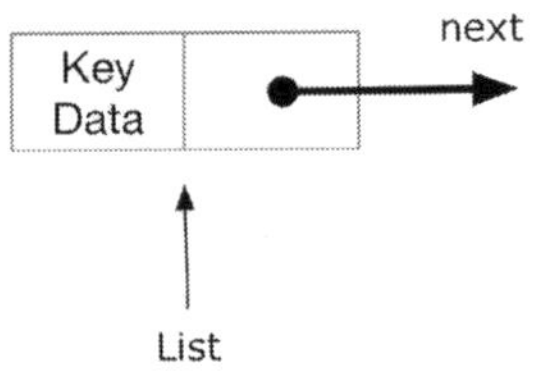


Figure 11.7 List Node

We won't follow up on this directly here, but will do something more sophisticated but that can be simplified if the above is all that is needed.

A node can have more than one reference to other nodes. A node with two such pointers is illustrated below, and a list could point to one of these, as shown.

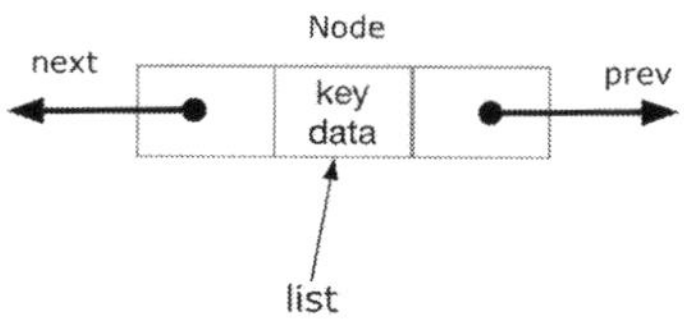


Figure 11.8 Double Linking

One of the implementations using such nodes is a doubly linked list in which these nodes point to other such nodes to "left and right", terminated with something like None. A list would then have two pointers, one to each end of the list of nodes so that new items could be inserted (pushed) or deleted (popped) at either end. If such a structure is used to push at one end (usually the tail) and pop at the other (the head) then it is known as a queue. The push operation is then normally called enque or enqueue and the pop is deque or dequeue. Queues are normally used for processing things that need to be processed in the same order they arrive. Arrival generates enqueue and processing happens after dequeue.

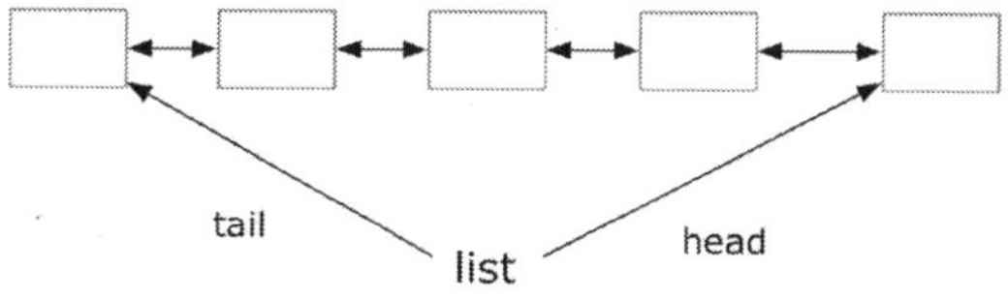


Figure 11.9 Deque

We won't show a program for this either. (Note: that in the above figure, the two headed arrows are drawn for convenience to represent a pair of opposite pointing arrows: next and previous.)

However, it is possible also, to connect the head and tail together, giving a circular structure as in Figure 11.10:

In this case, a list (CircularLinkedList) only needs one pointer, normally to the tail. The head is "previous" to the tail and the tail is "next" after the head. Pointing to the tail makes insertions and deletions at either conceptual end easier as we shall see. The cells themselves can contain arbitrary data, including key: value pairs. Following "next" arrows is moving in the clockwise direction.

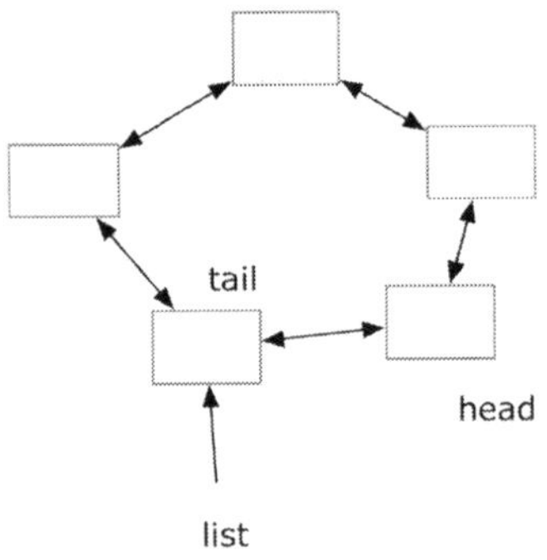


Figure 11.10 Circular Linking

We want to be able to push an item (new cell, actually) on to either end. To push at the head, just insert a new cell between head and tail, and adjust the next and previous pointers. There are four pointers to fix up. The head's "next" points to the new cell and the tail's previous also. The new cell's previous points to the current head and it's next points to the tail. That cell is then, automatically the new head. To insert at the tail (enqueue), do exactly the same thing and then make the list point to the new node, so that it is now the tail of the list.

We also want to be able to delete from either end. To pop (remove the head), make the tail's previous point to the current head's previous and make that cell's next point to the tail. Just two pointers to fix. To dequeue (remove the tail), just first make the tail point to it's own next node and then do just as we did for popping the head. Of course, we need to make special precautions when we empty a list or when we insert the first node into a list.

Here is a very complete Node class for a doubly or circularly linked list:

```
class Node:
    def __init__(self, data):
        self._next = self
        self._prev = self
        self._data = data
    def prevNode(self):
        return self._prev
```

```
    def nextNode(self):
        return self._next
    def data(self):
        return self._data
    def setPrev(self, node): # used in push
        self.prevNode()._next = node
        node._prev = self.prevNode()
        self._prev = node
        node._next = self
    def removePrev(self): # NOOP for a self pointing node
        prevNode = self.prevNode()
        if self != prevNode:
            prevNode._prev._next = self
            self._prev = prevNode.prevNode()
```

Note that it doesn't have setNext or removeNext methods, but they might be desirable for a doubly linked list. Our intention here is to build the circular list. This class will be nested within the CircularLinkedList class. For some applications it might also be desirable to have a *setData* method. The *setPrev* and removePrev capture important sequencing of operations so that they don't need to be repeated in other code. These two methods are used in *pushHead* and *popHead* of the CircularLinkedList class. An empty list will have its tail set to None and this will be updated on the first entry (pushHead or pushTail). The list will also keep track of its own length (size), increasing and decreasing as we push and pop.

```
def __init__(self):
    self._tail = None
    self._fromFront = True
    # convenience names for treating this as stack and queue
    self.push = self.pushHead
    self.pop = self.popHead
    self.enqueue = self.pushTail
    self.dequeue = self.popHead
    self.dequeueTail = self.popTail
    self._size = 0

def head(self): #car
    if self._tail is None: return None
    return self._tail.prevNode().data()
```

```
def tail(self):
    if self._tail is None: return None
    return self._tail.data()

def pushHead(self, data):
    newNode = CircularLinkedList.Node(data)
    self._size += 1
    if self._tail == None:
        self._tail = newNode
    else:
        self._tail.setPrev(newNode)

def pushTail(self, data):
    self.pushHead(data)
    self._tail = self._tail.prevNode()

def popHead(self):
    val = self.head()
    self._size -= 1
    if self._size == 0: #empty
        self._tail = None
        return val
    self._tail.removePrev()
    return val

def popTail(self):
    self._tail = self._tail.nextNode()
    val = self.popHead()
    return val
```

As with most collection structures we want to be able to iterate through it. But, since the two ends are equally useful, it is useful to be able to iterate in either direction. The instance variable *_fromFront* controls the order of iteration and the list will iterate from the rear if it is False. A method to switch it is useful and easy to write as is the *size* method. Initialization of such an iterator is more complex that we saw above:

```
def __iter__(self):
    if self._tail == None:
        self._iterNode = None
    elif(self._fromFront):
```

```
            self._iterNode = self._tail.prevNode()
        else:
            self._iterNode = self._tail
        self._startNode = self._iterNode #used to signal end of iteration
        self._flagHalt = False
        return self
```

This introduces three new instance variables. The *_iterNode* is the current node and it is updated (by *__next__*) as the iteration proceeds. The *_startNode* and *_flagHalt* are used so that we end the iteration on one cycle through the list, so we don't keep going round and round forever.

```
    def __next__(self):
        if self._iterNode is None or self._flagHalt:
            raise StopIteration
        val = self._iterNode.data()
        if self._fromFront:
            self._iterNode = self._iterNode.prevNode()
            if self._iterNode == self._startNode: self._flagHalt = True
        else:
            self._iterNode = self._iterNode.nextNode()
            if self._iterNode == self._startNode: self._flagHalt = True
        return val
        raise StopIteration
```

On each call to *next*, say in a for statement, we move the _iterNode one direction or the other depending on the value of *_fromFront*. We signal halt when we come again to the *_startNode*.

There are some other useful method that can be included, but we leave it there.

### Dense Lists

A dense list is indexed by integers, starting with zero and can be iterated over. Access to individual elements is fast, unlike linked lists, which must be traversed to find individual elements. Dense lists may be expandable (like Python lists) or not (like traditional arrays). They can be homogenous or heterogeneous. In an interpreted (rather than compiled) language like Python, heterogeneity is normally easy to achieve, but requires some discipline on users when homogeneity is needed in an application.

In Python there is little need to build dense list structures since lists and tuples serve well, though efficiency can be improved with some implementations. The purpose of this section is to show how the Python list is built up and how it might be done in other languages. We will show an extendable list that, except for periodic reorganization, is quite efficient, though it will use Python lists internally. Consider it a demonstration of technique, nothing more.

The structure shown here will integrate well into the Python system generally, supporting several common techniques, such as iteration, the "in" operator, etc. We will use this structure, just as an example, in the Secondo Intermezzo later.

A dense list can be efficiently used as a stack, but less so as a queue without special techniques. The reason is that operations at one end are favored, due to efficiency considerations.

The class DenseList represents an expandable structure, so it needs both a size and a capacity. The size is the current number of elements and the maximum currently allowed subscript of an element is one less than the size. The capacity is the maximum number of elements we can append to the structure before it needs to be reorganized. (expanded). We won't implement shrinking of the structure so it will grow as needed, but if things are popped, it will retain its capacity. We will also use *args to permit initial loading of the structure:

```
d = DenseList(0, 1, 2, 3)
```

will create a DenseList with a minimum capacity (the first argument) and initial contents 1, 2, 3. By setting an initial capacity above the minimum (which is actually 1) we can anticipate use and minimize the number of reorganizations, improving efficiency. Again, as this is only a demonstration of techniques, we use Python lists which already have all of the capabilities we describe here, so we are being very redundant in actuality. However, a novice programmer needs to understand how to build such things, not only how to use them.

We will implement the following protocol

```
add(index, value)
append(value)
clear()
```

```
clone()-> DenseList
contains(value)-> bool
get(index) returns a value
indexCheck(index)-> bool
pop() returns a value
remove(index)
removeValue(value)
removeAll(value)
set(index, value)
size()-> int
showStore()
```

along with ten hidden methods `__init__`, `__add__`, `__contains__`, `__delitem__`, `__getitem__`, `__iter__`, `__len__`, `__repr__`, `__str__`, `__setItem__`, all of which are to make the structure fit the Python framework.

The constructor is:

```
class DenseList:
    def __init__(self, initialCapacity=1, *args):
        self._size = 0
        self._capacity = \
            initialCapacity if initialCapacity > 0 else 1
        self._store = [None]*self._capacity
        for i in args:
            self.append(i)
        self.push = self.append #defines a synonym
```

All of the arguments, if any are inserted into the list by appending them to the end, possibly causing an immediate reorganization unless the initialCapacity given is large enough to contain them as would be the case in the example given above.

Note that the _store is just a Python list initialized to several copies of None.

In many ways, the most important method to implement in any collection class is its iterator. For this class it is especially simple since _store is a list and lists have their own iterators. So all we need is:

```
def __iter__(self):
    return iter(self._store[:self.size()])
```

Note that it will iterate only over the portion of _store up to self.size(), not the entire capacity. We don't need a __next__ method in this case.

Once we have the iterator we can use it to build other methods of the class. For example, clone will return a faithful copy of the object with minimal capacity:

```
def clone(self):
    result = DenseList(self.size())
    for i in self:
        result.append(i)
    return result
```

We use append (or its synonym, push) to extend the list on the right. But we need to be careful since we must increase the size and possibly the capacity and the size of the _store.

```
def append(self, value):
    if self.size() == self._capacity:
        self._expand()
    self._size += 1
    self._store[self.size() - 1] = value
```

There are more sophisticated expansion algorithms, but we will just double the size of the _store (and the capacity) when reorganizing:

```
def _expand(self):
    newStore = [None] * (2 * self._capacity)
    for i in range(self.size()):
        newStore[i] = self._store[i]
    self._store = newStore
    self._capacity *= 2
```

First, it creates a new list twice as long as the current one, then copies everything in to it. The _store becomes this new list and the capacity doubles. This is the operation that is usually missing from the arrays of other languages, though one can implement such a thing when needed using the logic here.

Setting an item at a given index is straightforward, provided the index is valid (i.e. less than the size): A simple implementation uses indexCheck:

```
def indexCheck(self, index):
    return self.size() > index and index >= 0
```

and then:

```
def __setitem__(self, index, value): #enables a[x] =
    if indexCheck(index):
        self._store[index] = value
```

With this, we can write d[1] = 42, since 1 is a valid subscript in our example. Note that this does nothing for an out of bounds subscript.

In Python, the boolean expression

```
self.size() > index and index >= 0
```

can actually be written as:

```
self.size() > index >= 0
```

chaining the two comparisons. The latter is interpreted exactly as the former. There are a number of other, similar compact expressions that can be used as tests.

We would also like to be able to use subscripts from the right so that we can enable d[-1] to set the last value. We might also like to set several elements in a sublist starting with a given index and replacing elements from some other iterable. For example:

```
d = DenseList(0, 0, 1, 2, 3, 4, 5, 6)
print(d)
d[1:4:2] = (0, 0, 0, 0)
print(d)
```

We would like this to produce:

```
[0, 1, 2, 3, 4, 5, 6]
[0, 0, 2, 0, 4, 5, 6]
```

On the right side of the assignment you can provide more or fewer values than necessary for the replacements, but it needs to be iterable, even if we only say:

```
d[1:4:2] = 0, 0, 0, 0
```

The notation `[1:4:2]` is called a *slice,* starting at 1, ending just before 4 and iterating by 2. A range does something like this also: range(1,4,2), though with slightly different syntax. So, the actual implementation of __setitem__ is:

```
def __setitem__(self, index, value): #enables a[x] =
    if isinstance(index, slice):
        stop = index.stop if index.stop is None else len(self)
        step = 1 if index.step is None else index.step
        start = 0 if index.start is None else index.start
        for i, v in zip(range(start, stop, step), value):
            self[i] = v
    else:
        if index < 0:
            index += self.size()
        if index < 0 or index >= self.size():
            raise IndexError
        self._store[index] = value
```

The else part handles negative indexing, simply by adding the size to a negative supplied index. The if part is more complicated. First, it checks whether the index supplied is a slice such as `[1:4:2]`, and if so zips two iterables together and iterates over the result. That requires some explanation, of course. First, an explanation of the form of the for statement, with two variables (i, and v) given:

Suppose we have a list or tuple of pairs:

```
l = ((1, 2), (3, 4), (5, 6))
```

Then the simple iteration over this object will produce the pairs:

```
for a in l:
    print(a)
```

Produces:

```
(1, 2)
(3, 4)
(5, 6)
```

But a modification of the *For* statement will also separate the pairs into their components. So:

```
for a, b in l:
    print(a, b)
```

Yields, instead:

```
1 2
3 4
5 6
```

Next, the "zip" of two iterables is itself an object that can be iterated over. Its iteration length will be that of the shorter of the two (or more) components. The first element of each zipped component will be produced first, and so on, until one of the iterables is exhausted. In the above, we zip a range with the values produced on the right hand side of the example assignment. The requires looking inside the "slice" in order to produce a range.

Finally, a slice in Python, has *start*, *stop*, and *step* fields that we can extract from it. Any of them might be None and we can't specify a range with None as an argument, so we need to define local start, stop, and step to protect against that. Then we just zip a range with the values provided and iterate over that to find indices and values to write into the DenseList. Experiment a bit with zipping a couple or three of lists and printing the results to see how it operates.

The method __getitem__ has a similar structure, permitting retrieval with negative indices and getting the entries of a slice as an ordinary list. We leave it as an exercise.

Deleting (__delitem__ from a DenseList has an additional issue, since we can't leave a "hole" that a deleted entry occupied. The solution is to move all items to the right (larger indices) of the deleted item one slot left to fill it, thus reducing the size by one. This takes (linear) time, of course. But, it is also possible to delete slices. The shifting for a single element is just:

```
for i in range(index, self.size() - 1):
          self._store[i] = self._store[i + 1]
      self._size -= 1
```

The slice deletion is actually recursive, using the *del* operator defined by __delitem__ itself.

```
def __delitem__(self, index): #enables del(a[x])
    if isinstance(index, slice):
        stop = index.stop if index.stop is None else len(self)
        stop = len(self) if stop > len(self)
        step = 1 if index.step is None else index.step
        start = 0 if index.start is None else index.start
        indices = range(start, stop, step)
        for i in reversed(indices):
            del self[i] #recursion
        return
    if index < 0: #handle negative indices
        index += self.size()
    if index < 0 or index >= self.size():
        raise IndexError
    for i in range(index, self.size() - 1):
        self._store[i] = self._store[i + 1] #shift
    self._size -= 1
```

We leave the rest for you to do.

## 11.4 Tree Structures

A tree uses nodes much like those of a doubly linked list, though the pointers reference "child" nodes of a "parent" node, and there may be more that two children of any node. We will only look at binary trees here. The typical node names are _left and _right, however.

There are many variations. A binary tree can represent an arbitrary collection if it permits arbitrary insertions. It can represent a set if it doesn't permit duplicates. It can be a map if it stores key:data pairs as in the figure, and it can represent a sorted structure or not. A node might also have a link to the node above it in the tree: a parent node.

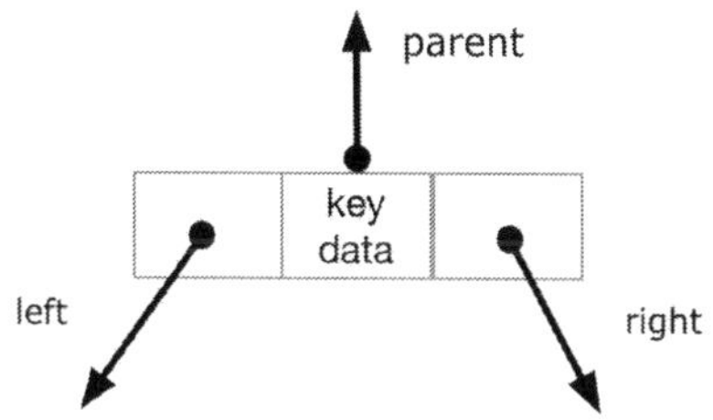


Figure 11.11 Binary Tree Node

A binary *search* tree stores its keys in order, so the keys need to be comparable in some way. It can be used to represent a sorted set (if no data is stored) or a sorted map, where the key:data pairs form the mapping. Here we show a binary search tree as a sorted map. Among other things it shows the usage of keyword arguments, which are used since there are many ways to tailor such a structure and positional arguments would become unwieldy. The map is sorted in order of the keys, which implies the keys need to have some notion of "size".

It also uses a quite general Node class as an inner class. This class is well encapsulated so that the BinarySearchTree itself calls its methods rather than referring directly to its "private" fields. In addition to the *left* and *right* links, this node also includes a *parent* link to point to the node above *self*. These parent links are only needed here for deleting nodes (and their values).

In the next chapter we will see how to document a class to make it easier for programmers to use this structure in other classes:

```
class Node:
    def __init__(self, val, data = None):
        self._left = None
        self._right = None
        self._parent = None #used in deletion
        self._key = val
        self._data = data
    def left(self):
        return self._left
```

```
    def right(self):
        return self._right
    def parent(self):
        return self._parent
    def key(self):
        return self._key
    def data(self):
        return self._data
    def newLeft(self, val, data = None):
        self._left = BinarySearchTree.Node(val, data)
        self._left.setParent(self)
    def setLeft(self, node):
        self._left = node
        node.setParent(self)
    def newRight(self, val, data = None):
        self._right = BinarySearchTree.Node(val, data)
        self._right.setParent(self)
    def setRight(self, node):
        self._right = node
        node.setParent(self)
    def setParent(self, node):
        self._parent = node
```

Note that when we place any node as, for example, the left child of the current node, that new "child" needs to point to the current node as its parent. Encapsulating that here makes it less likely to make an error later. Likewise, we encapsulate the creation of a new left or right child with given key (val) and data. Once again, it properly sets the parent of the new child.

The comparisons between keys might use the natural < operation, but that isn't guaranteed to work for all possible keys, so we provide the option of providing the compare operation to a new tree. We can also specify whether duplicates are permitted. An extension might also properly permit specification of whether or not reinserting a key will replace existing data or not. This implementation doesn't replace, which is probably a flaw.

```
def __init__(self, **kwargs):
    '''Construct a new empty BinarySearchTree
    @arg duplicates: whether or not to permit duplicate keys in tree
        (default is True)
```

```
    @arg compare: a function of two variables to control ordering of
        keys (a strategy). Default is the < operator.
    '''
    compare=lambda x, y: x<y
    if 'compare' in kwargs:
        compare = kwargs['compare']
    self._root = None
    self._compare = compare
    self._size = 0
```

We also show a multi line comment immediately following the method declaration. We will see this again in the next chapter. Note that it explains what keyword arguments will be processed and their meaning. It isn't implemented here, but it is possible to make the construction fail when a non-valid keyword argument is used.

Keyword arguments are presented to the body as a dict. So, we can use the "in" operator to determine whether any given keyword appears – as a string. Here is how to create a tree that won't permit duplicates but uses the default comparison:

```
tree = BinarySearchTree(duplicates=False)
```

Figure 11.5, above, shows a simple such tree with only keys represented, though there might also be data values stored in each node. If a tree is *balanced* then the path from root to leaf is always approximately the same, depending on the balancing. The figure shows one that is balanced, but that was serendipity since this implementation doesn't attempt that. For balanced trees, investigate Red-Black Trees or AVL Trees. In the sample above, 64 was the first insertion, followed by either 23 (less than 64) or 93 (greater), but we can't determine which. A balancing would potentially move nodes around so we couldn't predict order of insertion.

Before we start to build it, we need to understand the underlying idea of tree *traversal*. In a sorted tree, here sorted by keys, the normal traversal is called *inOrder*. For any node, starting at the root, before we "visit" the node, we first visit all of the nodes to the left (recursively). If there are no more nodes to process (visit) on the left, we then visit this node. Following that, we visit all the nodes to the right. For each node we visit we first do the left side, then the node itself, and then the right side. This is how the *insert* operation works, with the variation that we are seeking a node with a missing child to the left or right depending on the key values. If the key to be inserted is smaller than the node's key we go left if possible or else insert a new node there. If the new key is larger, then we work to the right. Since a map is a set, (of keys) we replace a value if we find an equal key. We will say more about traversals below, but that is enough to start.

Many binary tree operations are inherently recursive. If we attempt an operation at a node, but keys suggest that it is more properly applied to a child (or the parent, also), then we recurse on that node. Thus, *insert* will use a recursive (but private) helper function. Generally, operations on nodes will be private, but those on keys and data, public.

```
def insert(self, val, data = None):
    value = None
    if self._root is None:
        self._root = BinarySearchTree.Node(val, data)
        self._size += 1
    else:
        value = self.__insertHelper(val, self._root, data)
    return value
```

The helper will create a new node when needed. When it replaces a value when trying to insert an existing key, it returns the old value.

```
def __insertHelper(self, val, node, data = None):
    value = None
    if self._compare(val, node.key()):
        if node.left() is not None:
            value = self.__insertHelper(val, node.left(), data)
        else:
            node.newLeft(val, data)
            self._size += 1
    elif self._compare(node.key(), val):
        if node.right() is not None:
            value = self.__insertHelper(val, node._right, data)
        else:
            node.newRight(val, data)
            self._size += 1
    else: # Node has an equal key
        value = node.data()
```

```
            node.setData(data)
        return value
```

This method is executed with reference to a given node of the tree and depending on the comparison (with the *compare* function) we recurse to the left or right. Once we find the place where the insertion should occur we use the newLeft or newRight methods of the Node class to correctly insert a new node with the required key and data. We only insert at a node (left or right) if there is no Node there already, making the new Node a leaf of the tree.

We also assume that the compare method is a strict comparison, not including equality of the keys. This is why we separate out into three cases: compare(a, b), compare(b, a), and neither. The implementation (subject to change) permits doing something different in that last case, though we treat it here the same as a "right" insert. Think about how you might change this if we change the implementation to specify that subsequent insertion of an existing key would trigger replacement of the value in the existing node, or even replacement with a new Node.

The following method isn't especially helpful to tree operations, but it might be useful in your explorations. It gives the left-right path to any existing node as a list.

```
    def pathToKey(self, key):
        result = []
        node = self._root
        if node is None or node.data() == key: return result
        while node is not None:
            if self._compare(node.key(), key):
                result.append('right')
                node = node.right()
            elif self._compare(key, node.key()):
                result.append('left')
                node = node.left()
            else:
                return result
        return result
```

Think about what this would produce if you ask for the path to a non-existing key.

It is relatively easy to traverse a binary tree in key order and produce a list from the results. Again, a recursive helper is useful. It returns a list of tuples of key:data pairs

```
def __asList(self):
    result = []
    if self._root is not None:
        result = self.__getNextPair(self._root, result)
    return result

def __getNextPair(self, node, aList):
    if node is not None:
        self.__getNextPair(node.left(), aList)
        if aList is not None:
            aList.append((node.key(), node.data()))
        self.__getNextPair(node._right, aList)
        return aList
```

As with other collection classes, the iterator is one of the most important and useful methods. It can be very complicated to traverse such a structure one step at a time directly (think about how you might do it), but, using the above we can easily create a key-ordered list and use that for the iteration.

```
def __iter__(self):
    elements = self.__asList()
    return iter(elements)
```

With an iterator many other operations become easy.

For example, we can ask if a given tree contains a data value with:

```
def containsValue(self, value):
    for i in self: # i is a pair (key, data)
        if i[1] == value:
            return True
    return False
```

We can also produce a dictionary using the iterator, noting that duplicates are lost in the dictionary:

```
def asDict(self):
    result = {}
    allValues = list(self)
    for i in allValues:
        result[i[0]] = i[1] #dict insertion
    return result
```

Cloning a tree is also possible (and easy), though be careful about setting the tree parameters to those of the current tree.

## 11.5 Collections Exploration – Part 2, The MemoryManager

In the MemoryManager class of the French Military Game, we used two list-like structures, a list to hold *_thisGame*, the current game's moves, and *history*, another tuple of lists, to hold the complete history of all moves in all games. Both of these will benefit from transformations, but different transformations. Let's examine _thisGame first.

Like all two dimensional structures, _thisGame is a mapping between pairs of values, usually integers, the indices, to values of some kind, Here they were also ints, but the in general any element type may be used for such a structure.

For every move of the game, using the *record* method, we compute a tuple value with `(police.computeValueLocation(), fox.position)`. We then store that "move" in a list There was nothing particularly wrong with this, except that by using a list (naively) we possibly recorded the same positions multiple times if players return to earlier positions. For example, the first Police move could be from 1 to 2 and the Fox might retreat. If the Police then move back from 2 to 1 and the Fox moves back to 5, then we see the same position a second time. This has some implications for recording the history. Instead, we can use a *set* to record the individual game, since the ordering of the moves isn't material for our use. It might be, however, if we wanted to use it to "replay" a game. So, in initializing the MemoryManager, we now write:

```
self._thisGame = set({}) #set of moves
```

This will contain tuples (pairs, actually) but it is simpler than before. We just add a new move tuple to the set:

```
def record(self, fox:int, police):
 self._thisGame.add((police.computeValue(), fox))
```

Actually, we will later, in *summarize*, only process this set as an iterable:

```
def summarize(self, moves, outcome): #public
    for move in self._thisGame:
        police = move[0]
        fox = move[1]
        ... more – after we discuss the history.
```

We will get an even bigger benefit by changing the history structure to a dictionary, though that will also require changing how we read and write the history file. So, again in the initialization of the Memory Manager:

```
self._history = dict({}) #keys are (police, fox) pairs)
```

Recall that in our encoding of the police position values, there were only 165 possible outcomes, but they actually range between 7 and 1792. We didn't want to define an array that large to hold only 165 items so we used the reverse lookup technique to find a number in the range 0 .. 164 that was equivalent. But with a map, we don't need a cell for every possible value, only for the keys we actually want to save. So, the keys will contain (some of) the values between 7 and 1792, along with the fox position, and the values will be a code indicating whether the game was won or lost by the fox. Here is the new version of summarize.

```
def summarize(self, moves, outcome:int): #public
    for move in self._thisGame:
        police = move[0]
        fox = move[1]
        if not (police, fox) in self._history:
           self._history[(police, fox)] = 0
        current = self._history.get((police, fox))
        self._history[(police, fox)] = current + outcome
```

In the Python collections framework any iterable object can yield its contents one element at a time, as discussed above. Here everything matches up: *_thisGame* is a dictionary so it will yield move tuples.

The last statement of the above, inserts a new value into the dictionary with key (police, fox) and value current + outcome. The latter is just an integer. However, that key might not be in the dictionary at all, and so it might need to be initialized to zero, since we didn't try to add all keys originally.

You need to be careful with maps in this way. If you try to *get* a key that has not been stored you get None instead, so must normally check for it. This will occur elsewhere in this program.

The other important method of the MemoryManager, *smaller*, is used by the fox to evaluate possible moves. With the above changes it becomes:

```
def smaller(self, police, current, trial): #public
    currentVal = self._history[(police,current)] if \
        (police,current) in self._history else 0
    trialVal = self._history[(police, trial)] if \
        (police, trial) in self._history else 0
    return currentVal < trialVal
```

We have used a new form of the assignment statement here, resulting in long statements continued to the second line. You can assign one of two (or more) values to a variable with something like:

```
var = a if condition else b
```

Then var will be assigned either a or b, depending on the outcome of the condition. Also note that the condition is evaluated prior to evaluating either a or b, assuming they were more than simple values as they are here.

The methods *getMemory*, *saveMemory*, and *_readFile* also manipulated the history tuple in the original, and so require updates in this version. We leave *getMemory* to the reader. We want to write the contents of a dictionary to a text file and then read it later, reconstructing the dictionary. We need a format tailored to the contents of the dictionary, since that isn't the same for all such structures. Here the keys are pairs (police, fox) and the values are integers. So, the & character won't be in any of the data to be written, so we can use it as a separator.

```
def saveMemory(self):
    try:
        with open(filename, "w") as out:
            for i in self._history.keys():
                out.write(str(i) +'&'+ str(self._history[i]) + "\n")
            out.close()
    except Exception as e:
        print("Could not write the memory file.")
```

We use a *try* block, since the file might not be able to be opened. We also iterate naturally over the keys in the _history dict. We force the tuple i to be converted to a string, as we do to the integer value. Text files contain strings and you often need to do this conversion.

A very simple example of a history file would look like:

```
(25, 1)&1
(28, 0)&1
```

The police moves were 1 → 4, followed by 0 → 2, resulting in a loss.

Reading such a file is a bit complex as we need to parse those lines and create a dictionary entry for each. The separator is the key:

```
def _readFile(self, smart):
    memoryFile = None
    try:
        if smart:
            with open(filename, "r") as memoryFile:
                self._history = {}
                strings = memoryFile.read()
            lines = list(strings.split('\n'))
            for line in lines:
                if len(line)>0:
                    values = line.split('&')
                    key = literal_eval(values[0])
                    self._history[key] = \
                      literal_eval(values[1].strip())
    except Exception as e:
        self._history = dict({})
```

We read the entire file into a variable named strings and then split it into lines with split('\n'), giving a list. We then process each non empty line by again splitting it at the & character. The literal_eval function is in the ast library so we need to import: `from ast import literal_eval`

After we get the key, we use it to insert into the dictionary.

## 11.6 Collections Exploration – Part 3, The Police class

In the version presented in the Intermezzo, the police class used lists in two ways. First as a small, one dimension, list (_policePositions) to hold the three integers representing police board positions, and second, another one dimension list (_ALLMOVES) to do the reverse lookup. This list held the possible values of the police composite position and we searched for a cell holding one so that we could use its index as something like a key for storage in the history array of the memory manager. But this latter use simply disappears in this version since the history structure is now a map, not an array. So the _ALLMOVES list simply goes away, and the *computeValue* method will simply return the "raw" value of the sum of powers of the three police positions. We will wait to show this method for a bit, since we also want to change how the three police positions were implemented. Likewise the *computeValuePosition* will disappear since we are no longer indexing into a list.

According to the rules of the game, the player representing the police has three pieces on three different squares. Therefore, logically, the player has a mathematical *set* of positions chosen from the set of integers 0 through 10. But a Python *set* is like this also, and it is implemented, usually, as a specialized dictionary with only keys. Since we don't need these to be sorted, we just use a set to contain the Police positions. This works since they are guaranteed to be distinct.

We saw some possibilities for implementing sets above. A BinarySearchTree can implement a set if we don't permit duplicate keys, though we might have to do something about replacing and removing values. We will just use a Python *set* here.

We need to set this *set* up for the first and every subsequent game, so we do so in the init method as before.

```
def init(self):
    #  for a new game
    self._policePositions = {0, 1, 3}

def __init__(self):
    self.init()
```

This creates and adds elements to the set. It behaves like a set, of course, only permitting one copy of any object to be present. The computeValue method again gets quite simple:

```
def computeValue(self)->int: #the police positions as an int
    result = 0
    for i in self._policePositions:
        result += 2**i
    return result
```

Finally, here is the *moveIfLegal* method of the police class, which takes advantage of the new structures:

```
def moveIfLegal(self, from_, to, fox:object):
 if not MoveRules.legalPoliceMove(from_, to):
     self.warn()
     return False
 if fox.position() == to:
     self.warn()
     return False
 here = -1
 i = 0
 for i in self._policePositions:
     if i == from_:
         here = i
         break
 if here < 0:
     self.warn()
     return False
 for i in self._policePositions:
     if i == to:
         self.warn()
         return False
 self._policePositions.remove(from_)
```

```
        self._policePositions.add(to)
        return True
```

If we find that the potential move is legal, we remove the *from_* value (where the police player currently is) and add the *to* value (where it is moving to).

The other changes to the game are straightforward, though you are invited to complete them and then compare the two versions as a whole.

The Appendix has implementations of some classes that are similar to, but simpler than, some of the important classes of the Python collections framework.

## 11.7 Important Ideas From This Chapter

collection
natural order
iterable
Null Object Pattern
list
set
map
dense list
linked list
circular list
binary search tree
Iterator
comparator
comparable

## 11.8 Problem Set

1. Finish the modification of the FMG class discussed in this chapter

2. Do, or redo, problem 4 of the Primo Intermezzo.

3. Make the LispyList more Pythonic by adding an iterator and other methods to make it fit better with things like indexing and For statements.

4. Finish the implementation of DenseList.

5. Implement BinaryTreeMap.clone(). Be sure to set the keyword parameters the same as that of self. Note that the structure should be preserved, not just the contents. In particular the path to any key should be the same in the original and in the clone.

6. Implement BinaryTreeMap.__contains__(), which enables the "in" operator.

7. Implement BinaryTreeMap.__getItem__(), which enables tree[key] access.

8. The non-standard BinarySearchTree.__findNode(), is only partially implemented in the Appendix. Implement the helper structured like the insertHelper that returns a node with a given key if present, or None. We keep it private since it returns Nodes.

9. Give DenseList a *sort* method implemented with quickSort. The partition method can be private.

10. Explore binary search tree removal in the literature. Write one or two pages in your own words on how and why __delItem__ works in the BinaryTreeMap.

11. Explore, in the literature, the process of quicksort on a dense list. Once you understand how that works and can implement it. Consider the following, applied to a list.

```
def deSorter(aList, start, end):
    if end > start:
        midIndex = int((start+end)/2)
        mid = aList[midIndex]
        for i in range(midIndex, start, -1):
            aList[i] = aList[i-1]
        aList[start] = mid
        deSorterIP(aList, start+1, midIndex)
        deSorterIP(aList, midIndex+1, end)
```

Try it with a sorted array with, say, 7 or 15 elements such as:

```
aList = [1, 2, 3, 4, 5, 6, 7, 8, 9, 10, 11, 12, 13, 14, 15]
```

deSorter(aList, 0, 15); // "end" is initially the array length.

What happens if you take that modified list and iterate over its elements inserting them into a binary search tree?

12. Implement __eq__ for the DenseList class. Think first about what it should mean.

# 12 Testing and Documentation

It is hard to write programs. It is hard to understand them. It is hard to know when you got it right and when there are unintended consequences of what you have done. It is hard for teams to coordinate efforts. What to do?

## 12.1 Documentation Overview

Documenting a program or system of programs means providing natural language explanations of what it is, how to use it, and how it works. There are many different kinds of documentation. What is in the documents depends on the audience. If you create a program for end-users, you need to provide explanations of how to use it for common tasks, but you don't need to talk about its internal implementation. On the other hand, if you write a library of classes to be used by other programmers you need more detailed documentation. The explanations we gave in the Intermezzo, however, were neither of these. Rather we tried to provide an explanation of how it is built so that you can learn how to build and structure your own programs.

User level documentation for FMG would talk about how one plays the game, from the initial startup (how to invoke it), through the final end and shutdown. It would explain how to make a move and perhaps some things about strategy. It would explain that the input consists of two numbers in range 0..10 separated by one or more spaces. It would emphasize that the space is critical and that the numbers must be on the same line. Even better, of course, would be to provide more robust input mechanisms, but that is something other than documentation and we shall discuss that later in the chapter.

We are more interested here, however, in how to document a program so that it will be of use to programmers, including yourself. For this, Python two features that we shall discuss here. However, for the most part, we seek to write programs for which very little documentation is needed for other programmers, primarily because we choose both a structure and naming conventions that make it obvious to a skilled reader what is happening. We have tried to emphasize that throughout the book, but it is worth looking back at FMG to see what is working there and what could be improved in terms of having a *self-documenting* program.

The class names are probably fine in the main, *Police, Fox, MemoryManager,* etc. seem to be accurate names for what objects of the classes do. Most of the methods are fine. The *play* and *oneGame* methods are aptly named, etc. On the other hand, we have been suggesting you not abbreviate names, but *smaller* doesn't really make clear what is going on. Are there others? How hard is it to fix? Not very, it seems, especially with modern tools in which an editor can easily make global changes. One offender of naming here, is the local variable named just *a* in the *Police.computeValueLocation* method. Why this name? How is the name related to what it does? If you are trying to learn what the program does, does this name help?

One good reason for encapsulation, by the way, is that it limits the scope of names. We can choose names of things that will be used in smaller scopes and if we do it badly it will have a lesser impact on the overall program. The flip side of this is that names widely seen, such as class and public method names need to be chosen with great care. One convention is to use nouns for the names of methods that return values, with the name descriptive of the value returned. Methods that don't return values should have names that are verbs or verb phrases, describing the action. One reason we don't like methods that do both is that the programs that contain them are harder to reason about, but part of this is the difficulty of finding a good name. The method *moveIfLegal* of the Police class is such a dual purpose method. It tries to make a legal move and tells us if it did or not. So it is both an action and an accessor of information. You might be misled in your understanding of the program if it had a name implying it was just an information getter and later find that the program state was changed when it was invoked. It is difficult to overemphasize the importance of good names. This is especially true when you work in a team. Others need to understand your names, not just yourself.

Some people believe that every line of a program should have a comment on it explaining what it does. In actuality this is a terrible practice, since the program will probably be changed and the comments will probably not be kept in sync. Also, it is difficult to write non-technical comments that capture exactly what the statement does, but nothing more. Better is to have the statement explain itself, through clear naming and straightforward programming. Here is the worst example of per-line commenting:

```
c += 1  # increment c
```

Well, of course. If you know the language, you don't need the comment. But what does it *mean*? This one is a bit better:

```
c += 1  # increment the catheterCount
```

Ah, now we begin to have some understanding. But it should really say this:

```
catheterCount += 1
```

in which no comment is needed at all. The variable names a concept in the space of the problem itself. It helps you understand what is going on in this, presumably, medical related program. Strive for this.

## 12.2 Python *dir* and *help* – Automated Documentation

### dir

There is a form of programmer documentation, however, that is still needed, even if you write clearly. The purpose of each class and each method needs to be communicated to anyone who needs to work with your program. They need to know how a client needs to interact with your code, because they are likely interested in writing that client code. They therefore need to know what to expect.

If you have the name of a Python module or class (or even a variable) that is visible in your program, you can ask for its "directory" with the built-in *dir* function. It will produce a *list* of all features of the thing. So, *dir(FMGame)* produces a list of the classes defined in the module and *dir(FMGame.Police)* produces a list of the public features of the class. The list can be iterated over, of course. This can also be used for things that are part of the Python system itself, which is useful for discovering new things. If we iterate over the list produced for the Police class, printing each item we get all of the following along with many inherited items not listed here:

```
computeValueLocation
dumpAllMoves
holdingPosition
```

```
init
moveIfLegal
showPosition
warn
whereValue
```

**help**

There is another function, *help*, that is even more useful. We will show two things here that make it especially helpful. But, in addition, they make understanding the code easier as you read it.

The first idea is that you can document the expected types of function and method arguments and also the type of the value returned, if any. The notations we will see aren't required, and won't be enforced, but they need to be legal types. As a simple example, the declaration of the whereValue method of FMGame.Police could be written as:

```
def whereValue(L:int, M:int, R:int)->int:
```

This tells a reader that the three inputs should be int values and that it will return an int. But you can't write garbage instead of valid types. That will be caught.

Even more interesting and useful is the moveFox method of FMGams.Display:

```
def moveFox(self, fox:Fox):
```

This tells the reader that the *fox* argument is actually the fox object of class *Fox*, not the integer representing its current location. These notations can be very useful to avoid misunderstandings, just as good naming. They won't be enforced, however.

The second thing we want to do with public (at least) features in a module is to provide specific documentation strings, which are specially placed three quote comments: multiline comments. These are placed immediately after the declaration of the feature and will be read and printed by the *help* function.

Such comments appear in your code immediately after a class or method and they are just like ordinary multi-line Python comments and begin with ''' instead of only #. They end with ''' also. Within these comments there are certain things that are useful to provide to readers.

Let's look at an example, by going back and documenting the FMG. The Display class is short so we will use it as an example. First we look at the comment for the class as a whole. It is written immediately before the class header:

```
class Display():
    '''  The visual _display in ASCII art for the French Military Game.
         It shows the game board with the fox's current location marked.
    '''
...
```

A typical class comment begins with a sentence or two giving the purpose of the class.

Constructors and (public) methods should also be documented. Here is the constructor for this class along with its comment and part of the implementation:

```
    def __init__(self, theFox:int):
        ''' Create a _display for the French Military Game with an
            initial position for the fox
              @param theFox: the initial position of the fox player.
                  Usually 5.
        '''
        self._theFox = theFox
        where = Display.MAPPER[theFox]
    ...
```

Again, it just explains the purpose. @param is followed by the name of a parameter and that followed by some explanation of what the client code is expected to provide as an argument. It is just a hint to the reader about what is needed. Note that if you format the comment with spacing and such it will be preserved when we invoke the help function.

Methods that return values can also use @return to explain the nature of the value returned. The purpose of such comments, however, is to give logical meaning to those items. Note, though, that these '@' comments are just a style.

Method comments should also provide some explanation of any special algorithms used so that it will be easier for a reader of the code to get started.

It is possible to document private things as well, but this is of less use to most readers. The most typical usage is by someone who wants to use your code, and for this a discussion of public features is sufficient. In fact, too much documentation can get in the way of seeing the overall picture.

Once you have marked up your code with comments, preferably as you go, call the help function with the module, class, ... that you are interested in. So, *help(Display)* has:

```
Help on class Display in module __main__:

class Display(builtins.object)
 |  The visual _display in ASCII art for the French Military Game.
 |  It shows the game board
 |  with the fox's current location marked.
 |
 |  Methods defined here:
 |
 |  __init__(self, theFox: int)
 |      Create a _display for the French Military Game with an initial
 |      position for the fox
 |      * @param theFox: the initial position of the fox player.
 |            Usually 5.
 |
 |  moveFox(self, fox: Fox)
 |      Move the marked location of the Fox to a new position
 |      @param fox: the Fox object
 |
 |  show(self)
 |      Print the game board with current fox position marked
 |
 |
----------------------------------------------------------------------
 |  Data descriptors defined here:
 |
 |  __dict__
 |      dictionary for instance variables (if defined)
```

```
 |
 |  __weakref__
 |      list of weak references to the object (if defined)
 |
 |
----------------------------------------------------------------------
 |  Data and other attributes defined here:
 |
 |  MAPPER = ((3, 1), (0, 1), (3, 3), (6, 1), (0, 3), (3, 5), (6, 3), (0,
...
```

Note that this includes the multiline comments as well as the type notations.

The extensive Python libraries are all well documented with this technique.

## 12.3 Testing Overview

Just as is true of documentation, testing means several different things. Does a program meet the needs of its users and how can we know? Is the program error free? Does it meet the specification that was set for it when it was created? Is it fast enough to handle the required load? Does it make good use of available resources? All of these questions can be answered by testing of various kinds.

Some testing is just letting users use a program, perhaps only partly finished, and getting their feedback on its suitability for their needs and expectations. There is an entire field in the computing industry, *Human Computer Interaction* (HCI), that looks at programs from the user's standpoint.

Some testing, *load testing*, tries to break a program by overloading it with data to see how robust it is. Measurements are taken of the amount of work it can (safely) handle. Adjustments to the program may need to be made if we get unhappy results.

Some testing, especially of important programs, is done by specially trained professional testers who work with the finished program and its original specification to see if they match. Your professor does something like this with your programming assignments. He or she may run the program on specially devised data to see if it works in all situations as it should. Some testing, as in load testing, sets out to try and break a program by giving it unexpected inputs.

In fact, one of the major problems in the world of commerce is that too much software is insufficiently tested in this way and hackers gain access to systems by trying improper inputs until something breaks. Once this happens analysis can often show how to exploit the break with carefully crafted inputs. The solution to this problem is not just programmer vigilance, as no one is able to never make a mistake. The solution requires *defense in depth,* with programmer training, good language, good engineering practice, etc. all required to provide layers of safety, each of which is faulty, but in combination provide good security and safety.

However, none of the above testing techniques are very useful in helping a working programmer write good programs. They can tell you later that it is fine or that it is junk, but they don't give you feedback early enough that you can improve your product. So, the kind of testing we want to focus on here, is testing that matters to a working developer. How can you use testing to help you do a better job? One solution that has become popular, because it is both powerful and useful, is *Test Driven Development (TDD)*. TDD usually depends on special testing frameworks that you use as you develop and we will describe one in the next section, but first let's look at the process itself.

What we will describe will sound like more work than developing the application, but in the long run it saves work, as the most frustrating part of programming is finding, analyzing, and removing errors (bugs). TDD can give us the confidence to develop an application to solve a problem one step at a time, knowing that what we add in the next step doesn't break what we added in previous steps. However, like many good things, it takes discipline to become good at it. You don't become a good swimmer, for example, by taking short cuts in training.

Suppose you have a problem to solve and want to use TDD to help. The first step is to find some much smaller problem in the one you are given and think about solving that first. Pick something you know you will need and that you think you have a solution for. In the French Military Game, it would probably not be the memory manager. In fact it probably wouldn't be some particular class, since you are at the beginning and don't yet know what classes you might want or need. For FMG, you might try to first write the user input handler that will handle only one move, for example. You don't worry yet about how the Fox will respond to the move. You don't worry yet about how to represent the three Police pieces, etc. You just handle the input. Once you get that done, you might start to work on a framework for determining if it is a legal move. That doesn't mean getting all the logic right initially, but you will need some methods that will produce some outputs that tell you if a choice was valid or not.

Once you have a small problem within the bigger one that you will work on, the first thing you do is to write a test that, if it passes, will tell you that you got that problem correctly solved. You write the test before you create the solution. The test will initially fail, of course. Once you have a test, however, you then write enough of your application to make that test pass - and nothing more. Then try to think of another test for the same thing. What could go wrong at this point in my application? How will I know if it does? Write a test for that. Run the test. If it passes, good, but if it fails, write a bit more of your solution to make it pass - and nothing more. Once you can't think of how to break this little bit of code any more, and therefore can't think of any more tests, go on to the next little bit of your problem and do the same thing.

But, here is the important point. When you work on the second, third, ... parts of the program, run all of the tests for all of the parts at each stage. Then, if you do something today that breaks something you wrote yesterday, you will learn of it immediately. Moreover, since you have just now made only a small change to your program, it should not be too difficult to figure out why it broke. Programmers who write a lot before testing wind up with code that doesn't seem to work, its parts don't fit together, and it is difficult to know why or, more important, what to do. TDD is your friend here.

The real benefit of TDD is not that it helps you a lot in writing a small piece of code correctly the first time. Many programmers are good at that. If that is all it could do, it wouldn't be worth the effort. Where it pays you back, however, is learning immediately when you break something. It gives you the confidence to change a program knowing that it is already correct when you start, and that you will learn immediately if you put a bug into it.

A *suite* of tests that you can run repeatedly is what you want. This is called *regression* testing. It has been used for a long time in program maintenance of valuable programs, but it can also be used in the development of new programs, giving good feedback to the programmers that helps them measure their progress and their success. It is called regression testing, because when a test like this fails, you have *regressed*; gone backwards in your goal of creating a good program. We want to guard against changes making software worse.

Like HCI, there is a complete field of study on Software Testing. It is a viable career path for some people.

In the next section we will look at a tool that enables TDD in Python. Similar things exist for most computing languages. The Robot Programming Language has an extension that fits with this as well.

## 12.4 unittest – Automated Testing

### 12.4.1 Overview

In Python the tool for TDD is named *unittest*. It is part of the Python libraries: a module you import. There are similar "units" for most programming languages such as Java and C++. The module unittest provides a framework for programmer-written tests and was developed precisely to support Test Driven Development.

In TDD with unittest, the idea is to set up some scenario by creating an object or two and sending the objects a message or two and then making *assertions* about the result. An assertion is just a statement that something is true. The assertions are automated so that you don't need to look to see if they pass (statement true) or fail. If they pass, nothing in particular happens, but if they fail you are made aware of it. You can therefore execute a very large number of assertions about many objects in a few seconds and get confidence that your application passes all of its tests.

Python has a simple assert statement that when followed by an expression that can be interpreted as a bool, will halt the current execution with a message if the expression (an assertion) is False. But it is possible, also, for a user-defined class to provide specialized assertions to make testing with unittest much clearer.

The Monty Karel simulator has a class RobotTestCase (in its own module) that defines a specialized exception, RobotException as well as the class RobotTestCase, which, itself defines more than twenty assertions about a robot and its world (use *help* to see them all). An example of the use in an automated test is below.

There are three things that you need to do to write such an automated test; the setup, the messages in that context, and the assertions about the result. Part of what we need to write for this is determined by unittest, part from the application we want to test, and part from any extensions to unittest that we have created to simplify our process. One such assertion from the robottestcase module is RobotTestCase.assertFacingEast(self, robot). Here is how it might be used. When such an assertion fails (the robot isn't facing East) a RobotException is raised with an informative message: "Not facing east".

Let's suppose for an illustration that we are building the StairSweeper class of Chapter 2 of Monty Karel. Suppose again, that we have decided to write and test a turnRight command first. In unittest, the test class in its module would look like this:

```
import unittest
from karel.robota import East, South, West, North, world
from stairClimber import StairClimber
from robottestcase import RobotTestCase

class StairClimberTest(RobotTestCase):

    @classmethod
    def setUpClass(cls):
        pass

    def setUp(self):
        world.reset()
        world.readWorld("../stairs.kwld")
        world.setVisible(True)
        world.setDelay(0)
        self.karel = StairClimber(1, 1, East, 0, None)

    def testRightTurn(self):
        self.assertFacingEast(self.karel)
        self.karel.turnRight()
        self.assertFacingSouth(self.karel)
        self.karel.turnRight()
        self.assertFacingWest(self.karel)
        self.karel.turnRight()
```

```
        self.assertFacingNorth(self.karel)
        self.karel.turnRight()
        self.assertFacingEast(self.karel)
```

Classes that use unittest tests have names usually end in the word *Test* as above: StairClimberTest. The above is just part of the class, however, and we will add to it as we add more to the application. The class is a subclass of `RobotTestCase`, which is supplied with Karel. In turn, RobotTestCase is a subclass of unittest.TestCase. The object under test is declared as a field of the class but it is normally created in a *setUp* method that is part of the unittest infrastructure. The code you put in setUp will be executed immediately before any test is run and all of this and the running of the tests themselves will be done automatically.

The test method itself begins with the word test... as is necessary for unittest.main() to consider it a test: testTurnRight. This method does two things. First it exercises a method that we are about to create (turnRight) but have not yet written, and second it makes assertions about the results. In this case we want to show that a robot will correctly turn right no matter what position it is initially facing, so we make karel turn around the compass from East back to East.

We emphasize that this test is written before the *turnRight* method is begun, and when it passes (no assertions fail) we have confidence that we have done our job correctly.

We haven't yet shown the main function that runs this, but it looks like the following.

```
if __name__ == '__main__' :
    world.readWorld("../stairs.kwld")
    karel = StairClimber(1, 1, East, 0, None)
    world.showWorldWithRobots(1, 1, 5, 5)
    unittest.main()
```

Only the last command is needed in general. The first three will just show us the world and the initial position of the robot we are testing.

Running this will produce an application that runs all of our tests (just one here) and displays the results pointing to any assertion failures. Within any test method a test runs until the first assertion fails, but all of the tests are automatically run by unittest, even if some are failing. But note that since setUp is executed anew before running each test method, we start with fresh new objects for each test, since we did the delivery specification in setUp.

As the program develops, add more tests (testClimbStair....) to the above and all will be tested and you will be notified of errors in each of them. You can also collect a number of such testing classes into a *suite* (which you can explore) all of which will be run together.

Of course this tool is available for general programming as well as robot programming. The normal assertions you can make are that a Boolean expression is true, that two values are equal to one another, that a statement throws an exception, etc.

However, there are two restrictions. First is that you can only test public things. For the most part this means you can test visible methods that return something and look at the results. The exception to this is when the infrastructure builds in some helps, such as the special robot assertions in Karel. The second is that it is very difficult, though not impossible to test graphical programs and even the output to a console. The application should be developed apart from its presentation layer in any case, separating the *model* (or the logic underlying it) from the *view* (how it looks to the user). So unittest is most suitable for testing the model. In FMG, for example, the view is the FMG class, along with the Display. The model is everything else: The Fox, the Police, the MemoryManager, and the MoveRules. This is where the logic of the game is. The rest was just presentation. In fact, if we want a really clean separation between model and view, we could remove all of the methods of FMG model classes that write to the console and replace them with accessors of information that can be used by a view class such as FMG itself. The Fox.showPosition method would be replaced by, perhaps, Fox.getPosition, that returns a String, or even the cell number on which the fox resides. This provides cleaner separation of model and view, and also makes it easier to test, since we can invoke this method and make assertions about the result.

An interesting fact about testing, though, is that when well done, you will have about as much test code as application code; perhaps more. This is due to the fact that a lot of things can go wrong with software and you want to guard against all of them, especially when you are writing your programs a bit at a time, which is, really, the only sensible way to do it.

While this seems like a lot of extra work, it actually isn't, for the following reason. While you may have only a small part of your program to write at this moment, you still need to understand it and plan its solution. If it is at all difficult to understand you will need to ponder what to do. If you do this thinking while you have a test framework open in front of you, then you write tests as you think. You make the test framework part of your design process, capturing design decisions in tests as you go. Since you are writing tests that will exercise the code you are about to write, you get to see how the code looks in use before you actually write it.

For example, to write the turnRight command we need to think about the effect of it first, Then we can capture this in tests, designing its name and any needed parameters. Of course this case seems too simple to bother, but most are not, and the test will still be there to tell us later if we break something in adding a new feature later.

### 12.4.2 Testing Example – The Calculator Again

The CalculatorModel we examined in Chapter 9 was developed using TDD with unittest. Here we will show part of the process of development.

Imagine that we have not yet begun on the project, so have no code at all. We have a list of features that the calculator must have. We presented these as part of the discussion in Chapter 9. The first such *development story* was: *A new calculator should have a display of 0.* (See Section 9.6.1). Such stories are small and individually simple, but collectively they cover the necessary features of the application. We want to build the application one story at a time, though this sometimes makes it necessary for us to modify things we have done before. We pay that price to gain the benefit of being able to think in smaller parts, rather than try to juggle all of the requirements at once.

We start by creating a unittest test for an application that doesn't exist. It doesn't yet even have a name. We create a new file named calculatorTest.py and put the necessary imports in at the top. The name of the class is also related to but not exactly the same as our file name as usual:

```
from Calculator import CalculatorModel
import unittest

class TestCalculator(unittest.TestCase):
…
if __name__ == '__main__':
    unittest.main()
```

Note: it can be a problem if a module name is exactly the same as one of the classes within it. You want them different to aid import and avoid confusing things:

```
from TestCalculator import TestCalculator
```

uses the same term for two quite different things. Python is good, but not perfect about keeping these straight, but using (slightly) different names helps.

The next thing to do is to create an object to test, but we don't have the class name yet, so we think, think, think, and come up with *CalculatorModel*, for the reasons given back in Chapter 9. We then declare a new field of the test class of this new, as yet undefined, type. We also create the object in the *setUp* method:

```
class TestCalculator(unittest.TestCase):

    def setUp(self): #note bumpyWords used here. Run once per test
        self.calculator = CalculatorModel()

. . .
```

This doesn't run, of course, since CalculatorModel isn't defined yet, but it is useful to note that unittest can still process this file without error, though it will tell us that the file can't be run as CalculatorModel isn't defined.

We are now ready to write a test, though we could also build just enough of the calculator model to make this work. If you decide to do that, then create another file named Calculator.py with just this:

```
class CalculatorModel(object):
'''The model for a simple four function integer valued calculator
     It has no knowledge of operator precedence.'''
   pass
```

Everything will now work and if you run unittest at this point, it will tell you that there are no tests. Now we can attack the first story. The calculator needs to have a display of zero. Since we are building a model, this means that it should have a method (think of a name.... ah, *getDisplay*) that return zero immediately after a calculator is created. Well, we have just created the calculator in *setUp*, so we can write a test assertion that this, as yet undefined method, will return zero. So, we add the following to the CalculatorTest class:

```
    def testInitialDisplay(self):
     self.assertEquals(0, self.calculator.getDisplay(), \
         'Initial Display not zero')
```

This can't execute successfully yet, since there is no such *getDisplay* method in the CalculatorModel class, but the test *will* run and fail, saying that there is no getDisplay feature (AttributeError). So we can add getDisplay next. We want to write just enough code to make this test pass. There are a variety of ways to do this, some simpler than others, but we shall pick a middle ground here.

```
class CalculatorModel(object):
    '''The model for a simple four function integer valued calculator
    It has no knowledge of operator precedence.'''

    def __init__(self):
        ''' Create a calculator with display initially 0'''
        self._display = 0

    def getDisplay(self)->int:
        '''Get the current value of the display'''
        return self._display
```

If we run unittest.main() now, we will get 'success for 1 test: OK'. We have an absolutely minimal application, that implements one simple story, for which we have a test, and the test passes. We haven't even needed to look at the other stories, or think about how to build them. We just work in small increments and let the application grow, driven by the stories and the tests.

Now we can proceed to the next story: *Give the calculator keys like 5 and 3. When you hit a single key the value of the key should "show" in the display.*

Initially, we can give the calculator only those two keys and make them work for only single key presses. The other keys can be added later if we can add those successfully. Other stories will address multiple key presses. So, again, we have narrowed the scope of our development to the smallest possible step. So, we go back to the test class and write another test, or two.

```
def testPress5(self):
    self.calculator.pressFive()
    self.assertEquals(5, self.calculator.getDisplay(), \
     'Press 5 key fails')

def testPress3(self):
    self.calculator.pressThree()
    self.assertEquals(3, self.calculator.getDisplay(), \
     'Press 3 key fails')
```

Again, we have made a design decision here. The calculator will have a separate method for each key to press: *pressFive* and *pressThree*. In each test we started with a fresh calculator, since *setUp* is run between tests, We exercised the new functionality and then we made assertions about changes to the model.

Once we have the test, we can go back to adding methods to the application itself. So add the following to CalculatorModel.

```
def pressThree(self):
    '''Press the 3 key'''
    self._display = 3

def pressFive(self):
    '''Press the 5 key'''
    self._display = 5
```

Our tests will again pass since each of these sets the getDisplay field and the display method returns the current value of this field. We haven't considered other keys, nor multiple presses. Of course, this isn't the code we saw in Chapter 9, but this is just the first pass. This code will change as we go. We are willing to modify existing code as we learn that new things are required, but for now, we are meeting all requirements with a simple solution.

The third story talks about multiple key presses: *If you press a sequence of number keys, the results should accumulate in the display*. A 5 followed by a 3 should display 53. A test for this might look like the following. It is in the test class, of course.

```
def testAccumulate(self):
    self.calculator.pressFive()
    self.calculator.pressFive()
    self.calculator.pressThree()
    self.assertEquals(553, self.calculator.getDisplay(), \
     'Accumulation failure: 553')
```

Here we have shown a form of the assertEquals method of unittest.TestCase that has a message as the final argument. This message (str argument at the end) will be printed whenever the assertion fails. Also note that the expected value in an assertion comes before the tested value. This is just a convention, but it has proved useful in practice. The above test runs ok, since we have already built all of the methods it uses, but it will fail, since they don't yet do the right thing. So, we need to modify the *pressFive* and *pressThree* methods so that they do a better job. We examined the logic of the accumulation process in Chapter 9, so won't repeat it here, but as we start modifying the two methods we see that they both have to accumulate a value. It is therefore wise to factor this out (Say it Once) into a separate *accumulate* method of CalculatorModel.

```
def accumulate(self, value:int):
    '''Accumulate a new value into the display'''
    self._display = self._display*10 + value

def pressThree(self):
    '''Press the 3 key'''
    self.accumulate(3)
```

```
    def pressFive(self):
        '''Press the 5 key'''
        self.accumulate(5)
```

We still haven't gotten to the point at which we use objects to represent the keys, or to use strategies, but nothing in our stories yet requires anything like that. We also don't have a way to clear the display, but we have no requirement for that either. We now have eleven lines of code (not counting comments) and sixteen lines of test. But all the tests pass at this point, not just the newest one. The unittest will run them all so an OK message gives us confidence in out development process.

Note that each story is small. It leads to a small test or two, and that leads to a small change or addition to our code base. This is the essence of TDD. And notice how much of our design work is done while we are writing tests.

The fourth story is a bit more extensive: *Give the calculator a + key that adds the results of two operands. Other operator keys will be added later (-, *, /). Sum isn't done till you hit equals, though.*

At this point in thinking about how to proceed we discover that the numeric keys have to do two different things, depending on whether an operator key has just been pressed. We captured that in the first version of the state transition diagram (Figure 9.1). If we want to develop a polymorphic solution, we realize that we will need more than just the one class, CalculatorModel. So our next step is to *refactor* our code to enable us to move forward more easily. Refactoring is changing the structure of the code without changing its behavior, and we have tests in place to help us make sure we don't change the behavior. At this point we can introduce the class __NumberKey. Suppose we decide to make them inner classes of the CalculatorModel itself (as we did in Chapter 9).

```
    class __calculatorKey: # an interface
        def press(self):
            raise NotImplementedError("press not yet implemented.")

    class __NumberKey(__calculatorKey):
        def __init__(self, value, model):
            self.__value = value
            self.__model = model
```

```
    def press(self):
        self.__model.accumulate(self.__value)
```

We will then also need to create a Number key for the five key and another for the three key and connect them to the corresponding press methods of the CalculatorModel.

```
def __init__(self):
    ''' Create a calculator with display initially 0'''
    self._display = 0

    self._three = self.__NumberKey(3, self)
    self._five = self.__NumberKey(5, self)

def pressThree(self):
    '''Press the 3 key'''
    self._three.press()

def pressFive(self):
    '''Press the 5 key'''
    self._five.press()
```

We now have a larger collection of objects interacting to solve the current simple problem, but some of the objects (three and five) are hidden. The CalculatorModel can now be called a *façade* for the objects and we have an application of the Façade Design Pattern, the intent of which is to provide a unified face to a bunch of interacting objects. We haven't changed the behavior of the application in this change in its structure. How do we know that? The tests still pass. Now you can go on to implement the new story on this code base by adding strategies and it will be much easier than to do so on the earlier one. But it was the tests that gave us the confidence to make the changes to the new structure knowing that we couldn't break something unnoticed. This too is swell.

## 12.5 Important Ideas From This Chapter

model
view
documentation
unittest

TestCase
Test Driven Development (TDD)
Façade Design Pattern

## 12.6 Problem Set

1. Find one of your old Python programs and document it using unittest. Provide documentation for each class, each public method and for each parameter and return value of your methods.

2. Finish the development of tests for the CalculatorModel that was begun in Section 12.4.1

3. Write user level documentation for FMG explaining to a user exactly how to run the program and interact with it.

# Secondo Intermezzo – A Toy Computer

## 1 Introduction to Machine Language

In this second interlude we will discuss some very low level computer ideas by examining a simulation of simple hardware machine language. To give you an idea of how low level this is, we start by presenting a program that consists of a simple loop that will add some data and print it.

```
00:   zer
01:   push  104
02:   push  105
03:   subtr
04:   jnn   6
05:   jmp   16
06:   push  106
07:   ldd
08:   add
09:   push  104
10:   inc
11:   pop   104
12:   push  106
13:   inc
14:   pop   106
15:   jmp   1
16:   outp
17:   halt
```

Not easy to understand, of course. In fact, it isn't easy even if you understand the language. This language has absolutely no abstraction facility. You can't name a variable, or a method, or anything. You can make only the tiniest of steps at a time, and so the amount of detail required to do anything meaningful becomes overwhelming. Some of the words probably make sense; add and halt, for example, others are gibberish. Let's get started in trying to understand a system in which this can make sense. In a compiled language (Java), all of your computer programs are translated into something not too different from this. In Python, the interpreter is composed of similar things, though your programs might not be translated into such a low-level form.

Each line is an instruction, and even a simple Python program might require the execution of thousands of such instructions. This particular language, by the way, has no special merit. I just created it for purposes of this discussion. But it is similar to real *machine languages*.

First, the leftmost column is not part of the language. I've just labeled the lines, but the labels are significant. The 6 on the right of line 04 refers to line 06, in fact. The names in the middle column are called *opcodes* and a machine language comes with a fixed, not extendable, list of these. Each does some simple thing. The right column numbers are called *operands*, though not every opcode needs an operand. In this language an instruction consists of a single opcode and zero or one operands.

In reality it is even a bit harder than we have shown. The machine codes (opcodes) are really just numbers, though we have shown names above to make it a bit easier to follow below. We shall return to this idea, however.

## 2 The Memory and Its Contents

This computer has only a few parts. One is its memory, which is really just an array of cells. Each cell can hold either an *instruction* or a piece of *data*. The instructions are like those above. All of the operands in the right column of our program are actually indexes into this memory array. We normally call them addresses. The numbers in the left column, which label the instructions, are also addresses, and the implication is that at address 09 you will find the "push 104" instruction. Figure 1 shows the parts of this computer. The heavy line between the Stack and the Memory is a *data bus* that transfers data between the two. The PC (program counter) was discussed earlier, in Section 9.2. The meaning is the same here.

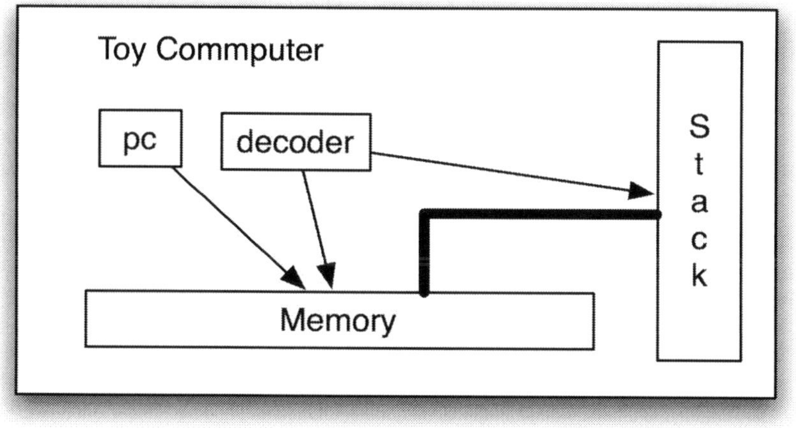


Figure 1. Schematic of the Toy Computer

The data used in this computer is of type *float*.

In Python, a float is (probably) a 64 bit number that represents an approximation to a real number with a decimal part. Some examples of floats are 65.3 and 3.1416. The most important thing to know about floats is that they really are approximations. It is not possible to represent all of the real numbers, even just those between 0 and 1, in a computer, since in any range of real numbers there are infinitely many values. But computers are finite.

An implication of this is that if you add up .01 a thousand times, you won't get 10 like you expect. Though you will get a number close to 10. Floats are good for measurements, such as temperature, which are seldom perfectly precise, but they are not good for things like money, which does require precision.

We will actually build a computer simulator that executes programs like those above. We will need some data structures to hold some of its elements, such as its memory. Rather than use a Python list, which would be a good choice, we will use instead the classes given in the Appendix and discussed earlier. These classes were built for no reason but to give you something to read that is fairly sophisticated, but a bit less so than those in the Python libraries. They are very similar to the corresponding Python collections and are in fact interchangeable with them for our purposes here. We will represent the memory of the computer with a DenseList, which is like a list as we saw in the previous chapter.

We will also encapsulate both the data stored in the array and the instructions in classes. They are quite simple. Since we want either of them to be storable in a memory cell. We have also provided documentation comments for the important parts.

```
class Data:
    def __init__(self, d:float):
        self.data = d

    def value(self)->float:
        return self.data

class Instruction:
    '''A machine language instruction with opcode and operand
        (if any)
    '''
    def __init__(self, operation:int, onWhat:int):
        self._opcode = operation
        self._operand = onWhat

    def opcode(self)->int:
        return self._opcode

    def operand(self)->int:
        return self._operand
```

So, Data has just a *value*, but an Instruction has both an *opcode* and an *operand*

The memory of the computer can now be defined as a DenseList of $1024 = 2^{10}$ cells, each of which can hold an item of type Data or type Instruction.

```
from denseList import DenseList
from instruction import Instruction
from data import Data
from flexStack import FlexStack

class Memory:
    ''' A memory structure for a toy computer. It can store both
        Data and Instruction cells but retrieval requires knowing
        which you expect as the protocols differ.    '''
```

```
    def __init__(self):
        self._memory = DenseList(1024)
        for i in range(1024):
            self._memory.append(0)

    def _get(self, address):
        return self._memory[address]

    def stack(self)-> FlexStack:
        '''Return a specialized stack within the structure'''
        flex = FlexStack(storage=self._memory, reverse = True)
        return flex

    def put(self, address:int, value):
        '''Insert a value at a given address.
        @param address: the location in which to insert the value
        @param value: either a Data or Instruction object
        '''
        self._memory[address] = value

    def getValue(self, address:int)->Data:
        '''Get a Data cell at a given address
        @param address: a valid location in the structure
        @raises TypeError if the location isn't a Data cell
        '''
        entry = self._get(address)
        if not isinstance(entry, Data):
            raise TypeError('address ' + str(address) + \
                " isn't a data value")
        return entry

    def getInstruction(self, address)->Instruction:
        '''Get an instruction object at a given address
        @param adress: a valid location in the structure
        @raises TypeError: if the location isn't an Instruction
        '''
        entry = self._get(address)
        if not isinstance(entry, Instruction):
            raise TypeError('address ' + str(address) + \
                " isn't an instruction")
        return entry
```

We can put something into memory by setting the DenseList cell with the new value. We don't record which kind of thing we put there, however, so if we want to retrieve it with one of our *get* methods, we need to know what we put in that cell. Nothing will help us keep track of this. This is one of the difficult features of low level programming; there is no nice language like Python to help keep you from misusing data.

## 3 The Execution Stack

The next major feature of our computer is its *stack*. A Stack is a data structure, that can be either densely stored or linked, but it has a special data protocol called Last-in, First-out, or LIFO. You insert data into a stack with a *push* operation, and it is then saved. For us the data will be floats. You retrieve data with a *pop* operation. And pop returns the item most recently pushed, as well as removing it from the storage. The name Stack is supposed to remind you of a stack of plates. You can put a plate on the top (push) but if you want a plate you normally retrieve (pop) the one most recently placed on the top. We will used the DenseList structure we've already seen, though a Python list would work as well. Since our DenseList is automatically expandable, so will the stack be. Note, however, that it is an error to try to pop from a stack that is empty. A push adds the new element at the end, and a pop retrieves it from the end, but also removes it. First we will use a separate stack (separate from the Memory) though a real computer will use memory cells to implement a stack. That is why our Memory will produce a *FlexStack* on demand. We save that discussion for later. Here is a simple Stack structure, though we could also use any of those we've seen before or a Python list. It should have no surprises so it in minimally commented. Our usage will be to store both int and float values. The int values will represent memory locations.

```
from denseList import DenseList

class Stack:
    '''A simple stack for use in the toy computer'''

    def __init__(self, size=100):
        self.storage = DenseList(size)

    def push(self, element):
        self.storage.append(element)
```

```
    def pop(self):
        if self.storage.size() == 0:
            raise Exception("Pop of empty stack")
        return self.storage.pop()

    def top(self):
        if self.storage.size() == 0:
            raise Exception("Pop of empty stack")
        return self.storage[-1]

    def isEmpty(self):
        return self.storage.size() == 0

    def clear(self):
        self.storage.clear()

    def __iter__(self):
        return iter(self.storage)

    def __str__(self):
        return self.storage.__str__()
```

The computer will have both a Memory and a Stack and the reason we want the latter is that is where all computation is done in this computer. To add two numbers you push both of them on to the stack and then issue an *add* instruction. The add instruction itself pops two items from the stack, adds them and pushes the result back onto the stack. The size of the stack shrinks by one in this operation, of course. This also explains why the add instruction at location 08 of our little program didn't need any operands. They are implicit, being the two top stack cells. A computer like this is called *stack-based*. The high level language Forth is based on similar principles, in fact, and almost all high level languages need a stack for such things as functions, especially when recursion is allowed.

## 4 The Toy Computer

The only other important piece of our computer is an int called the *pc* (program counter), previously discussed in Section 9.2. Normally we spell out the names of things in programming, but the name *pc* has become so entrenched among people who do this kind of programming that we will keep it. The idea is that the pc always maintains the address of the next instruction to be executed. When our computer starts, the pc is always 0, meaning that the instruction in memory cell 0 will always be the first one executed. The pc then steps through the program to execute the instructions one after the other. Some instructions can change this order of execution, as we shall see.

With this background we can explain some of the instructions in our program. Instruction *zer* pushes 0.0 onto the stack. Instruction *inc* adds 1.0 to whatever is on top. Recall that the stack contains (mostly) float data. Instruction *push* of the ToyComputer has an operand and the meaning is that the operand represents the *address* of a data cell in memory and the contents of that cell, a float, are to be pushed. The contents of the original cell are not modified, however. Only the stack changes. Note that the operand here is quite different from that of the stack operation with the same name.

Notice that in our definition of *Instruction*, the opcodes are represented as ints. here is a complete listing represented as Python constants. Following is part of the constructor of the ToyComputer

```
class ToyComputer:
     '''Create a computer simulator
     @param trace: if True, a trace of the program will be
      shown on execution
     '''
  def __init__(self, trace = False):
      self._memory = Memory()
      self._stack = Stack()
      self._loadAddress = 0
      self._running = False
      self._pc = 0
      self._decoder = None
      self._trace = trace

      self.push = 0
      self.pop = 1
      self.toss = 2
      self.outp = 3
      self.dupl = 4
      self.add = 5
      self.subtr = 6
      self.halt = 7                 # more...
```

```
        self.inp = 8
        self.jmp = 9
        self.jnn = 10
        self.ldd = 11
        self.zer = 12
        self.inc = 13
        self.lda = 14
```

We have used simple names here since the user needs to refer to them in building programs. So, the first instruction in the sample program is really just the value 12, which is the value given to the *zer* instruction that pushes 0.0 onto the stack.

However, in order to simulate the execution of a program like the one we began with, we need methods in the computer simulator to carry them out. These are part of the class *ToyComputer*, as are the constants above. The comments explain each operation.

```
    def _push(self, mem:int):
        '''extract a value from memory and push onto stack
        @param mem: the memory location of the source'''
        val = self._memory.getValue(mem).value()
        self._stack.push(val)

    def _pop(self, mem:int):
        '''Pop the stack and insert the result into memory
        #param mem: the location to store the value'''
        val = self._stack.pop()
        self._memory.put(mem, Data(val))

    def _toss(self, unused=0):
        '''Discard the top of the stack'''
        self._stack.pop()

    def _outp(self, unused=0):
        '''pop the stack and print the result'''
        print(self._stack.pop())

    def _dupl(self, unused=0):
        '''duplicate the stack top, pushing a new copy of the top'''
        self._stack.push(self._stack.top())
```

```
def _add(self, unused=0):
    '''Pop two elements from the stack and push their sum'''
    self._stack.push(self._stack.pop() + self._stack.pop())

def _subtr(self, unused=0):
    '''Pop two elements from the stack and push their
difference (first - second)'''
    self._stack.push(self._stack.pop() - self._stack.pop())

def _halt(self, unused=0):
    '''halt the current program'''
    self._running = False

def _inp(self, unused=0):
    '''Read a float form the input and push it onto stack'''
    self._stack.push(float(input()))

def _jmp(self, address:int):
    '''Jump to a given location in the program'''
    self._pc = address

def _jnn(self, address:int):
    '''pop the stack and if that is not negative, jump to address'''
    if self._stack.pop() >= 0:
        self._pc = address

def _ldd(self, unused=0):
    '''Pop an address from the stack and extract the value at that
     address from memory. Push that value onto the stack'''
    addr = int(self._stack.pop())
    val = self._memory.getValue(addr).value()
    self._stack.push(val)

def _zer(self, unused=0):
    '''Push a zero onto the stack'''
    self._stack.push(0.0)

def _inc(self, unused=0):
    '''add 1.0 to the stack top'''
    val = self._stack.pop() + 1.0
    self._stack.push(val)
```

```
    def _lda(self, address:int):
        '''Push the memory address of some location onto the stack
        @param address: the address to be loaded'''
        self._stack.push(float(address))
```

Next, we need a way to actually load the memory preparatory to running a program. Both the program and the data it will manipulate need to be loaded in to the memory. Since this simple device isn't connected to a disk drive we need some way to put instructions and data into individual memory cells. In the early days of computing, this was done using strictly numeric codes, 1 instead of pop, for example. They were entered physically using a set of switches on the front of the computer. Here we have three methods for handling this. They depend on a field called the *loadAddress* that represents the next cell into which to put an instruction. It is automatically incremented each time you put in an instruction, and it always starts from zero. Data cells are put into cells specified in the method itself, however.

```
    def loadInstruction(self, opcode, operand = 0): #default operand
        '''load an instruction with the given opcode and operand into the
        next available memory location
        @param opcode: the opcode of the instruction
        @param operand: the operand of the instruction
        '''
        self._memory.put(self._loadAddress, Instruction(opcode, operand))
        self._loadAddress += 1


    def loadData(self, data:float, location:int):
        '''place a data value at a given location in memory
        @param data: a data value
        @param location: where the data is to be placed
        '''
        self._memory.put(location, Data(data))

    def reset(self):
        '''reset the load address to the beginning of memory'''
        self._loadAddress = 0
```

Using this, our original machine language program would be loaded like this. I chose to load the data first, but it doesn't matter.

```
if __name__ == '__main__':
    computer = ToyComputer()

    computer.loadData(1.0, 100) # data to be added
    computer.loadData(2.0, 101)
    computer.loadData(3.0, 102)
    computer.loadData(4.0, 103)
    computer.loadData(0.0, 104) # control counter
    computer.loadData(3.0, 105) #const number of items - 1
    computer.loadData(100.0, 106) # data loc of beginning of data

    computer.loadInstruction(computer.zer)
    computer.loadInstruction(computer.push, 104)
    computer.loadInstruction(computer.push, 105)
    computer.loadInstruction(computer.subtr)
    computer.loadInstruction(computer.jnn, 6)
    computer.loadInstruction(computer.jmp, 16)
    computer.loadInstruction(computer.push, 106)
    computer.loadInstruction(computer.ldd)
    computer.loadInstruction(computer.add)
    computer.loadInstruction(computer.push, 104)
    computer.loadInstruction(computer.inc)
    computer.loadInstruction(computer.pop, 104)
    computer.loadInstruction(computer.push, 106)
    computer.loadInstruction(computer.inc)
    computer.loadInstruction(computer.pop, 106)
    computer.loadInstruction(computer.jmp, 1)
    computer.loadInstruction(computer.outp)
    computer.loadInstruction(computer.halt)

    computer.run()
```

See if you can now trace out this program using the definitions of the opcodes given in the comments. Its purpose is to add the data in cells 100 through 103 of the memory, printing 10.0 at the end.

## 5 Running the Program

Now that we have the program in the memory, let's look at how a computer actually executes a machine language program. Our simulation will be quite close to this. A computer is driven by a clock and we can think of the clock making four ticks per cycle. The computer also has a program counter (pc) that is always used to point to the next instruction to be executed as well as an instruction decoder that can hold one instruction: the one currently in execution.

On the first tick of the clock, the instruction in memory pointed to by the pc is loaded into the decoder. In our program an error will occur if that location doesn't hold an instruction, but in a real computer, it just loads whatever is there and will interpret it as an instruction even if it isn't. This tick is called *fetch*. The next, or *increment*, tick causes the pc to be incremented by one so that it now points to the next instruction in sequence. If we just loaded from cell 22, then the increment tick will put 23 into the pc. The third tick, *decode*, gives the computer a chance to extract the parts of the instruction and, in a real computer, start the electrical signals flowing through the machine. The last tick, *do*, is where the instruction is actually performed. The clock then goes around again, with a new *fetch* tick.

On the *do* tick, an add instruction causes two values to be popped from the stack and the result pushed back on. The only thing that is very different here, is what happens on *jump* instructions. Recall that the increment made the pc point to the next instruction after the current one. If a jump is executed, however, the pc itself may be modified. On an unconditional jump, *jmp*, the operand is written into the pc. Since this happens just before fetch, the next instruction executed will be the one whose address was in the *jmp*. Conditional jumps like *jnn* only write into the pc when their condition is met.

Here is the code that implements run. Note that we have broken the cycle down. The loop in *run* is potentially infinite, broken only by an error or by the execution of a *halt* instruction.

```
def run(self):
    self._running = True
    self._pc = 0
    while self._running:
        self.fetch()
        self.increment()            # more
```

```
            self.decode()
            self.do()

        def fetch(self):
         '''Fetch an instruction from memory and save it in the decoder
         The source is the program counter'''
         self._decoder = self._memory.getInstruction(self._pc)
         if self._trace: print('-------------------', \
             self._decoder.opcode(), self._decoder.operand())

    def increment(self):
        ''' increment the program counter'''
        self._pc += 1
```

The decoder, self._decoder holds an instruction object with both opcode (one of our fifteen codes) and an operand, such as an address. It will be used below when we execute *do*.

The *decode* operation selects from all of the operation methods, the one indicated by the corresponding numeric code. It actually sets a function object into a field `self._nextOperator`. The function will actually be executed by the *do* command. It is applied to the operand of the operation previously fetched.

```
    def do(self):
        self._nextOperator(self._decoder.operand())
```

The real work is done by decode, which simply translates opcodes to functions. Here we use a typical method, though we could also have stored the opcodes and corresponding functions in a dictionary or other map. You could do that as an exercise, of course.

```
def decode(self):
        instruction = self._decoder.opcode()
        self._nextOperator = None
        if instruction == self.push:
            self._nextOperator = self._push # a function
        elif instruction == self.pop:
            self._nextOperator = self._pop # a function
        elif instruction == self.toss:
            self._nextOperator = self._toss # a function
```

```
        elif instruction == self.outp:
            self._nextOperator = self._outp # a function
        elif instruction == self.dupl:
            self._nextOperator = self._dupl # a function
        elif instruction == self.add:
            self._nextOperator = self._add # a function
        elif instruction == self.subtr:
            self._nextOperator = self._subtr # a function
        elif instruction == self.halt:
            self._nextOperator = self._halt # a function
        elif instruction == self.inp:
            self._nextOperator = self._inp # a function
        elif instruction == self.jmp:
            self._nextOperator = self._jmp # a function
        elif instruction == self.jnn:
            self._nextOperator = self._jnn # a function
        elif instruction == self.ldd:
            self._nextOperator = self._ldd # a function
        elif instruction == self.zer:
            self._nextOperator = self._zer # a function
        elif instruction == self.inc:
            self._nextOperator = self._inc # a function
        elif instruction == self.lda:
            self._nextOperator = self._lda # a function
```

Note that it is the function itself that is stored. It isn't invoked yet.

## 6 More Convenient Programming – Assembly Language

Machine language has no programming abstraction facility. The only abstraction we have shown is names for opcodes. Real machine code doesn't have even this. If we extracted our program from the computer it wouldn't have the names of the operations, but their numeric opcodes:

```
12 0
0  104
0  105
6  0
10 6
9  16
0  106
```

```
11 0
5  0
0  104
13 0
1  104
0  106
13 0
1  106
9  1
3  0
7  0
```

Well, the original was bad enough. But we can do a bit better. Assembly language is an attempt to add a couple of simple abstraction facilities to machine code to make it a bit easier to understand. In addition to the names of opcodes, that we have already shown, but which are built in to the language, it is possible for a programmer in assembly code to give names to machine addresses also. This means that the 104 and 106 in the above program can be made a bit more decipherable. Here is an assembly program that has the same effect as our original, though slightly different structure, since it takes advantage of the new facility. It also shows a zero operand for those instructions that don't require an operand, but that is to make this easier to read by a program, the Assembler.

```
   zer 0
   lda data
   pop point
label loop
   push calc
   push stop
   subtr 0
   jnn more
   jmp done
label more
   push point
   ldd 0
   add 0
   push calc
   inc 0
   pop calc
   push point
```

```
    inc 0
    pop point
    jmp loop
label done
    outp 0
    halt 0
label data
    double 1.0
    double 2.0
    double 3.0
    double 4.0
label calc
    double 0.0
label stop
    double 3.0
label point
    double 0.0
```

As an historical note, Assembly language got its name from the way programs were submitted to computers in the early days of computing. Decks of *punch cards* were manually "assembled" with user code as well as system code and data and then read through card readers into the computer. The name has persisted.

This example shows not only the program, but also the data that it will manipulate. There are two new features here that are not part of machine code. A *label* is just a symbolic address. The first label, *loop*, will be associated with the address 3, since it immediately precedes the instruction that will be loaded into cell 3.

This sort of thing is much easier to understand, though still far from easy. The names let us decipher it a bit. The *data* consists of four values. The *calc* is where we shall save a counter that tells us when we have added enough values. *Stop* is the value of *calc* that will cause us to leave a counting loop, and *point* is going to be a pointer to the next data value to be added. The earlier labels are also supposed to be instructive. The label *loop* indicates that we return to it to complete a loop structure, The label *done* indicates that we have left the loop and want to output our result and exit. The *more* label is needed since the jnn instruction is a bit awkward for us in this program and we need to skip over the jmp instruction. This is a canonical two way branch in this language, similar to an IF-ELSE instruction in Python.

The second feature is the *double directive* that gives instructions to the assembler about what to do with the number that follows. It is not a machine instruction, nor does it correspond to one. Instead, it says that a float value is to be loaded into the computer memory at the current loadAddress. The first such, will be at the address specified by the *data* label, the next immediately after, etc. Label *data* will be 20, so the 1.0 will be at address 20, etc. The labels themselves are not instructions, so don't contribute to the instruction count.

We want to examine a program, the Assembler, that will translate this into machine code. The input will look like the above. But note that an assembler is very unforgiving. Errors will result in gibberish. We could provide output in many different forms. We could produce something like our first example in the intermezzo, or something like the first example in this section (real machine code), but we will actually do something much more useful. Our output will actually be a Python fragment that can be pasted into a main program of he ToyComputer and then run. Here is the output for the program above.

```
computer.loadInstruction(zer, 0);
computer.loadInstruction(lda, 20);
computer.loadInstruction(pop, 26);
computer.loadInstruction(push, 24);
computer.loadInstruction(push, 25);
computer.loadInstruction(subtr, 0);
computer.loadInstruction(jnn, 8);
computer.loadInstruction(jmp, 18);
computer.loadInstruction(push, 26);
computer.loadInstruction(ldd, 0);
computer.loadInstruction(add, 0);
computer.loadInstruction(push, 24);
computer.loadInstruction(inc, 0);
computer.loadInstruction(pop, 24);
computer.loadInstruction(push, 26);
computer.loadInstruction(inc, 0);
computer.loadInstruction(pop, 26);
computer.loadInstruction(jmp, 3);
computer.loadInstruction(outp, 0);
computer.loadInstruction(halt, 0);
```

```
computer.loadData(1.0, 20);
computer.loadData(2.0, 21);
computer.loadData(3.0, 22);
computer.loadData(4.0, 23);
computer.loadData(0.0, 24);
computer.loadData(3.0, 25);
computer.loadData(0.0, 26);
```

The version we will show here could use some fixing. While we will read an input file and write an output, we won't make this process very general or robust. Otherwise, this matches what happens in principle in a real assembler program.

Such a program is driven by a table, a map, actually, of symbols. The symbols are strings and the data are the numeric equivalents. When the assembler starts, the table is initialized with the opcode names and their values. We will use the classes from the Appendix for much of this, and show the use of a BinarySearchTree, as a map.

```
from denseList import DenseList
from stack import Stack
from binarySearchTree import BinarySearchTree

class Assembler:
    def __init__(self):
        self._instructionTable = { # a dict. Could be a
BinarySearchTree
              "push": 0,
              "pop": 1,
              "toss": 2,
              "outp": 3,
              "dupl": 4,
              "add": 5,
              "subtr": 6,
              "halt": 7,
              "inp": 8,
              "jmp": 9,
              "jnn": 10,
              "ldd": 11,
              "zer": 12,
              "inc": 13,          # more...
```

```
            "lda": 14,
            'double':0
        }

        self._dataPrefix = 'computer.LD('
        self._instructionPrefix = 'computer.LI('
        self._program = DenseList(50)
        self._translateOK = True
        self._translated = DenseList(50)
        self._table = BinarySearchTree(duplicates = False)
        self._numeric = DenseList(50)
```

We will read the assembly language program into the *_program* list, one token per entry. The *_translated* list will hold our output prior to writing it.

A typical assembler works in two steps, called *passes*. Each pass processes the input, which is why we capture it in a list. On the first pass, the program looks for symbols used in the program other than the opcodes and tries to give them numeric values. These values are always derived from the *instructionCounter* we discussed earlier, and which is used to assign instructions to addresses when loading. Something identical is used in the assembler to compute, on each pass, where each instruction will be put.

The assembler examines each instruction, one after the other. With the instruction counter initialized to zero it counts each instruction as it processes. Our sample program begins like this:

```
   zer 0
   lda data
   pop point
label loop
   push calc
   push stop
```

The instruction counter is 1 after processing the zer instruction, 2 after the lda, and 3 after the pop. So, when it encounters the label, it assigns 3 to the label named loop. The instruction counter is not incremented except for machine language instructions (which a label is not), so the label loop is actually the address of the push instruction. There is not much more to an assembler than this.

At the end of the first pass the program checks that all symbols used were actually put into the *_table*. If a symbol appears in an operand position before it appears in a label, we need to assure that the label eventually shows up.

At the beginning of the second pass, the *_table* should hold all symbols used in the program and the pass just uses this information to translate each label into numeric form. So all occurrences of *loop* in our program above will translate to 3 in the output.

Using traditional names for the passes, the main driver of the process, then is just this:

```
def assemble(self):
    print('running')
    self.readProgram()
    self.pass1()
    self.pass2()
    self.writeResult()
    self.printNumeric()
```

The structure of such an application is often called a *pipeline*. Each of the first four invocations advances the computation and hands off the results to the next piece. As was mentioned above, the read and write methods could use improvement, but here is what I used as this was developed:

```
def readProgram(self):
    try:
        with open("../prog.txt", "r") as file:
            for line in file:
                temp = line.strip().split()
                instr = (temp[0], temp[1])
                self._program.append(instr)
    except Exception:
        self._translateOK = False
        print('failed reading')
        return
```

This assumes each instruction line has two values, even for instructions like zer that don't require an operand. It could, therefore be improved. It reads the entire file in one read and then breaks it up into lines and the 'words'. Finally it extracts the first two words as the opcode and operand, stored in a tuple.

Writing is also straightforward but could be improved. In particular it assumes a particular filename.

```
def writeResult(self):
    print('writing')
    if not self._translateOK:
        print('failed')
        return
    with open("_translated.txt", "w") as writer:
        for instruction in self._translated:
            writer.write(instruction + "\n")
```

Given this, pass1 just fills the _table, being careful to count instructions as it goes. It is looking for labels, so it ignores the numeric values, but everything in the input file is a string, so it needs to try to extract integers from the operands to see if they really are integers encoded in the strings. If they really are integers, then we don't need to process them further, but if they are labels we need to assure that they are eventually defined. We put the string into some kind of list We used a stack for this, but don't really need it to be a stack. any iterable will do. A set would be better, actually, since we don't need duplicates. These saved operands are then checked at the end, when the first loop completes, to make sure they have been put into the table. The instruction counter is used to assign a value to each label that it finds as we discussed above.

```
def pass1(self):
    instructionCounter = 0
    toBeDefined = Stack()
    if not self._translateOK:
        print('failed')
        return
    for instr in self._program:
        opcode = instr[0]
        symbol = instr[1]
        if opcode.lower() == 'label':
            self._table.insert(symbol, instructionCounter)
```

```
        else:
            instructionCounter +=1
            if opcode.lower() == 'double': continue
            try:
                value = int(symbol)
            except Exception as e:
                toBeDefined.push(symbol)
    while not toBeDefined.isEmpty():
        value = toBeDefined.pop()
        if self._table[value] is None:
            print('Label ', value, ' not defined')
            print('failed in pass1')
            self._translateOK = False
```

Now, if there have been no errors, we can do the actual translation on pass 2. It is possible to produce many different output formats, as mentioned above. You can modify pass2 in a variety of ways to do this. In pass2, we again need to keep track of the instruction counter, for now it also determines where things are actually loaded. We have to process opcode lines and double directive lines differently, of course.

This is a process that has quite a lot of structure. At the limits of understandability. It would benefit by extracting helper methods, perhaps.

```
def pass2(self):
    if not self._translateOK:
        print('failed')
        return
    instructionCounter = 0
    for instr in self._program:
        opcode = instr[0]
        operand = instr[1]
        if opcode.lower() == 'label':
            continue
        else:
            if opcode.lower() == 'double':
                self._translated.append(self._dataPrefix + \
                    str(operand)+', '+ str(instructionCounter)+')')
                self._numeric.append(operand)
            else:
```

```
            value = 0
            try:
                value = int(operand)
            except Exception as e:
                value = self._table[operand]
            self._translated.append(self._instructionPrefix + \
                str(opcode)+ ', ' + str(value) +')')
            self._numeric.append((opcode, value))
        instructionCounter += 1
```

Note that we also save a listing of the numeric version of the program. It will be printed later, but more could be done with it, including directly loading it into the ToyComputer.

To use this, you just create the Assembler object and send it an *assemble* message, though it reads from a file with a fixed name and, likewise, writes to a fixed file. But you can then copy the output into a program that will drive the operation of the Toy Computer.

## 7 Important Ideas From This Intermezzo

Stack
Machine Language
Assembly Language
instruction counter
instruction
double

## 8 Problem Set

1. Make the Stack class here Iterable<T>, and give it an Iterator<T> returned from the iterator() method. A stack iterator should probably work from the top of the stack toward the bottom.

2. Give the machine language a new instruction *jez* that will jump if the stack top is zero, while also popping the stack.

3. Give the machine multiply and divide instructions: *mul* and *div*.

4. Modify the output of the Assembler so that it puts a comment to the right of each output line showing at what address that instruction or data cell will be loaded.

5. Modify the output of the Assembler program so that it writes a complete and correct Python class with a main function that can be directly executed. The current output is the only variable part of this output.

6. Write a program in our little assembly language to do the following. A section of memory has a sequence of values, starting at a known location. The last number in the sequence is 0.0, but there are no other zero values. Start at the beginning of this sequence and sum all of the values. Stop when you get to the zero and print the result. You might also print out the count of values. You then could modify the program to print the average. Assemble the program and run it on the simulator. Are there additional, simple, instructions that would help you do this exercise?

7. Modify the ToyComputer so that the mapping between opcodes and their corresponding functions are first stored in a dict and later extracted in decode.

8. Try to implement a FlexStack with the same protocols as the Stack shown here, but which has some additional functionality. First, instead of creating a Dense List, it can be given one as a constructor argument in which to operate. Second, it can be told whether to grow toward larger subscripts of the list or toward lower. If it grows toward lower, it can start with the last index in the list and pushes are toward the "left". Third, though not needed here, it can be told at which index to start its operation, so that you could start in the middle of a large list and increment either direction. Then, use this in the ToyComputer so that the Memory and the Stack occupy the same DenseList. This is a difficult exercise and you need to keep in mind that the Memory contains Code, which might be Data or not, but the Stack only contains Data. This requires adjustments to the code here.

9 Modify the assembler so that instructions like zer and ldd, which don't really have operands, don't need to have a "dummy" operand specified in the assembly instruction as we did above.

# 13 Queues, Priority Queues, and Huffman Coding

In this chapter we will examine two additional storage structures as well as get additional practice working with strings and floats. We shall see another application as well, one that tries to make data transmission as efficient as possible by carefully coding the information sent.

## 13.1 Queues and Priority Queues

In spite of the similarity of names, these are two quite different things. Normally the term queue refers to a First-in, First-out (FIFO) data structure in which the next item to remove is the one that has been stored the longest, but not yet removed. It is like a waiting line that one enters at the back (tail) and exits at the front (head). Queues are used in event simulation, such as a program that simulates the effect of customers arriving at a bank and waiting in line for service. The usual purpose of such a simulation is to determine average waiting times, for example. In the Python libraries, *queue* is a module with a *Queue* class, though it is intended for specialized use. It is actually a bit dangerous to use in general, since it you use the simple *get* operation on an empty Queue your call won't return anything and a process will be left waiting for some other process to put an element (but, see *get_nowait()*). Insertion into a Python Queue is with put().

The queue module also defines a deque, short for Double Ended Queue. In a deque (pronounced deck, as in deck of cards) an element can enter at either the front or rear and exit at either end as well. A deque that utilizes only one "end" behaves like a stack, in fact. And a deque is also like a deck of cards in that a card can easily be inserted at either the top or bottom and likewise removed from either end. In Python a deque is preferred when you want a simple queue. The operations on a deque are *append, appendleft, pop, and popleft*. Using only appendleft and pop gives you a queue.

Among our sample implementations, the CircularLinkedList is a classic deque since we can insert or remove from either the head or tail. Generally speaking a doubly linked list is a good candidate for implementing either a queue or a deque. It is possible to use array-like structures for these, especially when they only require a bounded number of elements, though the implementations are a bit tricky. Our DenseList favors operations at one end only, making it more suitable for a Stack.

The key operations on a queue are *put* (adds an element at the tail), *get* (removes and returns an item from the head). The operation get_nowait will get an item from the head of a non-empty Queue and raise the *Empty* exception if the Queue is empty.

A *priority queue* on the other hand, is not FIFO. The typical use of a priority queue is a situation in which a process has work to do but additional work comes in while the process works on the current item. When the process is ready for more work it goes to he queue to get the next item. However, in this case, it is better if the process work on high priority items, not just old items. In general terms, it *polls* the queue to get the desired, highest priority, item. But a Python PriorityQueue has no poll operation, so we need to improvise.

You can think of the insert point in a priority queue as the tail. However when you *poll* (or *get*) a priority queue the item you get is the one with smallest *priority*. This item is thought of as the head, but it need not have been in the queue the longest amount of time. The priorities are associated with the elements themselves and don't change while the item is in the queue. Module queue also has a PriorityQueue class. Its operations, like that of a Queue are get() and put().

In the Python implementation, Queue, queue, and PriorityQueue are all objects that wrap lists, providing the specialized operations associate with each structure. A PriorityQueue actually contains tuples, with the first component the priority, for example.

When implemented as a doubly linked list all of the major operations on a queue or deque take constant time. You simply need to add or remove a node. Priority queues, on the other hand are quite different and their operations are normally logarithmic in relation to the number of items stored. This is due to the fact that a priority queue is often stored as a height balanced binary tree (which may well be stored in an array in a certain way). The highest priority item (the smallest value) is always at the root of the tree, and when you insert or delete an element the tree is re-balanced and the new high priority item is brought to the root. This is typically explored in a *Data Structures and Algorithms* course.

A common implementation is called a Priority Heap which is a binary tree stored in an array. If you store root of a binary tree in cell 1 (not 0) of an array or dense list and store the children of the node stored in cell k in cells 2*k and 2*k +1, then it is easy to find both children and the parent from any given array cell, just knowing the index. It is also possible to do this with no empty cells in the array. We leave it to you to investigate this.

It won't have the same efficiency as a Priority Heap, but a BinarySearchTree can be used as a priority queue provided that it has a few features such as preventing duplicates and retrieval/removal of the item with the "smallest" key.

## 13.2 Huffman Coding – The Problem

Suppose you want to send textual information across a communication *channel*, such as downloading a message to a cell phone. Your channel may have lots of *bandwidth* (capacity), but never enough. So you would like to encode the information efficiently. The time it takes to transfer a message depends on the number of bits it contains, with each character of information normally requiring 8 or 16 bits, if normal encoding is used. In Python, the encoding of a character uses UNICODE, requiring 16 bits, though older systems still use something like ASCII, requiring only 8 bits, but less suitable for use in international commerce with many languages and therefore many alphabets. An 8 bit code only has room for $2^8 = 256$ different encodings. This is enough for English, but not for English and Swedish, Norwegian, Japanese, Urdu, etc. Therefore UNICODE is becoming more popular, though it has to make some compromises in the case of Chinese.

The problem we want to address, however, is that these codes all use a fixed number of bits for each character, but the relative frequencies of the various characters is not uniform. There are a lot more 'a' characters sent across the net than '%' characters. A key insight is that a code that uses fewer bits for frequently used symbols and longer codes for uncommon ones should be an advantage overall. The problem is knowing where such a character begins and ends within a stream of bits. The key trick for that is devising a code in which the coding of no character is the prefix of the coding of any other character. Thus, once you have discovered a valid code by reading a few bits, you can assume that you have what you want and go on from there for the next code.

To make it a bit more concrete, let's take an example. Here is the first paragraph of *The Adventures of Huckleberry Finn* by Mark Twain. Aside from being an interesting story, the book is noteworthy for its treatment of a variety of American English dialects of the early 19th century.

> YOU don't know about me without you have read a book by the name of The Adventures of Tom Sawyer; but that ain't no matter. That book was made by Mr. Mark Twain, and he told the truth, mainly. There was things which he stretched, but mainly he told the truth. That is nothing. I never seen anybody but lied one time or another, without it was Aunt Polly, or the widow, or maybe Mary. Aunt Polly--Tom's Aunt Polly, she is--and Mary, and the Widow Douglas is all told about in that book, which is mostly a true book, with some stretchers, as I said before.

This short paragraph contains 559 characters. but they are not evenly distributed. Here is what we mean (note that the newline is omitted here)

| char | freq | char | freq |
|---|---|---|---|
| ; | 1 | T | 7 |
| D | 1 | , | 11 |
| O | 1 | m | 12 |
| S | 1 | b | 14 |
| U | 1 | w | 14 |
| W | 1 | y | 15 |
| Y | 1 | d | 16 |
| I | 2 | l | 16 |
| ' | 3 | u | 16 |
| f | 3 | s | 20 |
| g | 3 | r | 21 |
| P | 3 | i | 22 |
| v | 3 | n | 24 |
| - | 4 | h | 30 |
| A | 4 | a | 34 |
| c | 4 | e | 38 |
| M | 4 | o | 39 |
| k | 6 | t | 47 |
| . | 7 | space | 110 |

So the space character alone accounts for nearly 20% of the text. A code that used a few bits for space, t, o, etc but more for semicolon, D, O, and the like might be advantageous. The method we will show can encode the 564 characters in 2492 bits, or about 4.4 bits per character, rather than the 8 of ASCII.

Here is the beginning of that 2492 bits of encoding:

```
11000001011111011001111101110000111010111111...
```

And it goes on for quite a while. It looks like gibberish, but the code itself, looks like this:

```
Char, Code
<ret> 1100001
<space>  00
' 11011000
- 0110100
, 110001
. 1111110
; 1100000110
A 0110101
D 1100000111
I 11000000
M 0110110
O 1111101100
P 11011001
S 1111101101
U 1111101110
T 1111111
W 1111101111
Y 110000010
a 1000
c 0110111
```

```
Char Code
b 01000
e 1010
d 01110
g 11011011
f 11011010
i 11010
h 0101
k 1111100
m 110111
l 01111
o 1011
n 11110
s 10011
r 11001
u 10010
t 1110
w 01001
v 11111010
y 01100
```

And the encoding begins with: `110000010 1111101100 1111101110`, which is YOU, using letters that were very infrequent and so with codes 10 bits long. The next two "bits" are 00, a space. And notice that 00 does not begin any other code. This is why it works. No character code is the prefix of any other.

We want to be able to create such a code and use it to encode and later decode texts. The process is named Huffman coding, named for its inventor, David A. Huffman. One interesting feature of a Huffman code is that it can be created tailored precisely to the text that will be sent. That is interesting, and achieves very good compression of the encoding, but leaves you with the problem that the receiver of the encoded text has to also have the key that encoded it in order to decode it and in the example we are using of encoding for data transmission it means that the code has to be sent along as well, lowering the benefit. It is also possible to create a general coding table based on a larger text that contains all characters that will be needed, and with typical frequencies. Then, the table (and the tree used to create it) can be sent once and for all.

Edgar Allen Poe wrote a story, *The Gold-Bug*, in which he discusses some similar things in a different context. Poe was interested in what was then known as Secret Writing, now known as encryption. Poe's discussion in The Gold-Bug is also based on relative frequencies of letters in text. If we devise a Huffman code for typical English (German, French, ...) text, rather than for a particular example of text, then the same encoder can be shared once and several different texts can be exchanged and decoded with some benefit. By the way, Poe's story is fun and interesting, but he got the relative frequencies for English wrong.

## 13.3 Huffman Coding – The Data Structures

We will require quite a few different ways of storing data for the creation of a Huffman coder. The main coding mechanism itself is a binary tree. The leaves of this tree are also referenced from a map. The tree has, in each node, a reference pointer to each child, but also a reference to the parent node (except at the root, of course). The way that a character is encoded is to work up the tree from leaf to root. The "turnings" at the nodes give us the bits of an encoding. For example, the t is encoded in a leaf that requires three right turns and one left turn to reach the root. A right turn moving upward means that the path is upward from the right child. The map referencing the leaves lets us easily find the beginning of a path for an encoding.

This tree will be purpose-built. There is no way to use a general purpose data structure for something like this. The operations are too specialized. It also will not be well encapsulated. Just the fact that we have references from outside the tree to the leaves makes this fairly obvious. The implication of this is that the programming we will do will be more error prone because we can't depend on abstraction and encapsulation to guide us. We have to "get it right" all the time.

The tree has two interesting aspects. One is that we can both encode and decode using the same tree. Encoding works up the tree from the leaves, so we require a map to find them, and decoding works down from the root. The other interesting aspect is that this tree will have "no missing nodes". A node is either a leaf or it has exactly two child nodes. The process we use to create it should make that obvious. A property of such trees is that they always have exactly one more leaf node than they do internal nodes. You can easily prove this by *mathematical induction* on the number of nodes in such a tree. Figure 13.1 shows a part of this resulting tree.

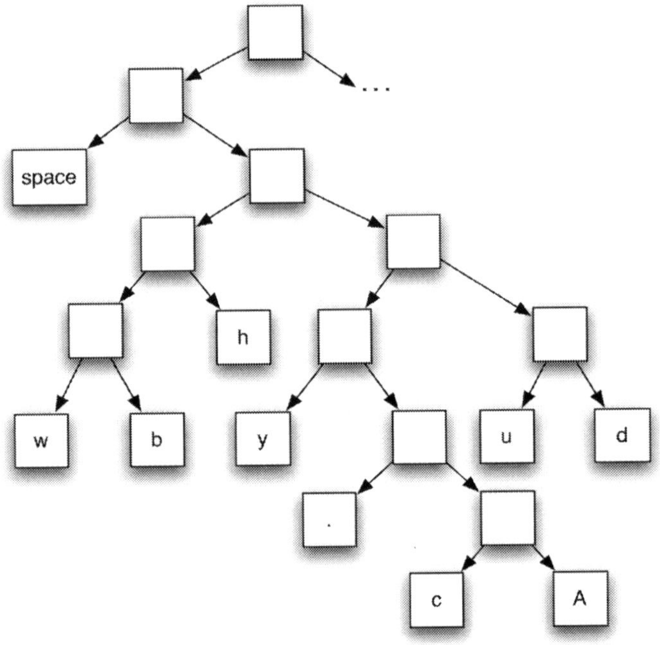


Figure 13.1. Part of the Huffman Tree

Note that the coding of 'h' is 0101, so it can be found from the root by moving left, right, left, right.

In order to create this tree, we need two additional structures. One will be a PriorityQueue (named, *_frequencyQueue*) and the other will be an ordinary Queue (the *_nodeQueue*). There are various replacements we could use for the PriorityQueue, but this one works for the purpose and you might enjoy thinking about what we could do to replace it. Recall that a queue has constant time operations. It is implemented as some kind of list, of course. The priority queue on the other hand has logarithmic time insertions and removals. This is not bad, but slower than constant time.

The *_nodeQueue* will hold partially built trees, along with priorities, and the final result is built up from those subtrees. The priority queue will hold leaf nodes and associated priorities, and since the tree itself isn't encapsulated, having a reference to any node means you have a reference to the "tree" that is rooted at that node. So, conceptually, the queue and priority queue contain trees. We also want to sort these trees (actually we sort the leaves) using the probability that the character represented by the node will occur in the text. Priorities are determined by the frequencies of the characters, with smaller relative frequency being higher priority.

We will also do a fair amount of processing of strings, but only one character at a time. Our inputs and outputs will all be represented as strings, though it would make more sense for the output (the encoded bit pattern of 0's and 1's) to be stored in something like int values with zeros and ones representing bits in the integer, similar to what we did to encode the Police in the FMG. For illustrative purposes, a String will serve.

Finally, node probabilities are numbers between 0 and 1 so we will represent them using float values. The probability is just the frequency of a letter in the text divided by the length of the text. These probabilities will be the basis for choosing the length of the coding of each character. A character with a high likelihood of appearing will get a short code, Infrequent characters get long codes. They get those longer codes by being farther from the root than others.

To store the leaves of the tree (as nodes) along with their frequencies, we use a specialized collection called a *defaultDict* (imported from collections). An ordinary dict will produce an error if you try to index a character (or any key) that isn't present. A defaultDict, on the other hand will produce a default value, here zero, in that case.

The coding tree will be built from the bottom up. We will start with the leaves. We will start processing the characters of lowest frequency and these will get more processing, meaning that the paths to them from the eventually created root node will be longer. This is how we achieve short codings for frequent items.

Suppose we put some things into a priority queue in arbitrary order, but all at once, and then retrieve them all. The results will be in sorted order from smallest priority to largest. If we enqueue n items and the time to enqueue or dequeue an item is proportional to lg(n) (the base two logarithm of n), then over all, the time is proportional to n*lg(n). This is about as good as you can do with a sorting algorithm. In fact we could have put the nodes in an ordinary list and sorted them to achieve the same effect as our use of the priority queue, but only since we insert them all at once.

It would be good to consider something important here. The Huffman coding process, if considered all at once, is quite difficult. but almost all of the difficulty is in managing the data. By using data abstractions, such as queue and priority queue we isolate our problem solving from the low level details of precisely where in the structure the next insertion should be placed so that we may think at a higher level. The priority queue object will get it right and we can think about what to do with the values we extract rather than the details of the storage. This is a very big idea.

The data declarations of our coder class are these:

```
class HuffmanCoder:
    '''Creates Huffman trees and translates text to
        bitstring-like strings. Can also decode the
        strings to the original'''
    def __init__(self):
        self._characterFrequencies = defaultdict(int)
        '''Among other things, int() is a function returning a zero:
            the default value of an int. Used here, it provides a
            default value for any missing key in a default dictionary'''
        self._nodeQueue = Queue() #roots of subtrees during build.
        self._encodings = {} #map of symbols to leaves
        self._frequencyQueue = PriorityQueue() # character frequencies
        self._codeTree = None #huffman tree will be built.
        self._translationTable = {} #dict of symbols to Huffman codes
```

The two queues will be called the *_nodeQueue* and the *_frequencyQueue,*. The *_encodings* map will be used as we compute frequencies, and the _nodeMap to keep the character codings in order. A "priority" of an internal node in the tree is the sum of the priorities of the nodes below it. The *_codeTree* is the goal of this processing. We want to create this tree, represented simply by its root node, without encapsulation.

## 13.4 Huffman Coding – The Process

The program we will build for this will also use a pipeline architecture. We will have a number of phases, run one after another to finally get the coding tree and associated structures. Then we will be able to encode the string whose frequencies defined that particular tree. We can encode other strings with the same tree as well, provided that they don't use additional characters than the original, but the savings in total bits won't be as large.

The class we will build will be called HuffmanCoder. The pipeline method, which is what you usually call, looks like this:

```
def encode(self, text:str)->str:
    '''Produces the bitstring version of the text
    The code tree will be built as a product
    @param text: the text to be encooded
    @return: an equivalent bitstring encoded in a string
    '''
    self._getFrequencies(text)
    self._makeLeaves(len(text))
    self._buildCodeTree()
    return self._mapIt(text)
```

The parameter is the string to be encoded and the return result is the encoding. First we read the original text and compute simple frequencies of the characters in it. A map is good for this. Next we will make all of the leaf nodes in the tree we are about to create by reading the _characterFrequencies and writing both the _encodings (map) and the _frequencyQueue (priority queue). There will be one leaf for each distinct character in the text. The one "space" node will represent all of the space characters in the text, etc. Our text has 38 different characters, not counting newline, but the process will discover that. Then we build the trees using the two queues and finally we use the tree in the *_mapIt* process to do the actual translation.

Getting frequencies is quite easy. We hold them in a defaultdict with the characters as keys and the current count of occurrence as the value.

```
def _getFrequencies(self, text:str):
    '''Builds a frequency map of the characters in a text'''
    for character in text:
        self._characterFrequencies[character] += 1
```

We use a defaultdict to make it easy to handle a character the first time we see it. It won't be in the map yet, so a standard map would return null from the get method or generate an error. Here we get back 0 instead with the character inserted. In any case we just increase the count and put it back with the same key. This process replaces the current entry in the map. When this completes, the map holds our frequencies. Next we want to create the leaves, one for each entry in the map.

The Nodes of the binary tree will hold a variety of things, but the leaf nodes represent individual (distinct) characters from the text and their probability of occurrence. The probability is just the frequency divided by the length of the text, but we need to be careful. We can't use an integer for this (or it would always be zero) so we need to force the division to be done with *floating point* values. The node will hold the probability value and the character the node represents.

To create the leaves we can iterate over the keys of the map, extract the frequency, compute the probability, create the node, and put it into the _frequencyQueue, which is a priority queue. We also put the character and the new leaf into the _encodings map so that we can later find the leaves from their associated character symbols. The _frequencyQueue contains triples, the last of which is a leaf node.

```
def _makeLeaves(self, textLength:int):
    '''Create the leaf nodes of the Huffman tree with
        frequencies noted'''
    for character, frequency in self._characterFrequencies.items():
        prob = frequency*1.0/textLength
        node = Node(prob, character)
        self._encodings[character] = node
        self._frequencyQueue.put((prob, character, node))
```

Note that in the above we compute: `frequency*1.0/textLength`. The reason we multiply by 1.0 is to force the computer to use floating point arithmetic. If we just compute `frequency/textLength`, where both operands are integer types, the arithmetic will be integer and the fractional part will be lost. But in this case the result will always be zero, since the textLength is larger than the frequency. Multiplying the numerator by 1.0 (before the division is done) yields a floating equivalent of the frequency and the division will then be done retaining the fractional part. This is a common trick when you need both integer and floating point data in the same program.

We also have an additional map called *_encodings* that we will later use to encode the characters. As was mentioned earlier, we encode a character of the text by moving upward from the leaf. This _encodings map makes it easy for us to get the leaf knowing the character. Once we have the leaf we can move upward in the tree (Node) structure by following *parent* references.

The fact that the leaves are also in a priority queue using a comparison that gives the smallest probability the highest priority is also important. We want to process the leaves from least to most likely, which will have the effect of giving the unlikely characters longer codings. Alternatively we could sort the leaves, but the priority queue works just as well for this, with about the same amount of time required. You can experiment with this of course. A list in Python can be easily sorted, using methods you write yourself, or using the *sorted* function of Python lists.

Comparing nodes uses their value() attribute, which will be a character relative frequency for leaves and the sum of the values of subtrees for other nodes.

Finally we reach the real goal: creating the tree itself.

We start with all the leaves in the *_frequencyQueue*, a priority queue, effectively sorted by priority. High priority for a priority queue means small value, which exactly matches our problem. The *_nodeQueue* is empty, but we will put things in to it. In fact, we will put things in to it in order of increasing size. In fact, we want the contents of both queues sorted, but for the *_nodeQueue* it will be automatic. So, as we go along, there will be entries on both queues and if we *peek* at either queue (look at its head without removing it) we will see the smallest value in that queue. The *_nodeQueue*, unlike the other, will have nodes in it but they won't always be leaf nodes. At the end of the process the first element in that queue will be our coding tree.

The process itself is quite simple. Of all the nodes we have created (leaves or not) we select the two with the smallest probability value. From these we create a new node (non-leaf) with these two as children, but with a value equal to the sum of the probabilities of the two children. We put the result into the *_nodeQueue*. If you think about this for a moment it should be clear that larger values are going in to this queue than what it holds already, since we work from smallest value up. The process ends when there is only one node left. It will be in the *_nodeQueue*, of course, and we set this to be the value of the codeTree field.

```
def _buildCodeTree(self):
    '''Builds the Huffman tree'''
    while self._frequencyQueue.qsize() + \
            len(self._nodeQueue.queue) > 1:
        small = self._getNode() #node with smallest value
        next = self._getNode() #node with next smallest value
        newNode = Node(small.value() + next.value(),'-')
        newNode.setLeft(small)
        newNode.setRight(next)
        self._nodeQueue.put(newNode)
    self._codeTree = self._nodeQueue.get()
```

Here, whenever we create a Node, we immediately attach a left and right child. Thus, the tree winds up with no missing nodes. While leaf nodes have characters as their "symbol" we use '-' for internal nodes, though that isn't really needed. We depend on a private method *_getNode* that retrieves the smallest value from either of the queues:

```
def _getNode(self)->Node:
    '''Get the smallest available node from one of the structures'''
    if  len(self._frequencyQueue.queue)==0:
        return self._nodeQueue.get_nowait()
    elif  len(self._nodeQueue.queue) == 0:
        triple = self._frequencyQueue.get()
        return triple[2]
    triple = self._frequencyQueue.queue[0] #peek
    if triple[0] < self._nodeQueue.queue[0].value():
        self._frequencyQueue.get()
        return triple[2] # a Node
    else:
        return self._nodeQueue.get_nowait()
```

Strange, perhaps, that this is the longest method we have seen so far. While we are doing something quite profound, the methods that achieve it are extremely simple. But this one has several cases to consider, hence its structure. Unfortunately the Queue and PriorityQueue don't let us "peek" at the head of the queue, so we need to dig into the implementation somewhat. Both of them have an internal structure called the *queue* and this can be indexed directly. The "zero" element will be the one we need for each, and with these we can do the comparisons to find the smaller.

The tree has a leaf for each character, plus newline, so 39 leaves and 38 internal nodes. The codes we saw in Section 13.2 actually tell us where these leaves appear in the tree. The space node, with code 00 appears down two nodes to the left from the root: the leftmost grandchild of the root. To find the "Y" node, different from the 'y' node, with code `110000010`, you need to descent 2 levels moving to the right, then five to the left, right again for one, and finally one more to the left. This is what makes the code work: purely the structure of the tree and nothing else.

But moving down the tree is useful for finding a character knowing it's code, We first want to go in the other direction to discover the code for a character. So here is the final step in our pipe line. It uses a helper that does all the work. We left the helper public in this case, since it is useful for finding codes of individual characters.

```
    def _mapIt(self, text:str)->str:
        '''Produces the actual bitstring
        @param text: the text to be encooded
        @return: an equivalent bitstring encoded in a string
        '''
        print(text)
        result = ''
        for i in text:
            code = self.codeFor(i)
            result += code
            self._translationTable[i]=code
        return result

    def codeFor(self, ch)->str:
        '''Walks the tree bottom up to get the encodings'''
        result = ''
```

```
        node = self._encodings[ch]
        if node is not None:
            result = node.code()
            while node.parent() is not None:
                node=node.parent()
                result = node.code() + result
        return result
```

Because of the way we created the tree and filled the encodings map, we should never see None for the node. That would imply we see a character in the text that doesn't have a node. This might occur only if you try to use a Huffman tree to encode a text other than the one it was created from and it has additional characters not in the original.

So *codeFor* just walks up the tree, from leaf to root, extracting one bit for each step. The code extracted from each node will be just a zero or a one and we just catenate them together. Since we work up the tree, we attach the new code "bit" to the left, rather than the right of the result. The code stored in the root is the empty string, by the way.

But wait, there is magic here. What is this *code* method? We haven't seen anything like that yet! And the *parent*. We talked about that, but haven't seen it yet.

All of that his handled internally by the tree nodes themselves. Each node in the tree (except the root) knows whether it is the left or right child of its parent. Left children have a 0 for the code and right children have a 1. Note that in general, nothing in Python does this automatically and you have to set up structures so that a Node can know is location.

The complete Node class is below. We won't discuss much of it, as it is mostly just accessors for fields, but note that we have as few mutators as we can and still carry out the process in buildTrees.

The constructor creates only leaves. They are turned into non-leaves when the *setLeft* and *setRight* methods are called. Note that we didn't use a polymorphic solution here, instead using data to distinguish the kinds of nodes.

When a leaf is updated to a non-leaf, child nodes are attached to it. If they aren't None, then their codes are set depending on whether they are put to the left or right. It happens that it isn't important to the algorithm which of the two nodes goes to the left and which to the right, as long as we can remember which is which. Each such node is also given a parent when it is attached.

```
class Node:
    def __init__(self, value, symbol=None):
        '''A node in a Huffman tree - specialized'''
        self._value = value
        self._symbol = symbol
        self._left = None
        self._right = None
        self._parent = None
        self._code = ""

    def show(self, indent=''):
        '''Print the tree from this node downward'''
        if self.isLeaf(): print(int(len(indent)/3), end = '')
        print(indent, (self._symbol, self._value, self._code))
        if self._left: self._left.show(indent + '   ')
        if self._right: self._right.show(indent + '   ')

    def isLeaf(self):
        '''Return true iff this is a leaf node'''
        return self._left is None and self._right is None

    def code(self):
        '''An internal code indicating left (0) and right (1)
            children'''
        return self._code

    def setLeft(self, node):
        '''Set the node to be the left child of self and make
        self its parent'''
        self._left = node
        node._parent = self
        node._code = "0"

    def setRight(self, node):
        '''Set the node to be the right child of self and make
        self its parent'''
        self._right = node
```

```
            node._parent = self
            node._code = "1"

    def parent(self):
        return self._parent

    def value(self)->float:
        '''The relative frequency of the character in this node'''
        return self._value

    def symbol(self):
        '''A character from the text'''
        return self._symbol

    def left(self):
        return self._left

    def right(self):
        return self._right
```

Note that only leaf nodes have a meaningful *symbol*. The internal nodes are aggregate nodes over the probabilities of the children, rather than themselves representing any character.

## 13.5 Decoding the Result

All we have seen so far is the means of creating a coding from an original text. Presumably this code can be sent or stored somewhere, but eventually someone will want to see the original. So we need to decode the encoding to get back the original exactly. Our encoding, by the way, is called *lossless*. It loses no information at all in encoding in fewer bits. This is unlike something like mp3 music files or jpeg photo encodings, both of which are *lossy* compressions. You can't extract the original exactly from either of these formats. But a Huffman encoding loses none of the information in the original text.

We decode a Huffman encoding using the same tree that encoded it, just walking the tree from top down, rather than bottom up. The input is the 0-1 encoded version and the output should be the original. We look at each bit in the input, a 0 or a 1. Starting at the root of the tree a 0 tells us to move down to the left child, and 1 to the right. We keep this up until we reach a leaf and then we output the *symbol*() from that (attach it to the result) and start over at the root of the tree, looking at the next bit of input. Note that the input *bit stream* isn't divided up in to characters, It is just a continuous stream of 0's and 1's. It is the prefix property of the encoding that keeps us out of trouble in this. When we reach a leaf we have a character and it is the only one possible for that pattern of bits. No other character has a coding that begins with the 0-1 pattern we just followed to get to that leaf.

```
def decode(self, encodedText:str)->str:
    '''Decode a bitstring using the previously built tree
    @param encodedText: the bitstring produced by encode
    @return: the original text
    '''
    decodedText = ''
    currentNode = self._codeTree
    length = len(encodedText)
    i = 0
    while i < length:
        count = 0
        while not currentNode.isLeaf():
            bit = encodedText[i]
            if bit == '0' :
                currentNode = currentNode.left()
            else:
                currentNode = currentNode.right()
            i += 1
            count += 1
            if i >= length:break
        if i <= length: decodedText += currentNode.symbol()
        currentNode = self._codeTree
    return decodedText
```

We must note here for completeness, that we have encoded our 0-1 "bit stream," not as actual bits, but as characters in a string. As such we haven't really saved anything since, in Python, a 0 takes at least 16 bits to store. However, Instead of using string as our output type, we could, with minor modifications (and some change in the methods) used something called a BitSet instead and then we would see the savings. BitSet isn't part of the libraries, however.

There is a peculiarity in the code above, however. Perhaps you noticed that we have nested while loops. The outer loop counts characters, but the counter is actually incremented in an inner loop, making it possible for the counter, i, to exceed the length of the string before the test to stop the loop. We therefore need to intervene when this happens, once to break the inner loop, and again to avoid appending a nonsense character at the end of our translation. This is tricky and error prone programming, actually.

Also note that this decode method is part of the HuffmanCoder, which has the original tree already built from the original text. It won't do for a receiver of a coded message the other end. We need to do more.

## 13.6 Encoding the Translation Tree – More Recursion

There is a bit of a flaw in our scenario above. We talk about sending the encoded bit-stream across the net for to save time of transmission by sending fewer bits. But we also made clear that you need the same tree to decode the text that you used to encode it. So somehow, the tree needs to get to the receiver as well. There are a variety of ways to handle this, and we will see an additional application of recursion here. Indeed recursion is often used to process linked structures such as linked lists and trees. In processing of binary (especially) trees, there are four orderings that we can think of for the nodes. They are called pre-order, post-order, in-order, and level-order. The first three are similar to each other and often useful in following a tree. The last, level-order is important in priority queues as it is the means of taking a binary linked tree and mapping it to an array in an especially efficient way.

In each of the first three orderings of a tree, we will walk through the structure following the parent and child relationships (which may be represented by links). We shall pass by each node more than once, perhaps, but one of these is distinguished, and called the *visit*. Any action we perform at the node occurs during the visit. With that concept is mind, we *traverse* a binary tree in pre-order, by visiting a node and then traversing the tree rooted at its left child (also in pre-order) and then traversing the tree rooted at the right child.

To make it more explicit, consider the following tree.

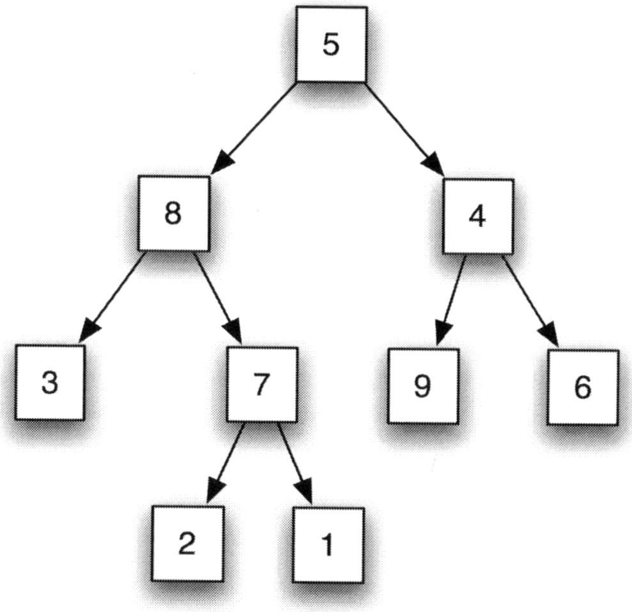


Figure 13.2. A Simple Binary Tree

To walk this in pre-order we start at the root and visit it. Here that means we just report the node. So 5 is our first node. Then we traverse the left tree rooted at 5 so we next visit 8. But then, since we are doing this recursively, after we visit the root of that tree we traverse its left tree, so visit 3. We are now done with the left child of 8 so we visit 7 and then 2 and, after the 2, the 1 node since it is the right child of the 7. But now we have completed the right child of the 8 node as well and thus the left child of the 5 so we can begin on the right child. We next visit 4 then 9 and finally 6: So, in all: 5, 8, 3, 7, 2, 1, 4, 9, 6. Make sure you can follow this. Preorder in a binary search tree will produce the node values in order.

Post-order, on the other hand, visits a node after traversing both the left and right trees. So in post order, we start with the left tree and get to the 8, but don't visit it yet, since we haven't yet traversed the sub-trees. We then get to 3, which has no children so we visit it. We now begin on the right child of 8 and visit these nodes in order 2 then 1 and finally 7. Now, having traversed both sub-trees of the 8 we can finally visit the 8 and then start on the right sub tree of the 5 without yet visiting it. We let you fill in the rest, but the result is 3, 2, 1, 7, 8, 9, 6, 4, 5. Is it clear why pre-order is sometimes called top-down, and post-order called bottom-up? Think about it and become familiar with the terminology. A post-order walk on a binarySearchTree produces the values in reverse order.

In-order traversals visit a node between traversing its left and right child trees. So in particular the 8 will be visited between (though not immediately between) the 3 and 7 nodes. The order here is 3, 8, 2, 7, 1, 5, 9, 4, 6.

Finally level order reports the nodes by height, and moving left to right within a level. It doesn't follow the links at all. Here the root is reported, then its children (left to right) then their children, etc. 5, 8, 4, 3, 7, 9, 6, 2, 1.

All of these are important for various reasons. Level order is useful in priority queues, for example.

What we want to do here with our code tree is create a version of it that can be sent across a transmission line and then re-constituted at the other end. The tree will be encoded as a character stream (a String) that "knows" the structure of the tree. What we will do is a recursive pre-order traversal of the code tree, outputting information about each node we visit and the path we take. It is actually a common processing method. In fact, compilers that translate languages like Python into a lower level form use something like this.

Not to lose focus, here, now we are going to encode the tree itself that was used to encode the text. It uses a completely different process than we have seen so far.

Here *visiting* a node will simply be represented by a recursive invocation in which the node is an input parameter. As part of this, and the basis of the recursion, the same method will be invoked on both the left and right children. We show two versions of this. The first, though longer may be easier to decipher. The method is called *encodeTree* and it invokes itself twice. This is a method of the HuffmanCoder class. The second return statement is especially long, so broken over two lines

```
def encodeTree(self, node:Node, soFar:str='')->str:
    '''Produces an encoding o the Huffman tree that can be used
    to reproduce it. Highly recursive on nodes
    @param node: originally the root of a Huffman tree
    @return: the tree structure encoded as a string
    '''
    if node.isLeaf():
        return soFar+'L'+node.symbol()
    return soFar + '0' + self.encodeTree(node.left(), soFar) + '1'+\
         self.encodeTree(node.right(), soFar) +''
```

The original invocation of this, assuming our HuffmanCoder object is *coder*, is

```
coder.encodeTree(coder._codeTree, '')
```

So, the first node we visit is the root of the codeTree, and the *soFar* parameter is the empty string. It is intended to be the tree encoding we have created "so far." Perhaps it is easiest to understand this if we look at the last line first. What we will do in between is create an encoding of the left child of the current node and an encoding of the right child and then just paste them to the end of what we have done so far. For a leaf node, the encoding is just the letter "L" followed by the character in the Node itself. Recall that these were the characters from the original text that form the leaf nodes of our code tree. For a non-leaf node we recursively process the left and right sub-trees, with, for example

```
encodeTree(node.left(), soFar),
```

but we also mark the left tree with a "0" and the right tree with a "1", just as we marked the nodes themselves this way to enable decoding of our coded text. The output of this for our example tree is this:

```
00L 1000Lb1Lw1Lh100Ly100L-
1LA10LM1Lc10Ld1Ll1000La10Lu1Ls10Le1Lo1000000LI10LY10L;1LD1L
1L,1Lr10Li1000L'1LP10Lf1Lg1Lm10Lt10Ln100Lk10Lv100LO1LS10LU1LW10L.1L
T
```

This was written over three lines above, but that is an artifact. The first break is just because the rest of the first line is too long. The same is true for the last line. But the newline ending the second line represents the code in the tree for the newline character itself.

It isn't so easy to understand, but it really is an encoding of the tree. Notice for example, the 00 before the "space" leaf.

Because the encoding tree actually has no missing nodes, we should never wind up in either of the else clauses in the above, and never see an "x" in the encoding. It indicates an error somewhere. Because of that, the following is equivalent to the above. It is more compact, but probably less understandable.

```
def encodeTree2(self, node:Node, soFar:str = '')->str:
```

```
        if node.isLeaf():
            return soFar + "L"+node.symbol()
        return soFar + "0" + self.encodeTree2(node.left(), soFar) \
                   + "1" + self.encodeTree2(node.right(), soFar)
```

Here is a third, non-equivalent version, that will let you see where the sub trees begin and end in the encoding. This latter form could also be decoded, but we shall use the above.

```
    def encodeTree3(self, node:Node, soFar:str = '')->str:
        if node.isLeaf():
            return soFar + "L"+node.symbol();
        return soFar + "0(" + self.encodeTree3 (node.left(), soFar) \
                  + ")1(" + self.encodeTree3 (node.right(), soFar) + ")"
```

Here we just wrap parentheses around the result of each recursive call. The output then shows more clearly where the sub-trees begin and end. Each is within parentheses. The presentation here shows the break of the root node. The first two lines, beginning with 0 holds the entire left sub-tree. the first parenthesis matches the last on the second line. There is a space following the first L character, of course. The third line begins the right sub-tree (hence the 1), but it is much longer. The first parenthesis on that line matches the last in the entire string. While this may be slightly easier for you, the computer can process the shorter version above, and it is the one we will use.

```
0(0(L )1(0(0(0(Lb)1(Lw))1(Lh))1(0(0(Ly)1(0(0(L-)1(LA))1(0(LM)1(Lc))
))1(0(Ld)1(Ll)))))1(0(0(0(La)1(0(Lu)1(Ls)))1(0(Le)1(Lo)))1(0(0(0(0(
0(0(LI)1(0(LY)1(0(L;)1(LD))))1(L
))1(L,))1(Lr))1(0(Li)1(0(0(0(L')1(LP))1(0(Lf)1(Lg)))1(Lm))))1(0(Lt)
1(0(Ln)1(0(0(Lk)1(0(Lv)1(0(0(LO)1(LS))1(0(LU)1(LW))))))1(0(L.)1(LT))
)))))
```

Now, suppose that we have created the code tree and used it to encode the text and then used the above process to encode the tree itself. Then we send both across our transmission line and, at the other end, we want to be able to reconstruct the tree and then recover the original text.

This will also use a recursive process, but it will be recursive on the coded tree string. We want to start with the entire string and *consume* it, a character at a time (or two characters in case of a leaf node), re-creating left and right sub trees as we see 0's and 1's respectively. This will also be a top down tree traversal, except that we will be creating the tree as we go, not just walking an existing tree.

We have considered the possibility of error in the following, so it is a bit longer than it should be, but the errors indicate bugs in the program, though they could also indicate that the tree coding wasn't received accurately.

We want to start with the entire string and gobble up characters of it from the beginning, creating nodes as we go, passing the remainder to recursive calls, rather than the whole. We create new strings for each recursive call, but that creates a lot of objects that will be almost immediately discarded. We have seen above the slice objects and will use them here "Karel"[2:0] will strip the first two characters from the string, returning a new string: 'rel'.

Previously we created the HuffmanCoder class. Here we see the companion HuffmanDecoder. It contains the decoder method we saw previously, to re-create the text, but two methods to re-create the tree.

The first method is just an organizer for the main work. It begins by creating a new non-leaf node, that has null child nodes to be filled in as we go, and passes this and the encoded tree to the *_recodeTree* method which does the work recursively.

```
class HuffmanDecoder:
    '''Decoder for a given Huffman tree created from a
    representation
    '''
    def __init__(self, tree:str):
        self._codeTree = None
        self._createCodeTree(tree)
        self._temp =''

    def _createCodeTree(self, codedTree:str):
        '''Recreate the code tree from its encoding'''
        self._temp = codedTree
        self._codeTree = self._recodeTree(Node(0.0, '-'))
```

The next, recursive method does the work.

```
def _recodeTree(self, node):
    '''Recursively walk the encoding and recreate the tree'''
    if self._temp:
        ch = self._temp[0]
        if ch == 'L':
            symbol = self._temp[1]
            self._temp = self._temp[2:]
            return Node(0.0, symbol) #leaf
        if ch == '0':
            self._temp = self._temp[1:]
            another = Node(0.0, '-')
            node.setLeft(self._recodeTree(another))
        else:
            print("error l")
        ch = self._temp[0]
        if ch == 'L':
            symbol = self._temp[1]
            self._temp = self._temp[2:]
            return Node(0.0, symbol)
        if ch == '1':
            self._temp = self._temp[1:]
            another = Node(0.0, '-')
            node.setRight(self._recodeTree(another))
        else:
            print("error r")
    return node
```

Once we have the tree, we can use it to decode the original message created by the encoder.

```
def decode(self, coded:str)->str:
    '''Uses the created tree to decode a text
    @param coded: the bitstring previously encoded
    @return: the original text'''
    result = ""
    node = self._codeTree
    length = len(coded)
    i = 0
    while i < length:
        while not node.isLeaf():
            if i<length and coded[i] == '0':
```

```
                node = node.left()
            else:
                node = node.right()
            i += 1
        if i <= length: result += node.symbol()
        node = self._codeTree
    return result
```

When *_recodeTree* is invoked, sending a node, it will either send back the original node with child nodes attached to it, or it will return a leaf node instead, Don't forget this important fact. When it is invoked the original tree encoding may have been partially consumed already, of course, in previous invocations. If in the current state we see an "L" character at the beginning of what remains of the encoding we get the next character and create a leaf node with it as symbol, and return it. But we also must consume the two characters that we processed. This is key to understanding how it proceeds. We advance the computation by consuming the input. If we forget to do this, our program will fail. We give 0.0 as the probability here, since we no longer need it. That was only used to create the tree from the original frequencies of the text, but we are beyond that now.

If we don't see an "L" at the beginning then it is either a 0 or a 1. In fact a 0 will be followed by a tree encoding followed by a 1 followed by another. At any point, that "tree" could be a leaf or not, and if not, another 0, etc.

So, if we see a "0" then we create another empty, but non-leaf, node and recurse, getting back either a completed tree (completed by further recursions) or a leaf. Since we saw a 0, we attach the result as the left child of the current node. This recursion, of course, consumes more of the input, so it is no longer the same as what we sent. In fact, it should have consumed one sub-tree worth of characters. If we were using the parenthesized version of the coding, it would process everything up to the matching parenthesis.

After processing the left child (starting with the 0) we expect a right child as well, since the tree has no missing nodes. But this child might itself be a leaf, so we have to repeat that logic.

When the process completes we have in the decoder program a codeTree that is identical in structure to the one that was used in the coder program. Therefore we can now take the coded text and re-create the original.

## 13.7 Important Ideas From This Chapter

queue
priority queue
Huffman tree
coding
decoding
recursive tree processing
in-order
pre-order
post-order
level-order

## 13.8 Problem Set

1. We built the Huffman tree using frequencies derived from a specific text. Modify the program by making it possible to use a set of predetermined frequencies instead.

2. Instead of walking the tree for each occurrence of a character while encoding a text, do this instead. Provide a hash map of with character keys and the encodings as values. Then just look up the code while encoding. Given what you know about trees and maps, which of these would be faster. Suppose you take into account the fact that you also need to create the map.

3. Provide a polymorphic solution for Nodes, distinguishing Leaf and NonLeaf Nodes. Why are the Leaf Nodes not an instance of the Null Object Pattern?

4-7 Completely distinct from providing a means of encoding, the Huffman tree provides a bit of raw material on which to practice recursive programming. The next few exercises explore this.

4. Write a recursive pre-order tree walk that will count the number of nodes in the Huffman tree (or any binary) tree. The prototype for this method follows. It is invoked by sending the root node and zero for the count so far.

```
public int nodeCount(Node root, int count);
```

Try it again for a post-order walk. Do you need the count paramenter? Note that post-order tree walks are good for passing information up the tree from below.

5. Verify that the number of leaf nodes in the Huffman tree we created is one more than the number of internal nodes. Do this by actually counting them with recursive tree walks.

6. Verify, using mathematical induction, that the number of leaf nodes is one more than the number of internal nodes in any binary tree with the property that all nodes have either exactly two children or none.

7. Write a recursive tree walk that will print out the leaf nodes values of the Huffman tree. Note that this walk can use any of the tree walking protocols: pre-order, in-order, or post-order. You might try them all for practice.

8. Suppose that we want to encode a character using the Huffman tree, but, for some reason, have lost the encodings map. Start from the root of the tree, use a tree walk to search for your character, and return the encoding if you find it.

9. The tree encoding produced by HuffmanCoder actually has enough information in it to do more than produce a key suitable for decoding. You can also use it to reproduce the _encodings map and, hence, find the leaves of the Huffman tree so that you can encode with it. Modify the decoder to make this possible.

# 14 Project and Case Study – MiniKarel

This chapter presents a course-long project that can be carried out as you study the various chapters here. We will describe a robot world, similar to the Karel World. It won't be exactly the same, however. Some things will closely track the simulator you have been using and other things will differ greatly.

The project will start with a skeleton application that has some features already implemented. Your work will be to read and understand what is here, and then to extend it. Unlike the earlier chapters in which the exercises appear at the end, here they will appear in-line as it becomes feasible to do them. We will also arrange this according to the dependencies on earlier chapters. We will also ask you to do some investigations outside this book, using the official Python documentation. Some of the exercises here will depend on your having done earlier ones, as well.

This is how much real-world programming goes, by the way. You don't start with nothing, but with an application that may have been in use for a while and needs updating and extension. You might someday find yourself on a project that is new to you, but which has been in development for weeks or months.

## 14.1 Overview

In this section we will see the basic skeleton of the robots and the world.

We need a way to represent robot directions. The module for this defines a few things, but not a class.

```
North = 0
West = 1
South = 2
East = 3

left = (West, South, East, North)
nextDirection = {North: West, West: South, South: East, East: \
                    North}
directionName = {0: 'North', 1: 'West', 2: 'South', 3: 'East'}
```

As a robot turns left, its next direction is `(direction + 1) % 4`, where *direction* is the current direction the robot is facing.

In addition, there is a *directionName* method, so direction.name[0] will return the String "North" but 'North' itself would then return 0;

The simplest robot type here is called MiniKarel and it is like UrRobot in the Monty Karel system. It implements *move, turnLeft, pickBeeper, putBeeper,* and *turnOff,* nothing more, except a report method that gives you information about the robot's state. None of these methods have arguments and pickBeeper, putsBeeper, and move might fail when executed depending on their current state and the state of the *World* object. The initialization of a MiniKarel is a bit different, however, as it specifies a name for a robot, not necessarily the same as the name of the variable that references it, and a world as well.

Without the method bodies, but with the needed comments, it looks like this:

```
from world import World, world
from directions import North, East, South, West, nextDirection,
directionName
from robotAssertion import RobotAssertion

INFINITE = -1

class MiniKarel(RobotAssertion):
    def __init__(self, name:str, street:int=1, avenue:int=1, \
         direction=North, beepers:int=0, world:World=world):
        pass

    def move(self): #check front is clear
        '''Move one block in the current direction or fail if
                  blocked'''
        pass

    def turnLeft(self):
        '''Turn 90 degrees to the left'''
         pass
```

```
    def putBeeper(self):
        '''Put one beeper on the current corner or fail if none
                available'''
        pass

    def turnOff(self):
        '''Turn off, making all other actions no-ops'''
        pass

    def report(self):
        '''Report the current state of the robot'''
        pass
```

Some of these methods will raise Exceptions if their action is illegal. An Exception's message should say why the action failed. If a robot tries to move through a wall, for example, we will raise an Exception.

To avoid confusing things too much, the simplest kind of robot here is called MiniKarel. Here is the complete class in this skeleton form. Some of the methods are incomplete as noted. This will be work for you to do. We also give a string *name,* to each robot as we create it. This will be useful in reporting the state of a robot, especially if your robot program has more than one robot.

```
class MiniKarel(RobotAssertion):
    def __init__(self, name:str, street:int=1, avenue:int=1,
         direction=North, beepers:int=0, world:World=world):
        self._name = name
        self._myWorld = world
        self._currentStreet = street
        self._currentAvenue = avenue
        self._direction = direction
        self._onState = True
        self._beepers = beepers

    def move(self): #check front is clear
        '''Move one block in the current direction or fail if
            blocked'''
        if not self._onState: return
        if self._myWorld.canMoveFrom(self._currentStreet,\
                self._currentAvenue, self._direction):
```

```
            if self._direction == North:
                self._currentStreet += 1
            elif self._direction == East:
                self._currentAvenue += 1
            elif self._direction == South:
                self._currentStreet -= 1
            elif self._direction == West:
                self._currentAvenue -= 1
        else:
            self.turnOff()
            raise Exception("Can't move from", \
                self._currentStreet, self._currentAvenue, \
                directionName[self._direction])

    def turnLeft(self):
        '''Turn 90 degrees to the left'''
        if not self._onState: return
        self._direction = nextDirection[self._direction]

    def pickBeeper(self):
        '''Pick one beeper from the current corner or fail if none
                available'''
        if not self._onState: return
        if self._myWorld.hasBeepersAt(self._currentStreet, \
                self._currentAvenue):
            pass # finish this
        else:
            pass # finish this

    def putBeeper(self):
        '''Put one beeper on the current corner or fail if none
            available'''
        pass # finish this

    def turnOff(self):
        '''Turn off, making all other actions no-ops'''
        self._onState = False

    def report(self):
        '''Report the current state of the robot'''
        print(self._name+': street:', self._currentStreet, \
```

```
            'avenue:', self._currentAvenue)
        print('  facing:', directionName[self._direction])
        print('  beepers:', 'yes' if self._beepers>0 or \
                self._beepers==INFINITE else 'no')
        print('  running:', self._onState)
```

Note that the methods like *move* raise Exceptions when they can't be properly executed. Some of them need to interact with World objects as well. Each robot created is also told what world it will be delivered to. This is different from what we have seen before. You can modify this so that a robot also prints out its progress each time it executes one of the methods using the report method.

And all of the commands first check that the robot is still in the _onState.

We will discuss the superclass *RobotAssertion* presently. It enables test directed development with unittest but is also useful in checking the correctness of your robot programs.

Robots need to exist in a World, of course. The world maintains information about beepers and walls. It can also keep information about what streets and avenues are legal and a variety of other information. Default dictionaries and Sets are discussed in Chapter 11. As you begin simply note that a *set* is much like a mathematical set. It holds elements that you can insert and remove. A dictionary is a set of associations between *keys* and *data*. Knowing a key gives you access to the data using the *get* method or using the key as an index.

```
from collections import defaultdict
from worldAssertion import WorldAssertion
from directions import North, East, South, West

class World(WorldAssertion):
    INFINITE = -1
    def __init__(self): #specify size??
        self._beepers = defaultdict(int) #Dict[pair, int] = {}
        self._eastWestWalls = set({}) #Set of pairs
        self._northSouthWalls = set({}) #Set of pairs

    def placeBeepers(self, street:int, avenue:int, howMany:int=1):
        where = (street, avenue)
        current = self._beepers.get(where)
```

```
        if current == World.INFINITE: return
        if current is None:
            self._beepers[where] = howMany
        else:
            self._beepers[where] = howMany + current

    def removeBeeper(self, street: int, avenue: int) -> None:
        where = (street, avenue)
        howMany = self._beepers.get(where)
        if howMany == World.INFINITE: return
        if howMany is not None and howMany>0:
            self._beepers[where] = howMany - 1
        else:
            raise RuntimeError \
               ("Tried to remove a beeper that wasn't there")

    def hasBeepersAt(self, street, avenue)->bool:
        return self._beepers[(street, avenue)]>0 or \
               self._beepers[(street, avenue)] == World.INFINITE

    def _placeWallEastWest(self, northOfStreet:int, \
            blockingAvenue:int):
        self._eastWestWalls.add((northOfStreet, blockingAvenue))
    def placeWallNorthOf(self, street, avenue):
        self._placeWallEastWest(street, avenue)
    def placeWallSouthOf(self, street, avenue):
        if street <= 0: return
        self.placeWallNorthOf(street-1, avenue)

    def _placeWallNorthSouth(self,blockingStreet:int, \
            eastOfAvenue:int):
        self._northSouthWalls.add((blockingStreet, eastOfAvenue))
    def placeWallEastOf(self, street, avenue):
        self._placeWallNorthSouth(street, avenue)
    def placeWallWestOf(self, street, avenue):
        if avenue <= 0: return
        self.placeWallEastOf(street, avenue-1)

    def wallOnStreetEastOf(self,street: int, avenue: int) -> bool:
        return (street, avenue) in self._northSouthWalls
```

```
    blockedToEast = wallOnStreetEastOf

    def wallOnAvenueNorthOf(self,street: int, avenue: int) -> bool:
        return (street, avenue) in self._eastWestWalls

    blockedToNorth = wallOnAvenueNorthOf

    def wallOnStreetWestOf(self,street: int, avenue: int) -> bool:
        if avenue == 1: return True #boundary
        return (street, avenue-1) in self._northSouthWalls

    blockedToWest = wallOnStreetWestOf

    def wallOnAvenueSouthOf(self,street: int, avenue: int) -> bool:
        if street == 1: return True #boundary
        return (street-1, avenue) in self._eastWestWalls

    blockedToSouth = wallOnAvenueSouthOf

    def numberOfBeepersAt(self,x: int, y: int) -> int:
        return self._beepers.get((x, y), 0)

    def canMoveFrom(self, street:int, avenue:int, direction:int):
        if direction == 0: #North
            return not self.blockedToNorth(street, avenue)
        elif direction == 1: #West
            return not self.blockedToWest(street, avenue)
        elif direction == 2: #South
            return not self.blockedToSouth(street, avenue)
        elif direction == 3: #East
            return not self.blockedToEast(street, avenue)
        else:
            raise Exception('Illegal direction in move check')

    def infinite(self) -> int:
        return World.INFINITE

#The following are exercises, but not at the moment

    def readWorld(self, filename):
        pass
```

```
    def writeWorld(self, filename):
        pass

    def showWorld(self, streets:int, avenues:int):
        pass

world = World()
```

These skeletons form the basis of a simulator that you can extend by doing the exercises in the next sections.

Note that some of the operations are no-ops if they don't make sense. And this class defines an object of the class: World.world that robots can use after building up necessary walls and placing beepers as needed prior to execution.

## 14.2 State, Building MiniRobot

The exercises here are all accessible after you have worked through Chapter 9.

Exercise 14.1 Create a main driver to create and test the above code so that you understand how it operates. Note that some of the operations aren't yet implemented completely. Once you understand it, modify move, turnLeft, pickBeeper, and putsBeeper so that they raise exceptions when executed but not in the _onState. This gives you more feedback in a developing program.

Exercise 14.2 Create an inner (nested) class *RobotState* within MiniKarel. It's fields should form a snapshot of the state of the containing robot when the RobotState object is created. Its constructor should initialize all fields. There should be an accessor for each field, but no setters at all. It looks like the following:

```
class RobotState:
    def __init__(self, robot): # may require more arguments
        self._robot = robot
        pass

    def getCurrentState(self):
        '''Obtain a snapshot of the current state of the robot
         as a dictionary
         '''
```

```
        print(self._robot._name, 'to be done')
        return None
```

Create a new *currentState* method of MiniKarel by creating and returning a RobotState object.

Exercise 14.3 Complete the MiniRobot class, which extends MiniKarel, building all methods. Each uses *currentState* to get a snapshot of its own state as the basis for making its decision. Here is skeleton code for this class:

```
from miniKarel import MiniKarel
from world import World, world
from directions import North, East, South, West, directionName

class MiniRobot(MiniKarel):

    def __init__(self, name:str, street:int=1, avenue:int=1,\
            direction=North, beepers:int=0, world:World=world):
        super().__init__(name, street, avenue, direction, \
            beepers, world)

    def anyBeepersInBeeperBag(self)->bool:
        '''Return True iff the robot has beepers'''
        state = self.currentState()
        raise Exception("To be done anyBeepersInBeeperBag")
        return False

    def nextToABeeper(self)->bool:
        '''Return True iff there are beepers on the current
            corner'''
        state = self.currentState()
        raise Exception("To be done nextToABeeper")
        return False

    def facingNorth(self)->bool:
        '''Return True iff the robot is facing North'''
        state = self.currentState()
        raise Exception("To be done facingNorth")
        return False
```

```
    def facingWest(self)->bool:
        '''Return True iff the robot is facing West'''
        state = self.currentState()
        raise Exception("To be done facingWest")
        return False

    def facingSouth(self)->bool:
        '''Return True iff the robot is facing South'''
        state = self.currentState()
        raise Exception("To be done facingSouth")
        return False

    def facingEast(self)->bool:
        '''Return True iff the robot is facing East'''
        state = self.currentState()
        raise Exception("To be done facingEast")
        return False

    def frontIsClear(self)->bool:
        '''Return True iff the robot can move in the current
        direction'''
        state = self.currentState()
        raise Exception("To be done frontIsClear")
        return False

    def running(self)->bool:
        '''Return True iff the robot is currently running'''
        state = self.currentState()
        return state['running']
```

Give it a main function and use it to test what you have built.

## 14.3 Two Dimensional Structures and I/O, Extending the World

The exercises here apply to the material in Chapter 10 especially, as well as the Primo Intermezzo.

Exercise 14.4 The constructor of MiniKarel robots wasn't careful enough. It is possible to pass null as the world, for example, or to initialize a robot on an illegal corner. In reality the constructor should throw an exception when this sort of thing happens. Make these changes, and search the code for other opportunities to improve its safety of use. Which class should be responsible for knowing what is a legal corner?

The RobotAssertion class inherited by MiniKarel defines a set of assertions that can be implemented by the MiniKarel class to make it easy to make assertions about the state of robot programs as they run:

```
class RobotAssertion:

    def assertOnStreet(self, street:int):
        '''Assert that self is on a particular street and
        raise an informative Exception otherwise'''
        if not self._currentStreet == street:
            raise Exception(self._name+' is not on street '+str(street))

    def assertOnAvenue(self, avenue:int):
        raise Exception("To be done assertOnAvenue")

    def assertHasNoBeepers(self):
        raise Exception("To be done assertHasNoBeepers")

    def assertHasBeepers(self):
        raise Exception("To be done assertHasBeepers")

    def assertFrontIsClear(self):
        raise Exception("To be done assertFrontIsClear")

    def assertFacingNorth(self):
        raise Exception("To be done assertFacingNorth")

    def assertFacingWest(self):
        raise Exception("To be done assertFacingWest")

    def assertFacingSouth(self):
        raise Exception("To be done assertFacingSouth")

    def assertFacingEast(self):
        raise Exception("To be done assertFacingEast")
```

Exercise 14.5 Build all of the required methods of RobotAssertion. They raise Exceptions if their assertion fails, but do nothing otherwise.

Exercise 14.6 Give the World class a method

```
def readWorld(self, filename):
    pass
```

that will read world files and insert the walls and beepers specified there into the world. A sample such file appears in Section 10.3. It should raise an Exception if the file can't be found.

Here is a sample world file:

```
KarelWorld
Streets 6
Avenues 5
northsouthwalls 4 2 3
beepers 3 4 3
eastwestwalls 3 2 4
```

Except for the first line, the order of the others is irrelevant. The beepers specification first gives the corner (street, avenue) and then the number of beepers. The eastwestwalls specification gives the corner just below the first segment, here (3, 2) and, using the same street, the corner just below the last: (3, 4). The northsouthwalls specification first names an avenue (careful here) and the two streets. The wall then extends just east of (2, 4) to just east of (3, 4). The result can be seen in Figure 14.1. It would be best if the method ignores case when reading.

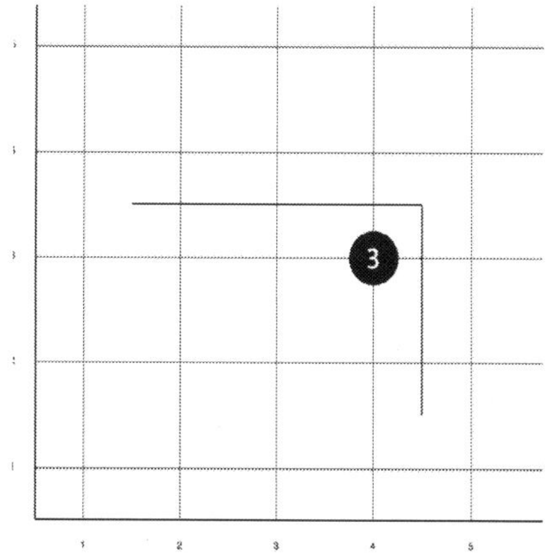


Figure 14.1. A Simple World Read From a File

Exercise 14.7 Finish the pickBeeper and putBeeper instructions. Be sure to throw informative Exceptions when the message is received in an illegal state. Don't forget to update the world in each of your methods also.

Exercise 14.8 Build the StairSweeper program of Chapter 3 and test it with this new environment.

Exercise 14.9 Give the World a method

```
def writeWorld(self, filename):
    pass
```

that will write files compatible with the Python World files using the current state of the world (walls and beepers). Robot are not written to such files.

Exercise 14.10 (After studying the Primo Intermezzo) Give the world a method

```
def display(self, startStreet:int, startAvenue:int, \
     streets:int, avenues:int):
    pass
```

that will print out an ASCII art representation of the world. Show corners as periods, walls as sequences of dashes (horizontal) or vertical bars (vertical), the beepers as *'s, and the robots using one of ^, >, V, <, according as the direction is North, East, South, or West, respectively. Here is a world with a beeper at 3, 3, a horizontal wall above 2, 1, a vertical wall East of 2, 2, and a North facing robot at the origin.

```
|
| .   .   .   .   .   .   .
|
| .   .   .   .   .   .   .
|
| .   .   .   .   .   .   .
|
| .   .   1   .   .   .   .
|___
| .   . | .   .   .   .   .
|       |
| ^   .   .   .   .   .   .
|____________________________

Lower left corner is street: 1 avenue: 1.
```

One good way to do this is to use a two dimensional list of characters with extra spaces between streets and avenues. Note that this exercise is quite challenging.

Exercise 14.11 Give the world a way to tell the robots whether they should be printing out their progress on every move, turnLeft, etc. The robots should actually consult the world to see if they should *trace*.

## 14.4 Collections, Neighbors

These exercises expand on your knowledge from Chapter 12.

The next few exercises detail changes that can form the basis of a graphic version of this, though we won't follow up on that. However, whenever a robot moves, for example, the world needs to know about it, and then inform a graphic layer to make the corresponding visual changes. This is actually how the Python simulator is built.

Exercise 14.12 Modify MiniKarel so that it extends Observable as discussed in Chapter 4.9. The *notify* method will have a RobotState object as the data parameter. See Exercise 14.15 below.

Exercise 14.13 Modify the methods of MiniKarel so that each method that causes a change in the state of the robot (such as move), sends itself the *setChanged* message and notifies all observers passing a new RobotState object.

Exercise 14.14 Modify the World so that it extends Observer from Chapter 4. The *update* method of the Observer class should, for now, just print something about the robot and its new state.

Exercise 14.15 Give the world a dictionary that maps robots to their locations and that keeps track of where each robot is. This map should be updated whenever any robot moves. The world will then know the locations of all robots as a program proceeds.

Exercise 14.16 Give MiniRobot a *nextToARobot* method to determine if the receiver is next to another robot. Implement it in MiniRobot.

Exercise 14.17 Provide for a method like *neighbors* as in Monty Karel. Create a collection "on the fly" to hold the current neighbors of the robot executing the method. Don't forget not to include the robot itself. Think about what sort of collection you should use. It needs to be iterable. The collection is not a permanent field but is created and returned within the method itself.

Exercise 14.18 Analyze the collections used in the World class for their appropriateness.

## 14.5 Documentation and Testing

These exercises apply to the material of Chapter 12.

The skeleton code was documented with Python documentation comments. You may not have kept these comments up to date as you worked. Now is the time to do that.

Exercise 14.19 Update documentation as needed for all of the methods you have created and/or modified.

We now have enough infrastructure, especially in the RobotAssertion class to do a good job of testing all of the code here. A simple unittest file has been provided that tests move. We want to extend that test class to provide good tests for all of the code, especially the MiniKarel code. Here is a start on your test class.

```
from miniKarel import MiniKarel, INFINITE
from directions import North
from world import world

class RobotTest(unittest.TestCase):

    @classmethod
    def setUpClass(cls):
        pass

    def setUp(self):
        self.chuck = MiniKarel("Charles", 1, 1, North, \
            INFINITE, world)
        self.sue = MiniKarel("Susan", 1, 1, North, 0, world)
```

```
    def populateWorld(self):
        pass

    def testTurnOff(self):
        '''Tests that exceptions are thrown'''
        self.sue.turnOff()
        try:
            self.sue.move()
            self.fail("Move")
        except Exception as e:
            if str(e) != 'Move after turnOff':
                self.fail("Exception should be raised: "+str(e))

    def testMoves(self):
        self.chuck.move()
        self.chuck.assertOnStreet(1)


if __name__ == '__main__' :
    unittest.main()
```

Make sure you follow the logic of the testTurnOff example. It shows how to handle the case in which an Exception should have been raised but was not. Note in particular the *fail* message and the not-equal operator. The exception that should have been raised here has the message 'move after turnOff'.

Exercise 14.20 Provide more elaborate tests in the RobotTest unittest test class for the move method of MiniKarel. Test the method in all possible configurations, including when the robot is not blocked and when it is, both by a boundary wall and by a wall within the world.

Exercise 14.21 Provide good tests for *turnLeft*. Check all possible turns.

Exercise 14.22 Provide tests for *pickBeeper*.

Exercise 14.23 Provide tests for *putBeeper*.

Exercise 14.24 In the same unittest test file or in another, if you prefer, test all of the methods of MiniRobot.

## 14.6 Dialogs, Refactoring, and Polymorphism

This section collects exercises of a somewhat more advanced nature.

Usually the main task block creates robots with invocations of the constructor directly. It is also possible, instead, to call for a dialog when you need a robot and have the user fill in the dialog with the delivery specification parameters. This might be useful in testing a robot in a number of initial configurations.

Exercise 14.25 Create a dialog for the initialization of a MiniRobot. The dialog will have input fields for street, avenue and number of beepers. You can explore various options for inputting the direction. The client of such a dialog will take the values entered to create a new MiniRobot.

Exercise 14.26 Note that both moving and turning depend on which direction a robot is facing in this implementation. We can delegate a lot of work to one or more strategy-like objects called DirectionManagers that implement this interface:

```
class DirectionManager:
    '''A way for robots to manage their direction
    '''

    def manageMove(self):
        pass

    def manageTurnLeft(self):
        pass

    def manageFrontIsClear(self):
        pass

    def manageFacing(self, direction):
        pass

    def manageAssertFacing(self, direction):
        pass

    def directionName(self)->str:
        pass
```

A robot will have four objects that implement this: northManager, etc. The manageTurnLeft in the northManager will set the currentManager to westManager (among other things, perhaps). The northManager will implement manageMove by increasing the street number by one, etc. The MiniKarel then delegates things like move and turnLeft to its current DirectionManager object. You might also want a map to associate managers with the corresponding directions. Note that now the "direction" implementation is really just the current direction manager. Externally the client code still uses North, etc, but internally it is the direction managers that handle everything. They have behavior, rather than just being tags. This might be an inner class of MiniKarel.

Exercise 14.27 Create a class diagram of all of the classes in your simple robot project.

# Bibliography and Resources

Web resources

Web searches for things that puzzle you can be helpful. Include "python" in your search terms. Often the questions (and answers) at

https://stackoverflow.com

which often show up in searches can be helpful.

Python official documentation:

https://www.python.org/doc/

Especially helpful might be:

https://docs.python.org/3/tutorial/datastructures.html

Less official, but often helpful is the W3schools site.

https://www.w3schools.com/python/default.asp

Wikipedia has information on many things discussed here. For example:

data structures (in general and specific cases)
balanced trees
FMG

A previous work by the same author: *Beyond Karel J Robot* covers approximately the same ideas, but tailored to the Java Programming Language.

# Appendix

## Python Operators

### Numeric Operators

+
-
*
/
%
//
**

### Assignment Operators

=
+=
-=
*=
/=
&=
//=
**=
&=
|=
^=
<<=
>>=

### Boolean Operators

and
or
not

Comparisons (bool result)

==
!=
<
<=
>
>=

Identity

is
is not

Membership

in
not in

Bitwise

#### Precedence of operators

Information about the precedence of all Python operators, such as those above can be found with the official documentation:

https://docs.python.org/3/reference/expressions.html#operator-precedence

#### Python special forms

Because of the way Python operates internally, there are a few "tricks" that can simplify the expression of some things, though with a possible cost in understanding when reading code. We present a few of them here

a<b<c as a test in an If or While statement, for example, is interpreted properly as a < b and b < c. You can even say a > b < c, which makes claims about a and b and about b and c, but not about a and c.

Similarly, in a test len(aList) == 0 is equivalent to just the name of the list: aList. So it is fine to say if aList: ... Empty lists will return true. Likewise a test such as if x !=

None: or if x is not None: will return the same results as if x: ... You need to think about that one so you don't get it backwards.

Remember that False has an int value of 0, which can be exploited in tests: if 0: is the same as if False:

Most things in Python support the hash function, but not lists, since they are fundamentally mutable and it would be difficult to find a valid hash for such an object.

Assignment generally results in nothing more than a new reference to an existing value, so an equality test will show them not only == but respond True to an 'is' test. Explicitly creating a new object will distinguish between the two forms.

## Simplified Data Structures

Here we will show some simplified implementations of a few of the important classes in the Python Libraries. We have left out quite a lot of things here, but the reader should get an idea about how to build such things from reading this code. Some of it is a bit complex, but most is easy.

Note as you read these that some of the methods are identical in quite different classes. That is because some of these are implemented in terms of others.

While we use these in sample code in the latter part of this book, the author recommends that you use these only for study, but build your own code using the official Python libraries.

## 1 A Dense List Implementation

Here we present a class that is a bit like the list class of the Python Libraries. It is, however, much less sophisticated. It has many of the frequently used methods. It expands as needed as you add items. The specification of these methods is close to that of the Python list.

```
class DenseList:
    '''An automatically expanding densely stored array-like structure
    '''
    def __init__(self, initialCapacity=1, *args):
        '''Create a DenseList with a given initial capacity and
        preloaded with a set of values
        @param initialCapacity: the initial capacity before expansion is
            needed
        @param *args: any number of initial values
        '''
        self._size = 0
        self._capacity = initialCapacity if initialCapacity > 0 else 1
        self._store = [None for i in range(self._capacity)]
        for i in args:
            self.append(i)
        self.push = self.append

    def add(self, index, value):
        '''Insert a value at a given index between 0 and current size -1,
            moving other items to the right to make room
        @param index: the index slot to put the value
        @param value: the value to put at the index
        '''
        if index < 0: index += self.size
        if index < 0 or index > self.size():
            raise IndexError
        if self._size == self._capacity:
            self._expand()
        for i in range(self.size() - 1, index - 1, -1):
            self._store[i + 1] = self._store[i]
        self._size += 1
        self._store[index] = value

    def fillRest(self, value = None):
        '''Fill the remaining capacity with a given value
        @param value: the value to be inserted
        '''
        i = self._size
        while i < self._capacity:
            self.append(value)
            i += 1
```

```
    def pop(self):
        '''Remove and return the item with the largest valid index
        '''
        where = self.size()-1
        val = self.get(where)
        self.remove(where)
        return val

    def showStore(self):
        print(self._store)

    def indexCheck(self, index)->:
        '''Determine the validity of a given index
        @param index: the index to be checked
        '''
        return self.size() > index and index >= 0

    def get(self, index): #unneeded
        '''Get an item at a given index. Note indexing can also
        be used
        @param index: the index from which to get a value
        '''
        return self.__getitem__(index)

    def clear(self):
        '''Make the structure empty with minimal capacity
        '''
        pass # TODO

    def append(self, value):
        '''Append (push) a value onto the right end, making room
        as needed. Return True if it completes properly.
        @param value: the value to be pushed
        '''
        pass # TODO

    def size(self)->int:
        '''The (logical) size of the structure'''
        return int(self._size)
```

```
def set(self, index, value): #unneeded
    '''Set a value into an existing slot, overwriting what is
    currently there. Note: indexing can also be used.
    @param index: the slot to be overwritten
    @param value: the value to replace current contents
    '''
    self.__setitem__(index, value)

def remove(self, index): #unneeded
    '''Remove an item from a given index, decreasing size
    Note that the del function also works
    @param index: the slot to be removed
    '''
    self.__delitem__(index)

def removeValue(self, value):
    '''Remove the first copy of a value from the structure,
        reducing size
    @param value: the value to be removed
    '''
    where = -1
    found = False;
    for i in self:
        where += 1
        if i == value:
            found = True
            break
    if where >= 0 and found:
        self.remove(where)

def removeAll(self, value):
    '''Remove all copies of a value from the structure, reducing size
    @param value: the value to be removed
    '''
    where = self.size()
    for i in self:
        where -= 1
        if i == value:
            self.remove(where)
```

```
    def contains(self, value):
        '''Determine whether a value is in the storage
        Note: the 'in' operator also works
        @param value: the value to be checked
        '''
        return self.__contains__(value)

    def clone(self):
        '''Create a faithful copy of the structure'''
        result = DenseList(self.size())
        for i in self:
            result.append(i)
        return result

  # more: addAll, removeAll ...

    def __len__(self): # enables len(x)
        return self.size()

  def __eq__(self, other):
        pass # TODO

    def _expand(self):
        newStore = [None] * (2 * self._capacity)
        for i in range(self.size()):
            newStore[i] = self._store[i]
        self._store = newStore
        self._capacity *= 2

    def __getitem__(self, index): # enables indexing on rhs
        if isinstance(index, slice):
            return [self[i] for i in range(*index.indices(len(self)))]
        if index < 0:
            index += self.size()
        if index < 0 or index >= self.size():
            raise IndexError
        return self._store[index]
```

```
def __setitem__(self, index, value): #enables a[x] =
    if isinstance(index, slice):
        stop = index.stop if index.stop is None else len(self)
        step = 1 if index.step is None else index.step
        start = 0 if index.start is None else index.start
        for i, v in zip(range(start, stop, step), value):
            self[i] = v
    else:
        if index < 0:
            index += self.size()
        if index < 0 or index >= self.size():
            raise IndexError
        self._store[index] = value

def __delitem__(self, index): #enables del(a[x])
    if isinstance(index, slice):
        indices = range(*index.indices(len(self)))
        for i in reversed(indices):
            del self[i]
        return True
    if index < 0:
        index += self.size()
    if index < 0 or index >= self.size():
        raise IndexError
    for i in range(index, self.size() - 1):
        self._store[i] = self._store[i + 1]
    self._size -= 1
    return True

def __iter__(self):
    return iter(self._store[:self.size()])


def __add__(self, other): #enables + operator extending the list
    c = DenseList()
    for x in self:
        c.append(x)
    for x in other:
        c.append(x)
    return c
```

```
def __contains__(self, value): # enables 'in' operator
    for i in range(self.size()):
        if self._store[i] == value:
            return True
    return False

def __str__(self):
    return "[" + ", ".join(str(self._store[i]) \
        for i in range(self.size())) + "]"

def __repr__(self):
    return "DenseList(" + ", ".join(str(self._store[i]) \
        for i in range(self.size())) + ")"
```

## 2 A Linked List Implementation

A linked list is built of nodes. First the Node class. This implementation is a circularly linked list with doubly linked nodes.

The Node class is actually an inner class to the main class.

```
class Node:
    def __init__(self, data):
        self._next = self
        self._prev = self
        self._data = data
    def prevNode(self):
        return self._prev
    def nextNode(self):
        return self._next
    def data(self):
        return self._data
    def setPrev(self, node): # used in push
        self.prevNode()._next = node
        node._prev = self.prevNode()
        self._prev = node
        node._next = self
```

```
    def removePrev(self): # NOOP for a self pointing node
        prevNode = self.prevNode()
        if self != prevNode:
            prevNode._prev._next = self
            self._prev = prevNode.prevNode()
```

Since this class has getters and setters for each field, it is not well encapsulated in spite of the private fields. It is really just raw stuff from which to build a list. It could be an inner class within the list itself. In a public form it is impossible to maintain invariants on it or on the class that depends on it.

```
class CircularLinkedList:

    class Node:
        omitted - see above



    def __init__(self):
        '''Create an empty list'''
        self._tail = None
        self._fromFront = True
        self.push = self.pushHead
        self.pop = self.popHead
        self.enqueue = self.pushTail
        self.dequeue = self.popHead
        self.dequeueTail = self.popTail
        self._size = 0

    def head(self):
        '''Return the value at the head of the list leaving
        it in place i.e. peek
        '''
        if self._tail is None: return None
        return self._tail.prevNode().data()

    def tail(self):
        '''Return the value at the tail of the list leaving
        it in place. peek
        '''
        if self._tail is None: return None
        return self._tail.data()
```

```
def pushHead(self, data):
    '''Add a new value to the head of the list
    @param data: the value to be pushed
    '''
    newNode = CircularLinkedList.Node(data)
    self._size += 1
    if self._tail == None:
        self._tail = newNode
    else:
        self._tail.setPrev(newNode)

def pushTail(self, data):
    '''Add a new value to the tail of the list
    @param data: the value to be added
    '''
    self.pushHead(data)
    self._tail = self._tail.prevNode()

def popTail(self):
    '''Remove and return the item at the tail of
    the list if any'''
    self._tail = self._tail.nextNode()
    val = self.popHead()
    return val

def popHead(self):
    '''Remove and return the item at the head of
    the list or None for an empty list'''
    val = self.head()
    self._size -= 1
    if self._size == 0: #empty
        self._tail = None
        return val
    self._tail.removePrev()
    return val

def size(self):
    '''Current size of the list'''
    return self._size
```

```
len = length = size #synonyms for size

def clear(self):
    '''Discard contents and make the list empty'''
    self._tail = None
    self._size = 0

def isEmpty(self)->bool:
    '''Determine if the list is empty'''
    return self._tail is None

def iterateFromFront(self, front = True):
    '''Set the direction of iteration: Default is from front
    @param front: True for front to back, False for back
    to front
    '''
    self._fromFront = front

def applyAll(self, fun = lambda x:x):
    '''Apply a function to every member, returning
        the results in a Python list.
    Note that returning a CircularLinkedList would be better:
        exercise
    @param fun: a function to be applied to each element
     '''
    res = []
    for i in self:
        res.append(fun(i))
    return res

def extend(self, iter = None):
    '''Push all of the items from the iterable (or an empty list
    @param iter: an iterable containing values to be pushed
     '''
    if iter == None: return
    for i in iter:
        self.push(i)

def copy(self):
    '''Create and return a copy of self'''
    pass #exercise
```

```
def asList(self): # not needed list(l) does the same
    '''Return a Python list with the elements in iteration
    order. Not needed as list(....) serves as well'''
    val = []
    for i in self:
        val.append(i)
    return val

def __iter__(self):
    if self._tail == None:
        self._iterNode = None
    elif(self._fromFront):
        self._iterNode = self._tail.prevNode()
    else:
        self._iterNode = self._tail
    self._startNode = self._iterNode #used to signal end of iteration
    self._flagHalt = False
    return self

def __next__(self):
    if self._iterNode is None or self._flagHalt:
        raise StopIteration
    val = self._iterNode.data()
    if self._fromFront:
        self._iterNode = self._iterNode.prevNode()
        if self._iterNode == self._startNode: self._flagHalt = True
    else:
        self._iterNode = self._iterNode.nextNode()
        if self._iterNode == self._startNode: self._flagHalt = True
    return val
    raise StopIteration

def __contains__(self, x):
    for i in self:
        if i == x:
            return True
    return False


def __repr__(self):
    return "CircularList" + str(self.asList())
```

```
    def __str__(self):
        return  str(self.asList())
```

## 3 A Tree Map Implementation

Here we present a very simple binary search tree. It makes no attempt to balance the tree, so can behave poorly if you add things in an order that puts it out of balance. The tree appears after the necessary node class. These nodes, like the list nodes are not well encapsulated. Note that the only real difference between list and tree nodes is the number of "next" references, here called children. The overall effect of this class is to create a sorted set-like class.

```
from circularLinkedList import CircularLinkedList

''' A binary search tree with keys that can be compared with <, =, and >
    So, all strings is fine as is a mix of int and float
    Recursive action demo
    Data can also be stored in order of the keys
    If it forbids duplicates, then
        it represents a sorted set if no data is permitted or
        a sorted map if it is.
    No balancing is attempted here
    Note that the parent link is used only for deletion, which is the
      most complicated method.
    The compare function is actually a strategy, though it doesn't
      change for a given tree.
    There is no remove operation since del will remove a node by key.
    Indexing by key will obtain data values.
'''

class BinaryTreeMap:

    class Node:
        def __init__(self, val, data = None):
            self._left = None
            self._right = None
            self._parent = None #used in deletion
            self._key = val
            self._data = data
```

```
    def left(self):
        '''get the left node if any'''
        return self._left

    def right(self):
        '''get the right node if any'''
        return self._right

    def parent(self):
        '''get the parent node'''
        return self._parent

    def key(self):
        '''get the key in this node'''
        return self._key

    def data(self):
        '''get the data value in this node'''
        return self._data

    def newLeft(self, val, data = None):
        '''create a new node with the given key and data and attach
           it at the left and set its parent to this node'''
        self._left = BinarySearchTree.Node(val, data)
        self._left.setParent(self)

  def setLeft(self, node):
        '''attach the given node at the left'''
        self._left = node
        node.setParent(self)

   def newRight(self, val, data = None):
        '''create a new node with the given key and data and attach
           it at the right and set its parent to this node'''
        self._right = BinarySearchTree.Node(val, data)
        self._right.setParent(self)

    def setRight(self, node):
        '''attach the given node at the right'''
        self._right = node
        node.setParent(self)
```

```
def setParent(self, node):
        '''set the parent of this node to the given one'''
        self._parent = node

def __init__(self, **kwargs):
    '''Construct a new empty BinarySearchTree
    @arg duplicates: whether or not to permit duplicate keys
     in tree (True)
    @arg compare: a function of two variables to control ordering
      of keys (a strategy)
    '''
    compare=lambda x, y: x<y
    if 'compare' in kwargs:
        compare = kwargs['compare']
    self._root = None
    self._compare = compare
    self._size = 0

def insert(self, val, data = None):
    ''' Insert a key and optional data into the tree
    @arg val: the key to be inserted also a key to determine
      the order
    @arg data: optional data to be stored in the node
    '''
    value = None
    if self._root is None:
        self._root = BinaryTreeMap.Node(val, data)
        self._size += 1
    else:
        value = self.__insertHelper(val, self._root, data)
    return value

def clear(self):
    '''Reset the tree to the empty state'''
    self._root = None
    self._size = 0

def size(self):
    '''current number of keys in the map'''
    return self._size
```

```
    def containsValue(self, value):
        ''' determine whether the tree contains a given data value'''
        for i in self: # i is a pair (key, data)
            if i[1] == value:
                return True
        return False

    def minimumValue(self):
        '''return the minimum data value
        Note that this is relative to the compare function'''
        node = self.__rootNode()
        if node is None: return None
        node = self.__minimumNode(node)
        return node.data()

    def minimum(self):
        '''return the minimum key in the tree'''
        node = self.__rootNode()
        if node is None: return None
        node = self.__minimumNode(node)
        return node.key()

    def maximumValue(self):
        '''return the maximum data value'''
        node = self.__rootNode()
        while node.right() is not None:
            node = node.right()
        return node.data()

    def maximum(self):
        '''return the maximum key in the tree'''
        node = self.__rootNode()
        while node.right() is not None:
            node = node.right()
        return node.key()

    def printTree(self):
        '''Print the tree to the console'''
        if self._root is not None:
            self.__printHelper(self._root)
```

```
def newPrint(self):
    '''Another way to print'''
    aList = list(self)
    for x in aList:
        print(x)

def pathToKey(self, key):
    result = []
    node = self._root
    if node is None or node.data() == key: return result
    while node is not None:
        if self._compare(node.key(), key):
            result.append('right')
            node = node.right()
        elif self._compare(key, node.key()):
            result.append('left')
            node = node.left()
        else:
            return result
    return result

def keyList(self):
    '''return all of the keys as a list'''
    temp = []
    result = []
    if self._root is not None:
        pairs = self.__getNextPair(self._root, temp)
        for i in pairs:
            result.append(i[0])
    return result

def clone(self):
    pass #TODO

def __contains__(self, x):
    pass # TODO

def __rootNode(self): # returns a node
    ''' Return the root node '''
    return self._root
```

```
def asDict(self):
    result = {}
    allValues = list(self)
    for i in allValues:
        result[i[0]] = i[1] #dictionary insertion
    return result

def levelOrder(self):
    result = []
    deq = CircularLinkedList()
    deq.enqueue(self._root)
    while deq.size() > 0:
        node = deq.dequeue()
        result.append((node.key(),node.data()))
        if node.left() is not None:
            deq.enqueue(node.left())
        if node.right() is not None:
            deq.enqueue(node.right())
    return result

def __findNode(self, val):
    ''' Find a node with a given key and return it (or None)
    @arg val: the key to search for
    @return: the first node found with that key or None
    '''
    if self._root is not None:
        return self.__findHelper(val, self._root)
    return None

def __findHelper(self, val, node):
    pass #TODO

def __minimumNode(self, node):
    while node.left() is not None:
        node = node.left()
    return node

def __iter__(self):
    elements = self.__asList() #keys if no data, or key data pairs
    return iter(elements)
```

```
def __insertHelper(self, val, node, data = None):
    value = None
    if not self._duplicates and val == node.key(): return
    if self._compare(val, node.key()):
        if node.left() is not None:
            value = self.__insertHelper(val, node.left(), data)
        else:
            node.newLeft(val, data)
            self._size += 1
    elif self._compare(node.key(), val):
        if node.right() is not None:
            value = self.__insertHelper(val, node._right, data)
        else:
            node.newRight(val, data)
            self._size += 1
    else: #both comparisons fail, duplicate key
        value = node.data()
        node.setData(data)
    return value

    def __asList(self):
    result = []
    if self._root is not None:
        result = self.__getNextPair(self._root, result)
    return result

def __printHelper(self, node):
    if node is not None:
        self.__printHelper(node.left())
        if node.key() is None:
            print(str(node.key()))
        else:
            print(node.key(), node.data())
        self.__printHelper(node._right)

def __getitem__(self, key):
    pass # TODO

def __getNextPair(self, node, aList):
    if node is not None:
        self.__getNextPair(node.left(), aList)
```

```
        if aList is not None:
            aList.append((node.key(), node.data()))
        self.__getNextPair(node._right, aList)
        return aList

def __transplant(self, u, v):
    node = u.parent()
    if node is None: self._root = v; return
    if u == node.left():
        node.setLeft(v)
    else:
        node.setRight(v)

def __delitem__(self, key):
    keyNode = self.__findNode(key)
    if keyNode:
        if keyNode.left() is None:
            self.__relink(keyNode, keyNode.right())
        elif keyNode.right() is None:
            self.__relink(keyNode, keyNode.left())
        else:
            y = self.__minimumNode(keyNode.right())
            if y.parent() != keyNode:
                self.__relink(y, y.right())
                y.setRight(keyNode.right())
            self.__relink(keyNode, y)
            y.setLeft(keyNode.left())
        self._size -= 1
        return keyNode.data()
    return None

def __repr__(self):
    return("BinarySearchTree"+ str(self.__asList()) )

def __str__(self):
    return str(self.__asList())
```

## 4 A Hashed Map Implementation

```
from denseList import DenseList

class HashMap:
    def __init__(self, buckets = 13):
        '''Create a hash map with a specified number of buckets
        @param buckets: the initial number of buckets. Default 10
        add will replace the value associated with a key
        '''
        self._bucketTable = DenseList(buckets)
        self._bucketTable.fillRest()
        self._size = 0
        self._primer = 3 #initial capacity of buckets
        self._scramble = 17

    def doHash(self, key):
        return (hash(key)*self._scramble) % len(self._bucketTable)

    def __iter__(self):
        self.currentIterator = None
        self.count = 0
        self.__curIterMax = 0
        self.__curIterCount = 1
        return self

    def __next__(self):
        if self.currentIterator is None or self.__curIterCount > \
          self.__curIterMax:
            while self.count < len(self._bucketTable) and \
                    (self.currentIterator is None or \
                  self.__curIterCount > self.__curIterMax):
                if self._bucketTable[self.count] is None:
                    self.count += 1
                    continue
                self.__curIterCount = 1
                self.__curIterMax = len(self._bucketTable[self.count])
                self.currentIterator = \
                   iter(self._bucketTable[self.count])
                self.count += 1
        if self.count > len(self._bucketTable):
```

```
            raise StopIteration
        self.__curIterCount += 1
        return self.currentIterator.__next__()

    def __contains__(self, key):
        bucket = self._bucketTable[self.doHash(key)]
        if bucket is None: return False
        for i in bucket:
            if i[0] == key:
                return True
        return False

    def __getitem__(self, key):
        bucket = self._bucketTable[self.doHash(key)]
        if bucket is None: return None
        for i in bucket:
            if i[0] == key:
                return i[1]
        return None

    def __setitem__(self, key, value):
        self.add(key, value)


    def __len__(self):
        return self._size

    def add(self, key, value=None):
        '''Insert a key:value pair into the map
        @param key: the hash key to the item
        @param value: an optional value to be stored with the key
        If the key already exists, replace the value
        '''
        bucket = self._bucketTable[self.doHash(key)]
        if bucket is None:
            bucket = DenseList(self._primer)
            self._bucketTable[self.doHash(key)] = bucket
            bucket.append((key, value))
        for pair in bucket:
            j = 0
            if pair[0] == key:
```

```
                bucket[j] = (key, value)
                return True
            j += 1
        self._size += 1
        return True

    def remove(self, key):
        '''Remove an item from the map
        @param key: the hash key of the item
        '''
        index = self.doHash(key)
        bucket = self._bucketTable[index]
        if bucket is None:
            return False
        try:
            j = 0
            for pair in bucket:
                if pair[0] == key:
                    bucket.remove(j)
                    if len(bucket)==0:
                        self._bucketTable[index]=None
                    self._size -= 1
                    return True
                j += 1
        except ValueError:
            return False

    def clear(self):
        '''Reset the map to the empty state'''
        self._bucketTable = [None] * len(self._bucketTable)
        self._size = 0

    def isEmpty(self):
        '''True if the map is empty'''
        return self._size == 0

    def __str__(self):
        return str(self._bucketTable)
```

## Classes Discussed

# Alphabetical Index

Made in United States
Orlando, FL
04 November 2026

90219750R00168